AF814220

Checkmate

Competency Based Questions

(CBQs)

Business Studies

CBSE Class 12

Checkmate

Competency Based Questions (CBQs)

Business Studies

CBSE Class 12

Author
Preeti Chaudhary
(M.A, B.Ed)
(PGT Business Studies)

arihant
SUCCESS AND NOTHING LESS

Checkmate

arihant

SUCCESS AND NOTHING LESS

ARIHANT PRAKASHAN (SCHOOl DIVISION SERIES), MEERUT

卐 **Administrative & Production Offices**

Regd. Office

'Ramchhaya' 4577/15, Agarwal Road, Darya Ganj, New Delhi -110002
Tele: 011- 47630600, 43518550

卐 **Head Office**

Kalindi, TP Nagar, Meerut (UP) - 250002
Tel: 0121-7156203, 7156204

卐 **Sales & Support Offices**

Agra, Ahmedabad, Bengaluru, Bareilly, Chennai, Delhi, Guwahati, Hyderabad, Jaipur, Jhansi, Kolkata, Lucknow, Nagpur & Pune.

卐 **PRICE** ₹ 245.00

卐 **PO No :** TXT-XX-XXXXXXX-X-XX

Published by Arihant Publications (India) Ltd.

For further information about the books published by Arihant, log on to www.arihantbooks.com or e-mail at info@arihantbooks.com

Follow us on

Checkmate **CBQs Series**

MASTER YOUR COMPETENCY!

01 **All types of Competency-Based Questions (CBQs),** including Multiple Choice Questions (MCQs), Assertion-Reason, Correct/Incorrect Statements, Case-Based/Source-Based, and Subjective/Open-Ended Questions, providing a well-rounded preparation.

02 Meticulously selected **competency-based questions from past exams** to ensure thorough preparation and familiarity with question formats.

03 **Detailed Solutions** for effective self-study and a deeper understanding of each topic, enabling you to learn at your own pace.

04 **Self Scoring feature** to track your performance and progress on your own, helping you identify strengths and areas for improvement.

05 **Indication of suggested time** with each set of questions to help you learn time management skills to maximize your efficiency and confidence during exams.

केन्द्रीय माध्यमिक शिक्षा बोर्ड

(शिक्षा मंत्रालय, भारत सरकार के अधीन एक स्वायत संगठन)

Central Boards of Secondary Education

(An Autonomous Organisation Under the Ministry of Education, Govt. of India)

CBSE/ACADEMIC/JS (SH)/2024/ 3rd April, 2024 Circulars No. Acad 30/2024

The changes for classes IX-XII year-end Board Examinations (2024-25)

(Classes IX-X)		
Particulars	**Academic Session 2023-24**	**Academic Session 2024-25** (No change from previous academic session)
Composition of question paper for year-end examination/ Board Examination (Theory)	• Competency Focused Questions in the form of MCQs/ Case Based Questions, Source-based Integrated Questions or any other type = 50% • Select response type questions (MCQ) = 20% • Constructed response questions (Short Answer/Long Answer Type Questions, as per existing pattern) = 30%	• Competency Focused Questions in the form of MCQs/Case Based Questions, Source-based Integrated Questions or any other type = 50% • Select response type questions (MCQ) = 20% • Constructed response questions (Short Answer/Long Answer Type Questions, as per existing pattern) = 30%

(Classes XI-XII)		
Particulars	**Academic Session 2023-24**	**Academic Session 2024-25**
Composition of question paper for year-end examination/ Board Examination (Theory)	• Competency Focused Questions in the form of MCQs/ Case Based Questions, Source-based Integrated Questions or any other type = 40% • Select response type questions (MCQ) = 20% • Constructed response questions (Short Answer Questions/Long Answer type Questions, as per existing pattern) = 40%	• Competency Focused Questions in the form of MCQs/ Case Based Questions, Source-based Integrated Questions or any other type = 50% • Select response type questions (MCQ) = 20% • Constructed response questions (Short Answer Questions/Long Answer type Questions, as per existing pattern) = 30%

Curriculum document released by the Board for the Academic Session 2024-25 and the Sample Question Papers may also be referred to for details of the QP design of individual subjects. Learning frameworks for various subjects for classes IX-XII are available at the link https://cbseacademic.nic.in for reference.

Contents

PART A Principles and Functions of Management

1. Nature and Significance of Management **3-21**
Multiple Choice Questions 4-9
Assertion-Reason Questions 10
Correct/Incorrect Statements 11-12
Case Based Questions 12-13
Subjective Questions 14-16
- Answers and Explanations 16-21

2. Principles of Management **22-41**
Multiple Choice Questions 23-29
Assertion-Reason Questions 30-31
Correct/Incorrect Statements 31-32
Case Based Questions 32-34
Subjective Questions 34-36
- Answers and Explanations 37-41

3. Business Environment **42-63**
Multiple Choice Questions 43-51
Assertion-Reason Questions 51-52
Correct/Incorrect Statements 52-53
Case Based Questions 53-56
Subjective Questions 56-57
- Answers and Explanations 58-63

4. Planning **64-81**
Multiple Choice Questions 65-70
Assertion-Reason Questions 71-72
Correct/Incorrect Statements 72-73
Case Based Questions 73-74
Subjective Questions 75-76
- Answers and Explanations 77-81

5. Organising **82-97**
Multiple Choice Questions 83-86
Assertion-Reason Questions 87
Correct/Incorrect Statements 88-89
Case Based Questions 89-91
Subjective Questions 91-93
- Answers and Explanations 93-97

6. Staffing **98-113**
Multiple Choice Questions 99-103
Assertion-Reason Questions 104
Correct/Incorrect Statements 105
Case Based Questions 106-107
Subjective Questions 108-110
- Answers and Explanations 110-113

7. Directing	**114-130**
Multiple Choice Questions	115-120
Assertion-Reason Questions	120-121
Correct/Incorrect Statements	121-122
Case Based Questions	123-124
Subjective Questions	124-126
• Answers and Explanations	126-130
8. Controlling	**131-146**
Multiple Choice Questions	132-136
Assertion-Reason Questions	137
Correct/Incorrect Statements	138
Case Based Questions	139-140
Subjective Questions	141-142
• Answers and Explanations	142-146

PART B Business Finance and Marketing

9. Financial Management	**149-164**
Multiple Choice Questions	150-155
Assertion-Reason Questions	155-156
Correct/Incorrect Statements	156-157
Case Based Questions	157-158
Subjective Questions	159-160
• Answers and Explanations	160-164
10. Financial Markets	**165-179**
Multiple Choice Questions	166-170
Assertion-Reason Questions	171
Correct/Incorrect Statements	172-173
Case Based Question	173-174
Subjective Questions	175-176
• Answers and Explanations	176-179
11. Marketing	**180-199**
Multiple Choice Questions	181-187
Assertion-Reason Questions	187-188
Correct/Incorrect Statements	188-189
Case Based Questions	190-191
Subjective Questions	192-194
• Answers and Explanations	194-199
12. Consumer Protection	**200-213**
Multiple Choice Questions	201-205
Assertion-Reason Questions	205-206
Correct/Incorrect Statements	206-207
Case Based Questions	207-209
Subjective Questions	209-210
• Answers and Explanations	211-213

Syllabus

Paper: One | Time: 3 Hrs | Max. Marks : 80

S.No.	Units	No. of Periods	Marks
Part A: Principles and Functions of Management			
1.	Nature and Significance of Management	12	16
2.	Principles of Management	14	
3.	Business Environment	12	
4.	Planning	14	14
5.	Organising	15	
6.	Staffing	16	20
7.	Directing	15	
8.	Controlling	12	
	Total	**110**	**50**
Part B: Business Finance and Marketing			
9.	Financial Management	20	15
10.	Financial Markets	18	
11.	Marketing Management	30	15
12.	Consumer Protection	12	
Part C: Project Work		30	20
	Total	**110**	**50**

PART A Principles and Functions of Management

UNIT 1 Nature and Significance of Management

- Management-concept, objectives, and importance
- Management as Science, Art and Profession
- Levels of Management
- Management Functions-planning, organizing, staffing, directing and controlling
- Coordination- concept and importance

UNIT 2 Principles of Management

- Principles of Management- concept and significance
- Fayol's principles of management
- Taylor's Scientific Management- principles and techniques

UNIT 3 Business Environment

- Business Environment- concept and importance
- Dimensions of Business Environment- Economic, Social, Technological, Political and Legal
- Demonetization - concept and features

UNIT 4 Planning

- Concept, importance and limitation
- Planning process
- Single use and standing plans. Objectives, Strategy, Policy, Procedure, Method, Rule, Budget and Programme

UNIT 5 Organising

- Concept and importance
- Organising process
- Structure of Organisation- Functional and divisional concept. Formal and informal organisation- concept
- Delegation- Concept, elements and importance
- Decentralization- Concept and importance

UNIT 6 Staffing

- Concept and importance of staffing
- Staffing as a part of Human Resource Management concept
- Staffing process
- Recruitment process
- Selection process
- Training and Development- Concept and importance, Methods of training- on the job and off the job - vestibule training, apprenticeship training and internship training

UNIT 7 Directing

- Concept and importance
- Elements of directing
- Motivation- Concept, Maslow's hierarchy of needs, Financial and non-financial incentives
- Leadership- Concept, styles authoritative, democratic and laissez faire
- Communication- Concept, formal and informal communication; barriers to effective communication, how to overcome the barriers

UNIT 8 Controlling

- Concept and importance
- Relationship between planning and controlling
- Steps in process of control

PART B Business Finance and Marketing

UNIT 9 Financial Management

- Concept, role and objectives of Financial Management
- Financial decisions- Investment, financing and dividend- Meaning and factors affecting
- Financial Planning- Concept and importance
- Capital Structure- Concept and factors affecting capital structure
- Fixed and Working Capital- Concept and factors affecting their requirements

UNIT 10 Financial Markets

- Financial Markets: Concept.
- Money market : Concept
- Capital market and its types (primary and secondary).
- Stock Exchange- Functions and trading procedure
- Securities and Exchange Board of India (SEBI) - Objectives and functions

UNIT 11 Marketing

- Marketing - Concept, functions and philosophies
- Marketing Mix – Concept and elements
- Product - Branding, labelling and packaging - Concept
- Price- Concept, Factors determining price
- Physical Distribution - Concept, components and channels of distribution
- Promotion – Concept and elements; advertising, personal selling, sales promotion, public relations

UNIT 12 Consumer Protection

- Concept and importance of consumer protection
- The Consumer Protection Act, 2019
- Meaning of consumer
- Rights and responsibilities of consumers
- Who can file a complaint ?
- Redressal machinery
- Remedies available
- Consumer awareness- Role of consumer organizations and Non-Governmental Organizations (NGOs).

UNIT 13 Project Work

PART A

Principles and Functions of Management

CHAPTER - 1

Nature and Significance of Management

Types & Nos. of Questions

Multiple Choice Questions	- 30
Assertion-Reason Questions	- 8
Correct/Incorrect Statements	- 8
Case Based Questions	- 2 Cases, *each with four Questions*
Subjective Questions	- 8

Trend Analysis

On the basis of analysis of last 2 years' papers, it is found that on an average 2 Multiple Choice Questions and 1 Short Answer Type Question are asked from this chapter.

Focus Topics of the Chapter

- Concept of Management
- Nature of Management
- Levels of Management
- Coordination: The Essence of Management

Multiple Choice Questions

No. of Questions : **30** Suggested Time : **45 Minutes**

Direction Each of the question given below is Multiple Choice Question (MCQ) i.e. there are Four Options/Choices for answer, out of which ONLY ONE is correct. You have to select the correct option.

A response box is given with each option, mark (✓) in the box of the correct option. For each correct answer you will get 1 mark, while there is no penalty for incorrect answer or missed out questions.

1. The technology landscape is constantly evolving with new trends, tools and platforms emerging regularly. Dynamic Tech Solutions must stay ahead of these changes to remain relevant and competitive.

Identify the characteristic of management reflected above.

(A) Management is continous ☐
(B) Management is pervasive ☐
(C) Management is dynamic ☐
(D) Management is multidimensional ☐

2.

Identify the characteristic of the management in the given diagram in which together everyone achieves more as a team.

(A) Management is a continuous process ☐
(B) Management is a dynamic activity ☐
(C) Management is all pervasive ☐
(D) Management is a group activity ☐

3. Different organisations have different goals. 'Zeepo' is an upcoming retail chain for providing consumer goods door-to-door, the objective of this organisation is to increase sales. 'Allie' is an educational organisation working with an objective of providing education to under privileged children of the society. Management of each of these organisations unite the efforts of their employees towards achieving organisational goals.

The characteristic of management discussed above is *[CBSE 2023]*

(A) management is goal-oriented ☐
(B) management is a continuous process ☐
(C) management is a dynamic process ☐
(D) management is an intangible force ☐

4. Over the past five years, there has been an exponential increase in the number of people practicing healthier lifestyles in India.

Doctors and nutritionists are advising people to reduce the daily intake of soft drinks as they are aerated, which can lead to obesity and other health issues.

In order to cope up with the setback in the demand from the consumers, "ENERGISE', a soft drink giant decided to introduce a tea brand named 'SFUR-TEA' and a wellness drink named 'FORTY PLUS' for women. The company received a hearty response from the consumers. Identify the feature of management reflected in the above paragraph.

(A) Management is intangible ☐
(B) Management is a dynamic function ☐
(C) Management is a group activity ☐
(D) Management is multidimensional ☐

5. There has been revelations that the production of cocoa in the Côte d'Ivoire involved child slave labour. These stories hit Cadbury especially hard. Cadbury's culture had been deeply rooted in the religious traditions of the company's founders and the organisation had paid close attention to the welfare of its workers and its sourcing practices.

The US Congress was considering legislation that would allow chocolate grown on certified plantations to be labelled "slave labour free," painting the rest of the industry in a bad light. Chocolate producers had asked for time to rectify the situation, but the extension they negotiated was running out. Students are asked whether Cadbury should join with the industry to lobby for more time.

Which objective has not been fulfilled by Cadbury?

(A) Organisational ☐
(B) Personal ☐
(C) Social ☐
(D) All of the above ☐

6. Mr. Anand Niketan has been successfully running a chain of restaurants in Delhi and Gurgaon for the past 15 years.

Aadhavan, his son, returned to India after acquiring a master's degree in social work. He suggested to his father that they should enter into a new line of business of Coffee Bars and provide employment opportunities to differently abled people and in the process create greater economic value for different sections.

After a lot of deliberation, Aadhavan opened his first Coffee Bar under the name of 'SPESH' near the college campus. The idea of taking orders was unique. The staff gave a pen and a pad and had codes on the menu in front of the dishes. On pressing the bell, the light would pop and the staff would come to assist customers. The users loved the concept and very soon 'SPESH' expanded its outlets to other parts of the city.

Aadhavan hired additional 70 employees to manage the new outlets. Identify the objectives that SPESH seeks to achieve through its new venture.

(A) Organisational and personnel objectives ☐
(B) Organisational and social objectives ☐
(C) Social and personnel objectives ☐
(D) Social objective ☐

7. 'Alfanzo Ltd.' is achieving all its objectives in an effective and efficient manner. It is earning enough revenue to cover costs and the risks of the business. Now the company wants to increase the sales volume, the capital investment, the number of employees and the number of products also.

By doing this, the management wants to achieve its following objective. *[CBSE 2023]*

(A) Survival ☐
(B) Profit ☐
(C) Personal ☐
(D) Growth ☐

8. Alo, a mobility platform, is in the process of laying-off 400-500 employees in a move aimed at driving cost efficiency. Which objective of management will the firm not be able to achieve by carrying out this process?

(A) Efficiency ☐
(B) Social ☐
(C) Profit ☐
(D) Survival ☐

9. Identify the importance of management highlighted in the picture below.

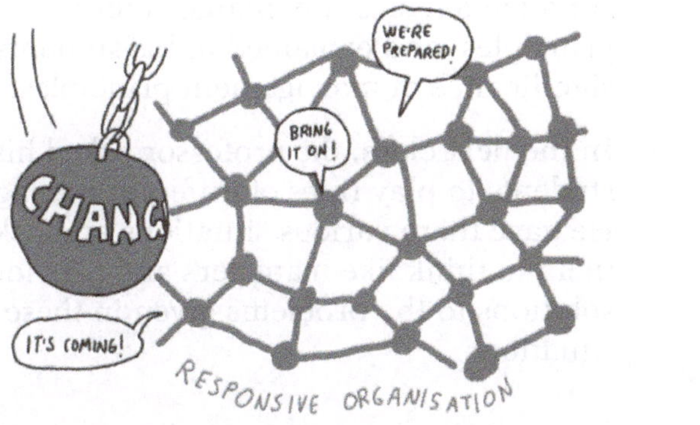

(A) Management helps in achieving personal objectives ☐
(B) Management creates a dynamic organisation ☐
(C) Management increases efficiency ☐
(D) Management helps in achieving group goals ☐

10. A multinational sweets and snacks company had been into catering business for the last many years. To add to its prospects and to grow in the long-run, it wants to increase its sales volume, the number of products and capital investment.

The organisational objective of management it seeks to achieve is [CBSE 2024]

(A) survival ☐
(B) profit ☐
(C) growth ☐
(D) corporate social responsibility ☐

11. 'Management has its own vocabulary of terms and concepts. Managers need to communicate with one another with the help of a common vocabulary for the better understanding of their work situation.'

Which characteristic of 'management as a science' is highlighted in the above statement? [CBSE 2023]

(A) Principles based on experimentation ☐
(B) Systematised body of knowledge ☐
(C) Universal validity ☐
(D) Personalised application ☐

12. Ram Murty, a professor of management conducted a class on 'management principles' and explained to his students the significance of management principles.

In the next class, the professor asked his students to play roles of different managers. He gave them various situations and asked them to think like managers and provide solutions to the problems given in these situations.

Each student applied the principles of management to the given situation in his own personalised manner, depending upon his creativity.

The nature of management highlighted in the above case is

(A) management as a science ☐
(B) management as an art ☐
(C) management both as an art and as a science ☐
(D) management as a profession ☐

13. Kamal, the CEO of Tech Innovations Inc, is responsible for setting the company's overall direction, goals and strategies.

He focuses on long-term planning, innovation and establishing partnerships with key stakeholders.

He makes high-level decisions that impact the entire organisation and set the tone for the company's culture.

Identify the level of management referred above.

(A) Top level ☐
(B) Middle level ☐
(C) Lower level ☐
(D) None of the above ☐

14. Identify the level of management which participates in such meetings as depicted in the below image.

(A) Middle level ☐
(B) Top level ☐
(C) Lower level ☐
(D) None of the above ☐

15. The company establishes a culture of continuous feedback and open communication, encouraging employees to share their ideas, concerns and feedback with management. Regular performance reviews and check-ins help to identify areas for improvement and provide support where needed.

Identify the function of management discussed above.

(A) Planning ☐ (B) Organising ☐
(C) Directing ☐ (D) Controlling ☐

16. Which function of management is highlighted in the below image?

(A) Controlling ☐ (B) Staffing ☐
(C) Planning ☐ (D) Directing ☐

17. "It is not something that happens by chance; it is a deliberate effort that requires clear communication, mutual respect and a shared vision. It is what transforms individual efforts into collective achievements."

Name the concept reflected in the statement.

(A) Management ☐
(B) Planning ☐
(C) Coordination ☐
(D) Directing ☐

18. GreenTech Solutions is a start-up specialising in sustainable energy solutions. Founded five years ago by a team of environmental engineers, the company has experienced rapid growth due to increasing demand for renewable energy technologies.

As GreenTech Solutions expands its operations and workforce, it faces challenges in managing growth effectively while maintaining its commitment to sustainability and innovation.

Identify the importance of coordination referred above.

(A) Growth in size ☐
(B) Functional differentiation ☐
(C) Specialisation ☐
(D) None of the above ☐

19. Cremica Corporation, a leading technology company, has recently launched a new product line aimed at revolutionising the healthcare industry.

The development and launch of this product require close collaboration among various departments, including Research and Development (R&D), marketing, sales and customer support.

However, each department operates independently, with limited communication and collaboration with other teams.

This siloed approach hinders information sharing and slows down decision-making processes.

Identify the aspect of management not followed here.

(A) Coordination ☐
(B) Planning ☐
(C) Directing ☐
(D) Controlling ☐

20. "Even where members of a department are willingly cooperate and work, coordination gives a direction to that willing spirit. Cooperation in the absence of coordination may lead to wasted effort and coordination without cooperation may lead to dissatisfaction among employees."

Identify the feature of coordination reflected in the above statement.

(A) Coordination is the responsibility of all managers ☐
(B) Coordination is a deliberate function ☐
(C) Coordination is an all pervasive function ☐
(D) Coordination integrates group efforts ☐

21. Light and Sound Pvt. Ltd. manufactures custom in ear monitors for musicians. Although it has been in the business for the last five years and has a considerable market share, on conducting an analysis it found that the company was spending almost 10% of the total cost on packaging. The company decided to outsource the packaging function to a professional packaging company.

The decision helped the firm to achieve its goals through greater customer satisfaction by timely delivery of orders and also helped the company in reducing the cost of packaging by 5%. After the implementation of the decision for outsourcing, the company has become

(A) effective ☐
(B) efficient ☐
(C) Both efficient and effective ☐
(D) Neither efficient nor effective ☐

22. "Some coordination is required by an independent person to reconcile the differences in approach, interest or opinion of the specialists."

Identify the importance of coordination reflected above.

(A) Specialisation ☐
(B) Functional differentiation ☐
(C) Growth in size ☐
(D) None of the above ☐

23. Choose the incorrect statement.

(A) Coordination is sometimes considered a separate function of management. ☐
(B) Management is implicit and inherent in all functions of an organisation. ☐
(C) Organisational efficiency is important to harmonise individual goals and organisational goals through coordination. ☐
(D) Specialisation arises out of the complexities of modern technology and the diversity of tasks to be performed. ☐

24. Choose the incorrect statement.

(A) Efficiency is also increased when for the same benefit or outputs, fewer resources are used and less cost is incurred. ☐
(B) People in organisations are performing diverse tasks but they are all working towards the same goal. ☐
(C) All organisations exist for the performance of some work. ☐
(D) Management of work implies dealing with employees as individuals with diverse needs and behaviour. ☐

25. Choose the correct statement.

(A) Management is multi-dimensional. ☐
(B) The management activities of all the organisations are similar whether the organisation is political, economic or social. ☐
(C) Management is considered as a full fledged profession. ☐
(D) Management principles are rigid and cannot be modified. ☐

26. Choose the correct statement.

(A) The social objectives of management include profit maximisation and growth. ☐
(B) The top level management is responsible for the welfare of the organisation. ☐
(C) The lower level management is responsible for the activities of the front line managers. ☐
(D) The directing function is responsible for recruiting suitable personnel. ☐

27. Match the following

	Column I		Column II
A.	Social objectives	(i)	Competitive salary, recognition
B.	Personal objectives	(ii)	Survival and growth
C.	Organisational objectives	(iii)	Creating employment opportunities

Codes

	A	B	C
(A)	(i)	(ii)	(iii)
(B)	(ii)	(i)	(iii)
(C)	(iii)	(i)	(ii)
(D)	(ii)	(iii)	(i)

28. Match the Column I with Column II in the following information.

Column I	Column II
A. They analyse the business environment and its implications for the survival of the firm.	(i) Supervisory level
B. It is responsible for implementing and controlling plans and strategies developed by top management.	(ii) Top level
C. Quality of output is maintained, wastage of materials is minimised and safety standards are maintained.	(iii) Middle level

Codes

	A	B	C
(A)	(ii)	(iii)	(i)
(B)	(i)	(iii)	(ii)
(C)	(iii)	(ii)	(i)
(D)	(ii)	(i)	(iii)

29. Match the Column I with Column II in the following information.

Column I	Column II
A. It can predict problems and prepare contingency plans to deal with them if and when they occur.	(i) Directing
B. It examines the activities and resources required to implement the plan.	(ii) Planning
C. It involves leading, influencing and motivating employees to perform the tasks assigned to them.	(iii) Controlling
D. Monitoring organisational performance towards the attainment of organisational goals is done.	(iv) Organising

Codes

	A	B	C	D
(A)	(ii)	(iv)	(i)	(iii)
(B)	(iv)	(ii)	(i)	(iii)
(C)	(iv)	(i)	(ii)	(iii)
(D)	(iii)	(i)	(ii)	(iv)

30. Match the Column I with Column II in the following information.

Column I	Column II
A. Doing the task correctly and with minimum cost.	(i) Process
B. The primary functions or activities that management performs to get things done.	(ii) Effectiveness
C. It is concerned with the end result.	(iii) Efficiency

Codes

	A	B	C
(A)	(iii)	(i)	(ii)
(B)	(i)	(ii)	(iii)
(C)	(ii)	(iii)	(i)
(D)	(i)	(iii)	(ii)

Assertion-Reason Questions

No. of Questions : **8** Suggested Time : **12 Minutes**

Direction Each of the question given below consist of the two statements; one labelled as **Assertion** (A) and other as **Reason** (R). List of common for each question is given below

(A) Both Assertion (A) and Reason (R) are true and Reason (R) is the correct explanation of Assertion (A)
(B) Both Assertion (A) and Reason (R) are true, but Reason (R) is not the correct explanation of Assertion (A)
(C) Assertion (A) is true, but Reason (R) is false
(D) Assertion (A) is false, but Reason (R) is true

You have to select the codes as *a, b, c* or d as your answer to the question by marking (✓) in the response box given against each option.

1. **Assertion** (A) Management is concerned with efficient used of resources.

   Reason (R) For management both efficiency and effectiveness need to be balanced.

   (A) ☐ (B) ☐ (C) ☐ (D) ☐

2. **Assertion** (A) Management helps in achieving personal objectives.

   Reason (R) A manager motivates and leads his team in such a manner that individual members are able to achieve personal goals while contributing to the overall organisational objective.

   (A) ☐ (B) ☐ (C) ☐ (D) ☐

3. **Assertion** (A) Mangement as an art and science are mutually exclusive, but not complement to each other.

   Reason (R) Managers can work better if their practice is based on the principles of management.

   (A) ☐ (B) ☐ (C) ☐ (D) ☐

4. **Assertion** (A) Management can be called an inexact science.

   Reason (R) Since management deals with human behaviour, the outcomes of these experiments are not capable of being accurately predicted and replicated.

   (A) ☐ (B) ☐ (C) ☐ (D) ☐

5. **Assertion** (A) Profession is a very personalised concept.

   Reason (R) A good manager works through a combination of practice, creativity, imagination, initiative and innovation.

   (A) ☐ (B) ☐ (C) ☐ (D) ☐

6. **Assertion** (A) Art presupposes the existence of certain theoretical knowledge.

   Reason (R) There is a lot of literature available in various areas of management.

   (A) ☐ (B) ☐ (C) ☐ (D) ☐

7. **Assertion** (A) The supervisory level performs the activities according to the plans of top and middle level management.

   Reason (R) The supervisory level motivates the employees and boosts their morale.

   (A) ☐ (B) ☐ (C) ☐ (D) ☐

8. **Assertion** (A) Coordination involves synchronisation of the different actions or efforts of the various units of an organisation.

   Reason (R) It is through the process of coordination that a manager ensures the orderly arrangement of individual and group efforts to ensure unity of action in the realisation of common objectives.

   (A) ☐ (B) ☐ (C) ☐ (D) ☐

Correct/Incorrect Statements

No. of Questions : **8**   Suggested Time : **12 Minutes**

Direction Each of the question given below consist of the two statements. List of common options applicable for each question is given below

(A) Statement I is correct and Statement II is incorrect
(B) Statement I is incorrect and Statement II is correct
(C) Both statements are correct
(D) Both statements are incorrect

You have to select the codes as *a, b, c* or *d* as your answer to the question by marking (✓) in the response box given against each option.

1. **Statement I** Management helps in achieving group goals.
   Statement II Management helps in the development of the society.
   (A) ☐ (B) ☐
   (C) ☐ (D) ☐

2. **Statement I** If an organisation has a good management team that is efficient and effective, it automatically serves society by providing good quality products at reasonable prices.
   Statement II Authority-responsibility relationship binds individuals as superiors and subordinates and gives rise to different levels in an organisation.
   (A) ☐ (B) ☐
   (C) ☐ (D) ☐

3. **Statement I** Management has to reconcile personal goals with organisational objectives for harmony in the organisation.
   Statement II A good manager works through a combination of practice, creativity, imagination, initiative and innovation.
   (A) ☐ (B) ☐
   (C) ☐ (D) ☐

4. **Statement I** Authority-responsibility relationship binds individuals as superiors and subordinates and gives rise to different levels in an organisation.
   Statement II Management cannot prevent problems, but it can predict them and prepare contingency plans to deal with them if and when they occur.
   (A) ☐ (B) ☐ (C) ☐ (D) ☐

5. **Statement I** Proper organisational techniques help in the accomplishment of work and promote both the efficiency of operations and the effectiveness of results
   Statement II Cooperation is implicit and inherent in all functions of an organisation.
   (A) ☐ (B) ☐ (C) ☐ (D) ☐

6. **Statement I** Any discrepancies between actual and realised activities are then taken care of at the stage of controlling.
   Statement II Coordination do not provide the requisite amount, quality, timing and sequence of efforts which ensures that planned objectives are achieved with a minimum of conflict.
   (A) ☐ (B) ☐
   (C) ☐ (D) ☐

7. **Statement I** Cooperation unifies unrelated or diverse interests into purposeful work activity.
Statement II Coordination in the absence of cooperation may lead to wasted effort and coordination without cooperation may lead to dissatisfaction among employees.
(A) ☐ (B) ☐ (C) ☐ (D) ☐

8. **Statement I** The process of linking the activities of various departments is accomplished by coordination.
Statement II Specialisation arises out of the complexities of modern technology and the diversity of tasks to be performed.
(A) ☐ (B) ☐
(C) ☐ (D) ☐

Case Based Questions

No. of Questions : **2** Suggested Time : **10 Minutes**

Direction This section contains 2 cases having 4 questions of 1 mark each. You have to write the answer of each question based on the context of the related case.

Case 1 Charminar Company, a medium-sized manufacturing firm, is facing challenges in its production department. Over the past year, there has been a decline in productivity, increased employee turnover and rising costs due to inefficiencies in operations.

The company's management recognises the need for intervention to address these issues and restore the department's performance to optimal levels. Employees within the production depart- ment are dissatisfied with their working conditions and lack of opportunities for growth, resulting in a high turnover rate.

The manager conducts a comprehensive review of existing production processes, identifies bottlenecks and inefficiencies and implements strategies to streamline operations. Key Performance Indicators (KPIs) are established to track progress and measure the success of implemented changes. The effective management practices implemented not only address the immediate issues facing the department but also lay the foundation for long-term success and sustainable growth within the organisation.

Questions

(i) "Employees within the production department are dissatisfied with their working conditions and lack of opportunities for growth, resulting in a high turnover rate."
Identify the objective of management not fulfilled in the above case.
(A) Organisational ☐
(B) Social ☐
(C) Personnel ☐
(D) All of the above ☐

(ii) "Key Performance Indicators (KPIs) are established to track progress and measure the success of implemented changes."
Which function of management has been referred above?
(A) Planning ☐
(B) Organising ☐
(C) Directing ☐
(D) Controlling ☐

(iii) Which level is responsible for all the activities of the business and for its impact on society?

(A) Top ☐

(B) Middle ☐

(C) Lower ☐ (D) All of these ☐

(iv) Identify the objectives discussed in the case above.

(A) Personal and social ☐

(B) Personal and organisational ☐

(C) Social and personal ☐

(D) Organisational and social ☐

Case 2 Sana is the branch manager of ABC Handicrafts Pvt. Ltd. The company's objective is to promote the sales of Indian handloom and handicraft products. It sells fabrics, furnishings, readymades and household items are made out of traditional Indian fabrics. Sana decides quantities, variety, colour and texture of all the above items and then allocates resources for their purchase from different suppliers.

She appoints a team of designers and crafts people in the company, who developed some prints for bed covers in bright colour on silk. Although the products looked very attractive and impressive, they were relatively expensive on the front of affordability for an average customer. Sana suggested that they should keep the silk bed covers for special festive occasions and offer the cotton bed covers on a regular basis to keep costs under control. *[CBSE QB]*

Questions

(i) "She appoints a team of designers and crafts people in the company, who developed some prints for bed covers in bright colour on silk."

Which function of management is highlighted in this context?

(A) Controlling ☐ (B) Staffing ☐

(C) Planning ☐ (D) Directing ☐

(ii) In the above case "company's objective is to promote the sales of Indian handloom and handicraft products."

The above line focus on which feature of management?

(A) Management is an intangible force ☐

(B) Management is a goal-oriented process ☐

(C) Management is pervasive in nature ☐

(D) Management is a continuous process ☐

(iii) With reference to the above case, at which level of management Sana is working?

(A) Lower level ☐

(B) Top level ☐

(C) Middle level ☐

(D) Shop floor ☐

(iv) "Sana suggested that they should keep the silk bed covers for special festive occasions and offer the cotton bed covers on a regular basis to keep costs under control."

Which function of management is highlighted in this context?

(A) Controlling ☐

(B) Staffing ☐

(C) Organising ☐

(D) Planning ☐

Subjective Questions

Free Response Questions, Open-ended Questions etc.

No. of Questions : **8** Suggested Time : **64 Minutes**

1. Big Pharma Pioneer Kesko focused on reducing their impact on the planet for three decades. Their initiatives range from leveraging the power of the wind to providing safe water to communities around the world. Their purchase of a privately-owned energy supplier in the Ixco Panhandle allowed the company to reduce pollution while providing a renewable and economical alternative to electricity.

The company continues to seek out renewable energy options with the goal of having 100% of its energy needs from renewable sources by next year.

However, it has been facing issues with employee morale and productivity due to poor working conditions. Complaints regarding inadequate facilities, safety concerns and lack of support have been increasing, leading to high turnover rates and decreased efficiency.

(i) Which objective of management is fulfilled by Kesko?

(ii) Identify and explain the objective of management which decreased employee morale and productivity.

2. Vakshu Properties and Infrastructure Ltd. is a well-known real estate company in India. The CEO of the company, Mr. Albert understands the importance of achieving a variety of objectives in all areas considering the interest of all stakeholders including shareholders, employees, customers and the government.

His job is complex and stressful, demanding long hours and commitment to the organisation. Mr. Albert also focuses on utilising human and material resources to the maximum possible advantage. He formulates overall organisational goals and strategies for the organisation.

With his dedication, the company is able to earn adequate revenues to cover costs. Its capital base, number of employees and production turnover has increased manifolds over the years. The rate of profitability of the business is also creditable.

The employees of the company are happy and satisfied with their remuneration, working conditions, promotion policy, etc. Vakshu Properties and Infrastructure Ltd. measures such as using natural resources for the construction, reducing waste, and using renewable energy sources.

(i) Identify and explain the various types of objectives of management being fulfilled by Vakshu Properties and Infrastructure Ltd. by quoting lines from the paragraph.

(ii) Identify and state the feature of management highlighted in the above para.

(iii) Also identify the level at which Mr. Albert works.

3. Sujot Ltd. is committed to sustainability and energy conservation, as reflected in their initiatives to reduce energy use. By implementing measures such as putting lights and HVAC systems on timers, swapping traditional light bulbs for LEDs and installing solar panels, Sujot Ltd. aims to minimise its environmental impact and contribute to a greener future.

This objective aligns with their broader goal of corporate social responsibility, demonstrating their commitment to environmental stewardship and sustainable business practices.

(i) Identify and explain the objective of business reflected here.

(ii) State the other two objectives of business.

4. Romilly was working in 'DESIGNCO', dealing in import and export. He found that the profits has started declining from the last six months. He is responsible for all the activities of the business and for its impact on society, so he analysed the business environment to find out the reasons for this decline.
   (i) Identify the level of management at which Romilly was working.
   (ii) State three other functions being performed by Romilly.

5. Mohan, a dedicated and experienced professional, holds a key role in the organisational hierarchy. He serves as a vital link between the strategic vision set by top management and the operational execution carried out by frontline employees.

   In his capacity, Mohan oversees the implementation and control of plans and strategies devised by top management, ensuring alignment with organisational goals and objectives.
   (i) At what level of management was he working?
   (ii) State any three functions he will perform.

6. Monika, Rashmi and Garima are childhood friends. After completing their education. Monika joined a school as a teacher. Rashmi joined a firm as a Chartered Accountant and Garima as a general manager in a multinational company. After a long time in a re-union function of the school, they met each other. Rashmi said that they were all professionals now. Garima told Rashmi that she can say this about Monika and herself, but not about her since manager is not considered a full fledged professional.

   Why did Garima say that she was not a professional? State any three points in support of your answer. *[CBSE 2023]*

7. Tech Target is a multinational corporation operating in the consumer electronics industry. It designs, manufactures and distributes smartphones, tablets and other electronic devices worldwide.

   With manufacturing facilities located in various countries and a complex global supply chain involving multiple suppliers, distributors and retailers, it is essential to ensure smooth operations and timely delivery of products to customers.

   The production manager aligns production schedules at different manufacturing facilities to meet demand forecasts and optimise efficiency while minimising inventory holding costs and production bottlenecks.

   Logistics department looks after transportation, warehousing and distribution activities to ensure timely delivery of finished products to regional distribution centers and retail stores while minimising transit times and transportation costs.

   Demand analyst collaborates with sales and marketing teams to accurately forecast demand for different products and regions, enabling proactive production planning and inventory management to prevent stockouts or excess inventory. The company is able to harmonise individual goals and organisational goals.
   (i) In the case of Tech Target, what specific aspect of management is highlighted in the company's operations, considering its global scale and complex supply chain?
   (ii) Elaborate on how the aspect of management demonstrated by Tech Target contributes to its success and competitive advantage in the consumer electronics industry, focusing on two key points.

8. Sam and Dave have been friends since childhood, growing up in the same neighbourhood and attending the same school.

   While Dave pursued higher education and eventually joined his family's hotel business in Dubai, Sam took a different path. Sam's family owned a small but successful retail business back in their hometown. Despite facing physical challenges due to a disability, Sam actively participated in managing the family business and played a significant role in its success.

Over the years, Sam developed exceptional management skills through hands on experience, learning the intricacies of operations, customer service and marketing. His ability to overcome obstacles and adapt to changing circumstances demonstrated his resilience and determination. Despite lacking formal education in management, Sam's practical knowledge and leadership qualities were evident to those who knew him well, including Dave.

When Dave, now a key figure in his family's hotel business, was looking to expand the sales and marketing division, he immediately thought of Sam. Knowing Sam's capabilities and character first-hand, Dave believed that Sam's unique blend of practical experience and personal qualities would be invaluable in the role of assistant manager.

Inviting Sam to join the team was not only a professional decision but also a personal one, driven by trust and loyalty.

However, Dave's father, a seasoned businessman with a more traditional perspective, expressed concerns about Sam's suitability for the position.

He emphasised the importance of formal education in management and questioned whether Sam's practical experience alone would be sufficient to excel in a managerial role.

Should Sam be appointed to the position of assistant manager in the sales and marketing division, considering his practical management experience and strong leadership potential?

Justify your answer.

Answers

If your answer matches with the answer given here then put (✓) in the box otherwise put (✗). In case you did not attempt the question leave the box blank.

Multiple Choice Questions

1. C ☐ 2. D ☐
3. A ☐ 4. B ☐
5. C ☐ 6. B ☐
7. D ☐ 8. B ☐
9. B ☐ 10. C ☐
11. B ☐ 12. B ☐
13. A ☐ 14. B ☐
15. C ☐ 16. D ☐
17. C ☐ 18. A ☐
19. A ☐ 20. B ☐
21. C ☐ 22. A ☐
23. B ☐ 24. D ☐
25. A ☐ 26. B ☐
27. C ☐ 28. A ☐
29. A ☐ 30. A ☐

Your Score__________ *(No. of Correct Answers)*

Assertion-Reason Questions

1. B ☐ 2. A ☐
3. D ☐ 4. A ☐
5. D ☐ 6. A ☐
7. C ☐ 8. A ☐

Your Score__________ *(No. of Correct Answers)*

Correct/Incorrect Statements

1. C ☐ 2. C ☐
3. C ☐
4. A ☐
5. A ☐
6. A ☐
7. D ☐
8. C ☐

Your Score__________ *(No. of Correct Answers)*

Case Based Questions

1. (i) C ☐ (ii) D ☐
(iii) A ☐ (iv) B ☐
2. (i) B ☐ (ii) B ☐
(iii) C ☐ (iv) A ☐

Your Score__________ *(No. of Correct Answers)*

Explanations

Multiple Choice Questions

1. (C) The statement reflects the dynamic nature of management, indicating the need for adaptation to the ever-changing technology landscape to stay relevant and competitive.
2. (D) Management is a group activity because it involves coordinating and directing the efforts of a team or group of individuals to achieve common goals and objectives.
3. (A) Managers play a crucial role in setting clear and achievable goals for their organisations.
   They coordinate and direct the activities of their teams, ensuring that all efforts are focused on attaining these goals.
4. (B) The feature of management reflected is management is a dynamic function, as 'ENERGISE' responds to changing consumer preferences by introducing new products to cope with setbacks in demand for soft drinks.
5. (C) Cadbury has failed to fulfill its social objective because it is facing allegations of child slave labour in its cocoa sourcing. This issue impacts the well-being of children and labour practices in the cocoa industry, which Cadbury had previously paid close attention to.
6. (B) SPESH aims to achieve both organisational goals like growth and profitability and social objectives such as providing employment opportunities to differently abled people.
7. (D) Growth in business typically refers to the expansion of various aspects of a company, such as revenue, market share, product lines, geographical reach and workforce size.
8. (B) The social objective of management entails fulfilling responsibilities towards society beyond profit-making, focusing on contributing positively to the welfare and well-being of various stakeholders, including employees, customers, communities and the environment.
9. (B) Management creates a dynamic organisation
10. (C) growth
11. (B) Management as a science entails a systemised body of knowledge that is based on principles, theories, models and empirical evidence. This body of knowledge is systematically organised to understand, analyse and predict managerial phenomena and outcomes within organisations.
12. (B) The students are asked to play role as managers and apply these principles to various situations in their own personalised manner, showcasing creativity. This demonstrates the artistic aspect of management.
13. (A) Top level management, including executives and senior leaders, sets the overall direction and vision for the organisation, formulates strategic goals and objectives and makes high level decisions to ensure the organisation's long-term success.
14. (B) Top level
15. (C) Directing involves guiding and motivating employees to achieve organisational goals. In the scenario described, the company is fostering a culture of open communication and feedback, which falls under the directing function.
16. (D) Directing
17. (C) Coordination refers to the intentional effort of bringing together individual actions through clear communication and shared vision to achieve collective success.
18. (A) As GreenTech Solutions expands its operations and workforce, coordination becomes crucial to manage the increasing size of the organisation effectively.
19. (A) Coordination involves ensuring that different departments and teams work together harmoniously towards common goals.
20. (B) Coordination is a deliberate function
21. (C) By outsourcing packaging, Light and Sound Pvt. Ltd. became both efficient, as it reduced packaging costs by 5% and effective by achieving greater customer satisfaction through timely delivery.
22. (A) Specialisation

23. (B) Management is not inherent in all functions of an organisation; rather, it is a distinct and essential activity that involves planning, organising, leading and controlling to achieve organisational goals.
24. (D) While good management acknowledges and considers individual needs to some extent, it primarily focuses on achieving organisational goals through the collective effort of its workforce.
25. (A) Management encompasses various dimensions such as planning, organising, leading and controlling, making it a multi-dimensional field of study and practice.
26. (B) Top level management typically holds the responsibility for setting the overall direction and goals of the organisation, as well as ensuring its overall welfare and success.
27. (C) (iii) (i) (ii)
28. (A) (ii) (iii) (i)
29. (A) (ii) (iv) (i) (iii)
30. (A) (iii) (i) (ii)

Assertion-Reason Questions

1. (B) Both Assertion (A) and Reason (R) are true, but Reason (R) is not the correct explanation of Assertion (A)
2. (A) Both Assertion (A) and Reason (R) are true and Reason (R) is the correct explanation of Assertion (A)
3. (D) Management as an art and science is not mutually exclusive; in fact, they complement each other.
   Management involves both the application of practical skills and the utilisation of scientific principles and theories to achieve organisational goals effectively.
4. (A) Both Assertion (A) and Reason (R) are true and Reason (R) is the correct explanation of Assertion (A)
5. (D) Profession is not inherently a personalised concept. A good manager indeed often relies on a combination of practice, creativity, imagination, initiative and innovation to effectively perform their role.
6. (A) Both Assertion (A) and Reason (R) are true and Reason (R) is the correct explanation of Assertion (A)
7. (C) The supervisory level typically implements activities according to the plans set by top and middle level management.
   However, while supervision may involve aspects of motivation and morale boosting, it's not the primary responsibility of this level of management.
8. (A) Both Assertion (A) and Reason (R) are true and Reason (R) is the correct explanation of Assertion (A)

Correct/Incorrect Statements

1. (C) Both statements are correct
2. (C) Both statements are correct
3. (C) Both statements are correct
4. (A) Planning cannot prevent problems, but it can predict them and prepare contingency plans to deal with them if and when they occur.
5. (A) Coordination is implicit and inherent in all functions of an organisation.
6. (A) Coordination provides the requisite amount, quality, timing and sequence of efforts which ensures that planned objectives are achieved with a minimum of conflict.
7. (D) Coordination unifies unrelated or diverse interests into purposeful work activity.
   Cooperation in the absence of coordination may lead to wasted effort and coordination without cooperation may lead to dissatisfaction among employees.
8. (C) Both statements are correct

Case Based Questions

1. (i) (C) The objective of management not fulfilled in the case is personnel. This is evident from the dissatisfaction among employees in the production department and the high turnover rate, indicating a need for addressing personnel related issues.
   (ii) (D) Key Performance Indicators (KPIs) are established to track progress and measure the success of implemented changes, which is a key aspect of the controlling function in management.
   (iii) (A) Top level management is typically responsible for setting the overall direction and policies of the organisation, including its societal impact.

(iv) (B) There is a focus on addressing personnel related issues such as dissatisfaction and turnover rate within the production department (personal objective), as well as implementing strategies to streamline operations and restore optimal performance (organisational objective).

2. (i) (B) Staffing involves selecting, recruiting, training and placing individuals in suitable positions within the organisation.

(ii) (B) Management is a goal-oriented process

(iii) (C) Middle level managers are responsible for implementing the policies and plans developed by top level management and supervising the activities of lower level managers.

(iv) (A) Controlling involves monitoring performance, comparing it with goals and taking corrective action as needed to ensure that objectives are achieved.

Subjective Questions

1. (i) **Social Objective is fulfilled by Kesko** It refers to consistently creating economic value for various constituents of society.

(ii) **Personal Objectives** This objective relates to the satisfaction of personal needs of the employees having different personalities, backgrounds, experiences and objectives.

Personal objectives include

(a) Financial needs, by giving competitive salary and perks.

(b) Social needs, by peer recognition.

(c) Higher level needs, by providing opportunities for personal growth and development.

2. (i) Vakshu Properties and Infrastructure Ltd. is fulfilling various types of management objectives

(a) **Organisational Objectives** The company is focused on achieving a variety of objectives in all areas, considering the interests of all stakeholders, including shareholders, employees, customers and the government.

This is evident from the statement, "Mr. Albert understands the importance of achieving a variety of objectives in all areas considering the interest of all stakeholders."

(b) **Personal Objectives** Mr. Albert's job is complex and demanding, requiring long hours and commitment to the organisation. Despite the challenges, he remains dedicated to utilising human and material resources to their maximum possible advantage, which fulfills personal objectives related to professional growth and achievement.

This is reflected in the paragraph, "His job is complex and stressful, demanding long hours and commitment to the organisation. Mr. Albert also focuses on utilising human and material resources to the maximum possible advantage."

(c) **Social Objectives** The company implements measures to promote environmental sustainability, such as using natural resources for construction, reducing waste and using renewable energy sources. This demonstrates a commitment to social welfare and environmental responsibility.

This is evident from the statement, "Vakshu Properties and Infrastructure Ltd. measures such as using natural resources for the construction, reducing waste and using renewable energy sources."

(ii) **Management is an Intangible Force** Management is an intangible force that cannot be seen but its presence can be felt in the way the organisation functions.

The effect of management is noticeable in an organisation where targets are met according to plans, employees are happy and satisfied, and there is orderliness instead of chaos.

(iii) **Top Level** He formulates overall organisational goals and strategies for their achievement.

3. (i) The objective of business reflected here is a social objective, specifically environmental responsibility and sustainability. This objective reflects a broader commitment to social welfare and environmental stewardship, aligning the company's operations with the values and concerns of the community and the planet.
 (ii) The other two objectives of business are
  (a) **Organisational Objective** This objective involves maximising profits and financial returns for the company's shareholders and stakeholders. Businesses aim to generate revenue and manage costs efficiently to ensure profitability and long-term financial sustainability.
  (b) **Personal Objective** These objectives in business refer to the goals and aspirations of individuals within the organisation. These objectives may include career advancement, skill development, job satisfaction and work life balance for employees.

4. (i) Romilly was working at top level of management.
 (ii) The three functions being performed by him at this level are outlined below
  (a) He is responsible for formulating the overall organisational goals and strategies.
  (b) He is responsible for all the business activities and its impact on society.
  (c) He has to coordinate the activities of different departments in pursuit of common goals.

5. (i) Mohan is working at the middle level of management.
 (ii) The three functions that he will have to perform at this level are stated below
  (a) He has to ensure that his department has the necessary staff.
  (b) He has to assign duties and responsibilities to the people in his department.
  (c) He has to motivate the people in his department to achieve the desired objectives.

6. Garima was correct. Management is not considered a full-fledged profession like legal and medical profession because of the following reasons
 (i) **Restricted Entry** The entry to any profession is restricted through a prescribed qualification. But there is no restriction on anyone being appointed as a manager in any business enterprise.
 (ii) **Professional Association** Though AIMA is an association for management graduates, it is not obligatory for managers to get registered with any professional body like the Medical Council or Bar Council of India, which regulates the professional conduct of doctors and lawyers respectively.
 (iii) **Ethical Code of Conduct** Legal and medical professions are bound by a code of conduct, which guides the behaviour of its members. AIMA has devised a code of conduct for Indian managers but there is no statutory backing for this code.
 (iv) **Service Motive** The motive of legal and medical profession is to serve their client's interests by rendering dedicated and committed service.
 The basic purpose of management is to help the organisation to achieve its goals by providing good quality products at reasonable prices. A manager is expected to adopt the service motive but the basic motive remains profit maximisation.

7. (i) Coordination aspect of management is highlighted in the given case. The company effectively aligns production schedules across various manufacturing facilities, manages logistics operations to ensure timely delivery and collaborates with sales and marketing teams for demand forecasting.
 (ii) The two points highlighting the importance of coordination are stated below
  (a) **Growth in the Size** With the growth in the size of an organisation, there is a proportionate increase in the number of its employees.
  So, there is a greater need to unify the efforts of diverse individuals towards the realisation of organisational goals.

(b) **Functional Differentiation** As a result of functional differentiation in an organisation, its people and activities get divided into small departments on the basis of functions like marketing, finance etc. Since each such department tends to formulate its own objectives, policies etc., there is a need to reconcile the goals pursued by each of such departments with the goals of the organisation as a whole.

8. Yes, Sam can be deployed at the post of assistant manager in sales and marketing division although he hasn't acquired any professional degree in management as management is not considered to be a full-fledged profession because of the following reasons

(i) **Restricted Entry** Unlike management, the entry to the other professions is restricted through an examination or eligibility criteria like specific percentage in a particular degree or diploma. However, management as a profession does not fulfill this criteria as anyone can be called a manager regardless of his/her academic qualifications.

(ii) **Professional Association** Unlike managers, all working professionals have to be a member of an affiliated professional association which regulates their entry, grants certificate of practice and formulates and enforces code of conduct.

For example, the practicing lawyers have to be a member of Bar Council of India, the practicing doctors should have membership of All India Medical Association, etc.

However, in case of management, although there exist several management association like the AIMA (All India Management Association), neither does it have any statutory backing nor is it mandatory for the practicing managers to a member of such associations.

CHAPTER -2

Principles of Management

Henri Fayol

Types & Nos. of Questions

Multiple Choice Questions	– 36
Assertion-Reason Questions	– 10
Correct/Incorrect Statements	– 10
Case Based Questions	– 2 Cases, *each with four Questions*
Subjective Questions	– 7

Trend Analysis

On the basis of analysis of last 2 years' papers, it is found that on an average 2 Multiple Choice Questions and 1 Short Answer Type Question are asked from this chapter.

Focus Topics of the Chapter

- Concept of Principles of Management
- Fayol's Principles of Management
- Taylor's Scientific Management

Multiple Choice Questions

No. of Questions : **36** Suggested Time : **54 Minutes**

Direction Each of the question given below is Multiple Choice Question (MCQ) i.e. there are Four Options/Choices for answer, out of which ONLY ONE is correct. You have to select the correct option. A response box is given with each option, mark (✓) in the box of the correct option. For each correct answer you will get 1 mark, while there is no penalty for incorrect answer or missed out questions.

1. Principles of management include contribution of the employee, paying capacity of the employer and also prevailing wage rate for the occupation under consideration.

   Identify the feature of principles of management discussed above.

   (A) Universal applicability ☐
   (B) Formed by practice and experimentation ☐
   (C) General guidelines ☐
   (D) Contingent ☐

2. Identify the feature of principles of management from the picture below

   (A) Providing managers with useful insights into reality ☐
   (B) Optimum utilisation of resources and effective administration ☐
   (C) Scientific decisions ☐
   (D) Meeting changing environment requirements ☐

3. Which of the following statements is incorrect?

   (A) A managerial principle is a broad and general guideline for decision-making and behaviour ☐
   (B) Management principles are as rigid as principles of pure science ☐
   (C) Management principles deal with human behaviour and thus are to be applied creatively given the demands of the situation ☐
   (D) The principles of management should be distinguished from techniques of management ☐

4. Which of the following statements is incorrect?

   (A) Management principles have been developed on the basis of observation and experimentation as well as personal experiences of the managers ☐
   (B) Derivation of the principle may be said to be a matter of science and their creative application may be regarded as an art ☐
   (C) Management principles are guidelines to action ☐
   (D) Management principles are general rules for behaviour of individuals in society formed through common practice ☐

5. Coca-Cola, an American company for soft refreshments, is known as a leading company for producing a variety of soft drinks. The firm has applied several changes in their management techniques to maintain itself in the global market.

The company faced many challenges and problems in many countries and faced aggressive competition from its biggest competitor such as Pepsico and other challenges from the political, social and economic environment.

The company met several internal difficulties in its production, marketing operations and developed multiple strategies to move from the uncertain situation by adopting change management models. The company handled many challenges of sustainable development. It produced its products in a recyclable way and compatible with customers' needs by making products free of sugars and sodium.

The company managed the Corona (Covid-19) crisis by reviewing its production, operations and supply chain and restructuring the company in more than one country to confront the pandemic and fulfill all concerned parties' desires.

Identify the importance of principles of management discussed above.

(A) Providing managers with useful insights into reality ☐

(B) Optimum utilisation of resources and effective administration ☐

(C) Meeting changing environment requirements ☐

(D) Management training, education and research ☐

6. Principles of management limit the boundary of managerial discretion so that their decisions may be free from personal prejudices and biases.

Which significance of principles of management is discussed here?

(A) Providing managers with useful insights into reality ☐

(B) Optimum utilisation of resources and effective administration ☐

(C) Scientific decisions ☐

(D) Meeting changing environment requirements ☐

7. Taylor called for complete mental revolution on the part of both management and workers. It meant that management and workers should transform their thinking. Management should share the gains of the company, if any, with the workers.

At the same time, workers should work hard and be willing to embrace change for the good of the company. The principle of management highlighted above is *[CBSE 2023]*

(A) science, not the rule of thumb ☐

(B) cooperation, not individualism ☐

(C) harmony, not discord ☐

(D) development of each and every person to his or her greatest efficiency and prosperity ☐

8. Companies outsourcing their non-core activities like share-transfer management and advertising to outside agencies is an example of one of the significance of principles of management, identify.

(A) Providing managers with useful insights into reality ☐

(B) Optimum utilisation of resources and effective administration ☐

(C) Scientific decisions ☐

(D) Meeting changing environment requirements ☐

9. Sirija Ltd. is a large company manufacturing electric motors. The company has several departments such as Production, Marketing, Finance and HR. Mr. Arun, CEO of the company set the target sale of ₹15 crore in a month. To increase the sales, the marketing manager, Mr. Sanyam insists on offering 10% discount to customers.

But the finance manager does not approve such discount as it would mean loss of revenue.

Because of dual subordination, the sales manager, Mr. Hritik could not achieve the sales target.

Which principle of management has been overlooked by this company?

(A) Discipline ☐

(B) Unity of direction ☐

(C) Unity of command ☐

(D) Subordination of individual interest to general interest ☐

10. Mr. Kautilya, the manager of Co-Co Ltd., found that Arpit, an employee is usually coming late to the office. Being new, he could not take strict action against him. Consecutively, other employees also started coming late.

Which principle of management Kautilya is not able to apply in the organisation?

(A) Unity of command ☐

(B) Discipline ☐

(C) Order ☐

(D) Authority and responsibility ☐

11. Cellulose Ltd. manufactures bikes and cars. It has two separate divisions for both of them. Each division has its own incharge, plans and executing resources. On no account, the working of two divisions overlap. There is systematic and efficient working. Along with that, people of various nationalities work together in a discrimination free environment.

Which principle of management is followed by Cellulose Ltd.?

(A) Unity of command and equity ☐

(B) Division of work and unity of direction ☐

(C) Unity of direction and equity ☐

(D) Esprit de corps and unity of direction ☐

12. The CEO of Radhe Cycles Pvt. Ltd. Mr. Kumar wants to get maximum output from the employees at a competitive cost. On the other hand Ramakaant, an employee of the company wants to get the maximum salary while working the least. The principle of management given by Fayol being violated by Ramakaant is ....

(A) remuneration ☐

(B) equity ☐

(C) discipline ☐

(D) subordination of individual interest to general interest ☐

13. "This principle will give rise to a spirit of mutual trust and belongingness among team members."

Which principle of management stated by Fayol is highlighted by this statement?

(A) Initiative ☐

(B) Esprit de corps ☐

(C) Equity ☐

(D) Remuneration of employees ☐

14. A traditional banking system is the one where the central authority manages all the transactions, maintains customer records and ensures compliance with regulations. Customers rely on the central authority to process transactions, store their funds and provide various financial services.

On the other hand, in a peer-to-peer file sharing network like BitTorrent, users can share files directly with other users without relying on a central server. Each user can download and upload files simultaneously, contributing to the network's overall file sharing capabilities.

Identify the management principle highlighted above.

(A) Scalar chain ☐

(B) Centralisation and decentralisation ☐

(C) Unity of direction ☐

(D) Unity of command ☐

15. The Fayol's principle of .... emphasises on kindliness and justice in the behaviour of managers towards workers.

(A) equity ☐

(B) discipline ☐

(C) esprit de corps ☐

(D) scalar chain ☐

16. Sangeeta visited 'Smile Dental Clinic' for treatment of toothache. She observed that the receptionist was seated at the reception desk, the place fixed for her.

Dental instruments were laid neatly in dental instrument trays and the used instruments were placed in the sterilisation area. There was a fixed place for everything and it was present there.

There was no hindrance in the work of the dentist and she was working with her maximum efficiency.

The principle of management followed at the 'Smile Dental Clinic' was [CBSE 2023]

(A) equity ☐
(B) discipline ☐
(C) order ☐
(D) initiative ☐

17. Pioneer Ltd. is dealing in fruit juices and hair oils. To ensure unity of action and coordination, it has made two separate divisions for each product. Each division has its own incharge, plans and execution resources. Thus, both the divisions are moving towards the same objectives through focused efforts.

Identify the principle of management followed by Pioneer Ltd. in the above case.

(A) Esprit de corps ☐
(B) Equity ☐
(C) Unity of direction ☐
(D) Authority and responsibility ☐

18. "A manager should have the right to punish a subordinate for willfully not obeying a legitimate order but only after sufficient opportunity has been given to a subordinate for presenting her/his case."

Identify the Fayol principle mentioned here.

(A) Scalar chain ☐
(B) Authority and responsibility ☐
(C) Subordination of individual interest to general interest ☐
(D) Discipline ☐

19. "Lazy personnel should be dealt with sternly to send the message that everyone is equal in the eyes of the management."

Identify the principle highlighted in the above statement.

(A) Equity ☐
(B) Remuneration of employees ☐
(C) Discipline ☐
(D) Subordination of individual interest to general interest ☐

20. Which principle of Fayol is depicted in the following image?

(A) Scalar chain ☐
(B) Remuneration of personnel ☐
(C) Equity ☐
(D) Simplification ☐

21. Identify the principle of management violated in the below picture.

(A) Subordination of individual interest to general interest ☐
(B) Esprit de corps ☐
(C) Unity of direction ☐
(D) Initiative ☐

22. Which of the following statements is correct?
(A) The principle of order ensures sense of fairness and justice to all workers. ☐
(B) A subordinate can receive orders from various superiors and can be efficient. ☐
(C) Every employee should be assigned one type of work to increase productivity. ☐
(D) None of the above ☐

23. Match the principles of management given in Coulmn I with their respective examples given in Coulmn II and choose the correct alternative

Column I		Column II
A. Division of work	(i)	After six months when the business was doing well, Nidhi awarded a cash bonus to each of the employees to honour her commitment.
B. Centralisation and decentralisation	(ii)	When it comes to settling the conflicts amomg employees, Reena tends to be more biased to her female employees.
C. Discipline	(iii)	The sales person are allowed to close a deal with a buyer by giving a maximum of 10 % discount, whereas the decision to give any further discount rests with Kamya as the final authority.
D. Equity	(iv)	For greater productivity, Neelam divides the work in smaller tasks.

Codes

	A	B	C	D	
(A)	(ii)	(iii)	(iv)	(i)	☐
(B)	(i)	(iv)	(ii)	(iii)	☐
(C)	(iv)	(iii)	(i)	(ii)	☐
(D)	(iii)	(i)	(ii)	(iv)	☐

24. Match the Column I with Column II in the following information

Column I		Column II
A. Any adhocism in this regard will create instability/ insecurity among employees.	(i)	Discipline
B. By following this principle, it ensures loyalty and devotion.	(ii)	Unity of direction
C. Workers and management both honour their commitments.	(iii)	Equity
D. All the units of an organisation should be moving towards the same objectives through coordinated and focussed efforts.	(iv)	Stability of personnel

Codes

	A	B	C	D	
(A)	(i)	(iii)	(iv)	(ii)	☐
(B)	(ii)	(iv)	(i)	(iii)	☐
(C)	(iv)	(iii)	(i)	(ii)	☐
(D)	(iii)	(i)	(ii)	(iv)	☐

25. Match the Column I with Column II in the following information

Column I		Column II
A. Centralisation	(i)	Dispersion of decision-making authority.
B. Decentralisation	(ii)	Decision-making authority at top level.
C. Scalar chain	(iii)	A clear line of authority from top to bottom.

Codes

	A	B	C	
(A)	(iii)	(i)	(ii)	☐
(B)	(ii)	(i)	(iii)	☐
(C)	(iii)	(ii)	(i)	☐
(D)	(i)	(iii)	(ii)	☐

26. 'Flavours of South' is a famous chain of South Indian restaurants. It believes in complete cooperation between the labour and management. It's management encourages the employees for their constructive suggestions. They take their employees into confidence for all important decisions.

Which principle of scientific management has been followed by 'Flavours of South'?

(A) Science, not rule of thumb ☐
(B) Harmony, not discord ☐
(C) Co-operation, not individualism ☐
(D) Development of each and every person to his or her greatest efficiency and prosperity ☐

27. Somesh works as a foreman in 'Lakshmi Automatives Ltd.', a company manufacturing cars. He is subordinate to Ramesh, who is the production incharge in the factory.

Somesh is incharge of timely and accurate completion of job by workers working in the production department.

There are three other foremen who work under the production incharge, while four other foremen work under Naresh, the planning incharge in the factory. Each of the eight foremen is a specialist in his area and gives orders to the workers relating to it. The technique of scientific management highlighted in the above case is

(A) method study ☐
(B) differential piece wage system ☐
(C) functional foremanship ☐
(D) standardisation and simplification of work ☐

28. Shreya Ltd., a well-established company has processes that are far too complex. Over time, these processes became a tangled web, persisting even when they are no longer effective or relevant. It tried to adjust and accumulate a variety of processes and procedures while adapting to changing circumstances. Raman, the manager suggested to the company to adopt a working model that simplifies the work process in a breeze, hence increasing productivity which also helps to remove the need for physical, stress and time-wasting meetings.

Identify the technique of Taylor adopted by Raman in the above para.

(A) Differential piece wage system ☐
(B) Functional foremanship ☐
(C) Standardisation and simplification ☐
(D) Time study ☐

29. Labour turnover and disengagement are the first indications that an employee is on the brink of quitting their job. To keep and retain your staff, companies are taking care about them.

Having opportunities to upskill oneself is now the number one characteristic that individuals feel, makes an excellent work environment.

Many industries and companies are investing their time and money in providing internal training to their employees through platforms like Coursera, Udemy, Youtube, and many off-job and on-job training methods.

Identify the scientific principle discussed above.

(A) Science not rule of thumb ☐
(B) Coordination not individualism ☐
(C) Harmony not discord ☐
(D) Development of personnel to their greatest efficiency and prosperity ☐

30. "Scientific management has, for its foundation, the firm conviction that the true interests of the two are one and the same; that prosperity for the employer cannot exist for a long time unless it is accompanied by prosperity for the employees and *vice-versa*."

Identify the scientific principle highlighted above.

(A) Science, not rule of thumb ☐
(B) Development of each and every person to his or her greatest efficiency and prosperity ☐
(C) Cooperation, not individualism ☐
(D) Harmony, not discord ☐

31. 'Brick layering' is an example of which technique of Taylor?

(A) Method ☐ (B) Motion ☐
(C) Fatique ☐ (D) Time ☐

32. "To establish standards of excellence and quality in materials" is one of the objectives of technique of scientific management.

Identify the technique of management.

(A) Functional foremanship ☐
(B) Differential piece wage system ☐
(C) Standardisation ☐
(D) Method study ☐

33. Identify the scientific method reflected below.

(A) Fatigue study ☐
(B) Method study ☐
(C) Motion study ☐
(D) Time study ☐

34. Which of the following statements is incorrect?

(A) Taylor was highly influential in reshaping the factory system of production ☐
(B) Taylor believed that contemporary management was amateurish and should be studied as a discipline ☐
(C) Personal experience is the basis of formation in Taylor's principles ☐
(D) Taylor wanted that workers should cooperate with the management and thus there would be no need of trade unions ☐

35. Match the Column I with Column II in the following information

	Column I		Column II
A.	These are procedures or methods, which involve a series of steps to be taken to accomplish desired goals.	(i)	Principles
B.	These have moral connotations.	(ii)	Techniques
C.	These are basic truths or guidelines for behaviour.	(iii)	Values

Codes

	A	B	C	
(A)	(i)	(ii)	(iii)	☐
(B)	(ii)	(i)	(iii)	☐
(C)	(ii)	(iii)	(i)	☐
(D)	(iii)	(ii)	(i)	☐

36. Match the Column I with Column II in the following information

	Column I		Column II
A.	Time study	(i)	Analysis of physical movements.
B.	Motion study	(ii)	Analysis of amount and frequency of rest intervals.
C.	Fatigue study	(iii)	Identification of most suitable way of doing a task.
D.	Method study	(iv)	Study of standard time to complete a task.

Codes

	A	B	C	D	
(A)	(iv)	(i)	(ii)	(iii)	☐
(B)	(ii)	(i)	(iv)	(iii)	☐
(C)	(iii)	(iv)	(i)	(ii)	☐
(D)	(i)	(iii)	(iv)	(ii)	☐

Assertion-Reason Questions

No. of Questions : **10** Suggested Time : **15 Minutes**

Direction Each of the question given below consist of the two statements; one labelled as **Assertion** (A) and other as **Reason** (R). List of common options applicable for each question is given below

(A) Both Assertion (A) and Reason (R) are true and Reason (R) is the correct explanation of Assertion (A)

(B) Both Assertion (A) and Reason (R) are true, but Reason (R) is not the correct explanation of Assertion (A)

(C) Assertion (A) is true, but Reason (R) is false

(D) Assertion (A) is false, but Reason (R) is true

You have to select the codesas *a, b, c* or *d* as your answer to the question by marking (✓) in the response box given against each option.

1. **Assertion (A)** The principles of management are intended to establish relationship between cause and effect so that they can be used in similar situation.

   Reason (R) Real business situations are predictable and perfect principles give solutions to the problems.

   (A) ☐ (B) ☐ (C) ☐ (D) ☐

2. **Assertion (A)** The principle of 'division of work' leads to specialisation and increases productivity.

   Reason (R) Division of work increases the scope of job rotation among employees.

   (A) ☐ (B) ☐ (C) ☐ (D) ☐

3. **Assertion (A)** The principle of 'scalar chain' refers to the chain of superiors ranging from the ultimate authority to the lowest rank.

   Reason (R) The scalar chain ensures that communication should follow the official chain of command.

   (A) ☐ (B) ☐ (C) ☐ (D) ☐

4. **Assertion (A)** The principle of 'unity of command' states that each employee should receive orders from one superior only.

   Reason (R) Unity of command prevents dual subordination and confusion among employees.

   (A) ☐ (B) ☐ (C) ☐ (D) ☐

5. **Assertion (A)** Centralisation refers to the concentration of decision-making authority at the top level of the management hierarchy.

   Reason (R) Decentralisation enhances the speed and quality of decisions made at various levels of the organisation.

   (A) ☐ (B) ☐ (C) ☐ (D) ☐

6. **Assertion (A)** The principle of 'equity' ensures fair treatment of employees by management.

   Reason (R) Equity is essential for creating dissatisfaction among employees.

   (A) ☐ (B) ☐ (C) ☐ (D) ☐

7. **Assertion (A)** The principle of 'order' states that there should be an orderly placement of men and materials.

   Reason (R) Orderly placement reduces wastage of resources and ensures smooth and systematic working of an organisation.

   (A) ☐ (B) ☐ (C) ☐ (D) ☐

8. **Assertion (A)** The principle of 'discipline' is essential for the smooth functioning of an organisation.

   Reason (R) Discipline means strict obedience to organisational rules and employment agreement.

   (A) ☐ (B) ☐ (C) ☐ (D) ☐

9. **Assertion (A)** The principle of 'remuneration of employees' states that the compensation for work done should be fair to both employees and the organisation.

   Reason (R) Fair remuneration helps in maintaining satisfaction and motivation among employees.

   (A) ☐ (B) ☐
   (C) ☐ (D) ☐

10. **Assertion (A)** If there is open communication system and goodwill, the workers desist from going on strikes; instead make trade unions to keep their demands.

    Reason (R) The principle of 'cooperation, not individualism' talks about complete cooperation between the labour and the management instead of individualism.

    (A) ☐ (B) ☐
    (C) ☐ (D) ☐

Correct/Incorrect Statements

No. of Questions : **10** Suggested Time : **15 Minutes**

Direction Each of the question given below consist of the two statements. List of common options applicable for each question is given below.

(A) Statement I is correct and Statement II is incorrect
(B) Statement I is incorrect and Statement II is correct
(C) Both statements are correct
(D) Both statements are incorrect

You have to select the codes as *a, b, c* or *d* as your answer to the question by marking (✓) in the response box given againest each option.

1. **Statement I** The principles of management are not rigid prescriptions, which have to be followed absolutely.

   Statement II They are flexible and can be modified by the manager when the situation so demands.

   (A) ☐ (B) ☐ (C) ☐ (D) ☐

2. **Statement I** Principles enable a better understanding of the relationship between human and material resources in accomplishing organisational purposes.

   Statement II Adherence to these principles will add to manager's knowledge, ability and understanding of managerial situations and circumstances.

   (A) ☐ (B) ☐ (C) ☐ (D) ☐

3. **Statement I** Management theory and management principles have also evolved in response to the demands.

   Statement II Scientific decisions must be timely, realistic and subject to measurement and evaluation.

   (A) ☐ (B) ☐ (C) ☐ (D) ☐

4. **Statement I** Principles equip the managers to foresee the cause and effect relationships of their decisions and actions.

   Statement II Wastages associated with a trial and error approach cannot be overcome.

   (A) ☐ (B) ☐
   (C) ☐ (D) ☐

5. **Statement I** The principle of unity of command states that each employee should receive orders from only one superior.

Statement II The principle of equity emphasises that employees should be treated fairly and impartially.

(A) ☐ (B) ☐ (C) ☐ (D) ☐

6. **Statement I** According to the principle of scalar chain, communication should follow a formal chain of command from the top level to the bottom level of the organisation.

Statement II The principle of division of work suggests that tasks should be divided into smaller and specialised components to enhance efficiency.

(A) ☐ (B) ☐ (C) ☐ (D) ☐

7. **Statement I** Centralisation refers to the concentration of decision-making authority at the top levels of management.

Statement II Decentralisation involves dispersing decision-making authority to lower levels of the organisation.

(A) ☐ (B) ☐ (C) ☐ (D) ☐

8. **Statement I** According to the principle of order, materials and personnel should be in the right place at the right time to ensure efficiency.

Statement II Stability of tenure of personnel suggests that management should strive to minimise employee turnover to maintain stability and continuity in operations.

(A) ☐ (B) ☐ (C) ☐ (D) ☐

9. **Statement I** Taylor is known for coinage of the term 'scientific management'.

Statement II Fayol broke up human activity into small parts and found out how it could be done effectively, in less time and with increased productivity.

(A) ☐ (B) ☐ (C) ☐ (D) ☐

10. **Statement I** Scientific management means knowing exactly what you want men to do and seeing that they do it in the best and cheapest way.

Statement II Taylor pioneered the introduction of the method of scientific inquiry into the domain of management practice.

(A) ☐ (B) ☐ (C) ☐ (D) ☐

Case Based Questions

No. of Questions : **2** Suggested Time : **10 Minutes**

Direction This section contains cases having 4 Questions of 1 mark each. You have to write the answer of each question based on the context of the related case.

Case 1 Mr. Roman Kumar is the managing director of a cosmetics manufacturing company. To boost sales, the board of directors decided to establish a full fledged marketing department. Mr. Kumar was entrusted with the task of finding a suitable candidate to head the proposed marketing department. After considering several candidates, he narrowed down his choices to two individuals: Biswajeet Dutt and Saurabh.

Mr. Biswajeet Dutt has an excellent track record in the company. During his ten years with the company, he has consistently shown a high degree of enthusiasm and initiative in his work. At 35 years old, he is dynamic and aggressive, focusing more on results than the means to achieve them. Despite occasional harshness, his leadership qualities are evident and he is willing to shoulder additional responsibilities.

He prefers a logical approach to business, recognising that it can lead to significant savings in human energy and time, rather than the hit and trial method.

On the other hand, Mr. Saurabh is known for his quick decision-making and proactive approach. During his 15 years with the company, he has earned the respect of his colleagues through his superior workmanship and pleasing manners.
He believes in employee participation in decision-making processes, fostering an environment where subordinates feel encouraged to share innovative ideas.

His leadership style has resulted in high job satisfaction among his team members and increased production in his department. He believed employees should be given reasonable time to show results. Any insecurity of job will result in high recruitment, selection and training cost.

Questions

(i) "During his ten years with the company, he has consistently shown a high degree of enthusiasm and initiative in his work." Identify Fayol's principle of management highlighted in the above lines.

(A) Discipline ☐ (B) Equity ☐

(C) Initiative ☐ (D) Esprit de corps ☐

(ii) "He believes in employee participation in decision-making processes, fostering an environment where subordinates feel encouraged to share innovative ideas."

Which scientific principle of management is being followed by Mr. Saurabh?

(A) Harmony, not discord ☐

(B) Development of each and every person to his or her greatest efficiency and prosperity ☐

(C) Science, not rule of thumb ☐

(D) Cooperation, not individualism ☐

(iii) "He prefers a logical approach to business, recognising that it can lead to significant savings in human energy and time; rather than the hit and trial method."

Which importance of principle of management is highlighted in this statement?

(A) Scientific decisions ☐

(B) Optimum utilisation of resources and effective administration ☐

(C) Providing managers with useful insight into reality ☐

(D) Fulfilling social responsibility ☐

(iv) "He believed employees should be given reasonable time to show results. Any insecurity of job will result in high recruitment, selection and training cost."

This statement relates to which of the following principles?

(A) Remuneration ☐

(B) Stability of personnel ☐

(C) Authority and responsibility ☐

(D) Esprit de corps ☐

Case 2 After completing her Bachelor in Fashion Designing from a well-known college in France, Aditi has opened a boutique in a posh market in Kolkata. She has divided the work in smaller units and each employee is well trained to perform his/her task efficiently. The sales persons are allowed to close a deal with a buyer by giving a maximum of 5 per cent discount, whereas the decision to give any further discount rests with Aditi as the final authority.

In the earlier period of her business venture, employees were asked to put in extra hours of work. In return she had promised to give them a special incentive within a year. Therefore, when the business was doing well, she honour her commitment by giving bonus to her employees. She also instructed her employees that communication from top to bottom should follow the official lines of command. However, she tends to be more biased towards her female employees, when it comes to solve the conflicts among employees. *[CBSE QB]*

Questions

(i) Aditi has divided the work in smaller units and each employee is well trained to perform his/ her task efficiently.

Which principle of management is being followed here?

(A) Centralisation and decentralisation ☐
(B) Division of work ☐
(C) Discipline ☐
(D) Order ☐

(ii) "The sales persons are allowed to close a deal with a buyer by giving a maximum of 5 per cent discount, whereas the decision to give any further discount rests with Aditi as the final authority." Identify the principle of management being followed here.

(A) Centralisation and decentralisation ☐
(B) Authority and responsibility ☐
(C) Unity of command ☐
(D) Unity of direction ☐

(iii) "Therefore, when the business was doing well, she honoured her commitment by giving bonus to her employees." Which principle of management is being highlighted here?

(A) Discipline ☐
(B) Order ☐
(C) Remuneration to employees ☐
(D) Unity of direction ☐

(iv) Aditi tends to be more biased towards her female employees, when it comes to solve the conflicts among employees. Which principle is being violated here?

(A) Discipline ☐
(B) Order ☐
(C) Equity ☐
(D) None of the above ☐

Subjective Questions

Free Response Questions, Open-ended Questions etc.

No. of Questions : **7** Suggested Time : **56 Minutes**

1. Kansal consulting firm, specialising in providing management consulting services, experienced communication breakdowns and delays. The lack of a defined hierarchy and communication protocol led to inefficiencies, missed deadlines, and confusion among team members.

   Without a clear chain of command, important information often got lost or delayed as it moved through various levels of the organisation. Decisions were frequently stalled as there was no designated authority responsible for approving and implementing them.

   Team members were uncertain about whom to report to or seek guidance from, leading to role confusion and inefficiencies. Ambiguity in reporting lines and decision-making authority increased the risk of operational errors.

   Identify and explain the principle of management violated by the company?

2. ABC Manufacturing Company recently implemented the principle of 'discipline' in its operations, aiming to positively impact employee behaviour and performance.

   Through clear communication of company policies, expectations and consequences for non-compliance, employees are now more aware of their roles and responsibilities.

   Regular training sessions on workplace conduct and adherence to safety protocols further reinforce the importance of discipline in maintaining a safe and efficient work environment.

As a result, employees demonstrate greater punctuality, attendance and adherence to quality standards, leading to improved overall productivity and morale.

Additionally, ABC Manufacturing has adopted a performance based remuneration system aligned with the principle of 'remuneration.'

Under this system, employees receive financial incentives based on their individual and team performance, productivity, and contribution to achieving company goals.

By tying compensation directly to performance outcomes, employees are motivated to enhance their discipline and productivity levels to earn higher rewards. This approach fosters a culture of accountability, where employees take ownership of their work and strive for continuous improvement to maximise their earnings.

As a result, ABC Manufacturing experiences higher levels of employee engagement, efficiency and competitiveness in the market.

(i) How can the principle of 'discipline' positively impact employee behaviour and performance in the manufacturing company?

(ii) Explain how a performance based remuneration system aligns with the principle of 'remuneration,' and how it can motivate employees to improve their discipline and productivity.

3. The manager of a retail store has a team of ten sales associates. To improve efficiency, she decides to implement the principle of 'division of work' and delegate specific tasks to each team member. However, one sales associate is unhappy with his assigned responsibilities and believes he should have more authority in decision-making.

(i) How can the principle of "division of work" help improve the store's efficiency and productivity?

(ii) How can the manager balance the delegation of tasks while ensuring appropriate authority is given to each team member? Explain in three points.

4. Flavours Ltd. was engaged in the business of making handmade chocolates. Lately, the business was expanding due to good quality and reasonable prices. As the demand was increasing, Flavours Ltd. decided to explore bakery products as well.

In order to make bakery products the company directed its workforce to work overtime but this resulted in multiple problems.

Due to increased pressure the efficiency declined and the workers had to take orders from more than one superior. Workers were overburdened and their health was also affected.

Gradually the quality of the products begins to decline and market share also, went down. The company realised that they had implemented changes without waiting for the required infrastructure.

Identify and explain the principles/ technique of Taylor/Fayol referred to in the above para.

5. Sanya, the production manager, disregards the organisation and coordination of human activities in the workplace, resulting in uncontrolled employee performance.

His employees often express concerns about inefficiencies due to disorganisation, lack of proper assignment of tasks and absence of a structured work schedule.

This disorganisation leads to wasted time and effort, as employees struggle to find tools and materials, ultimately decreasing productivity and prolonging production lead times.

Which principle of management is being violated in this scenario and how?

6. Acme Corporation, a large manufacturing company, faced stagnation and resistance to change due to entrenched attitudes and outdated practices among its workforce. Recognising the need for a cultural shift, the company focused on transforming mind sets and behaviours to embrace innovation and adaptability.

Employees felt more engaged and motivated, as they were empowered to contribute their ideas and make a meaningful impact on the organisation's success.

The transformative power of mind set shifts helped in organisa- tional change and achieving positive outcomes.

The general environment in the company is very supportive to the employees. The employee turnover ratio is very low.

(i) Which concept of management is discussed here?

(ii) Identify the scientific principle which follows the concept identified in (i).

(iii) Which principle of management is followed by Acme Corporation, considering the supportive environment and low employee turnover ratio?

7. Ankur Sachdeva did his MBA from ITB University. He decided to apply his knowledge of scientific management in the fast food restaurant chain Coffee Bean' set up by him. This restaurant was providing burgers, fries, shakes etc as a part of its menu.

Now-a-days people are quality conscious, so he was using standardised raw materials, processes, methods, working conditions, machinery etc.

The objective was to establish standards of excellence. By doing this, he was not only able to reduce the cost but was also able to provide new varieties of burgers, fries and shakes leading to increased turnover.

Ankur Sachdeva also believed that there was only one best method to maximise efficiency. As a result he developed best way of grilling burgers, cooking fries and preparing shakes. His main objective was to maximise the satisfaction of customers, which he was able to achieve.

Not only to learn the best way of doing a job, but to perform their tasks efficiently, Coffee Bean regularly invests in training and development programmes to equip employees with the necessary skill and knowledge. Coffee Bean believed that efficient employees will produce more and earn more. This will ensure their greatest efficiency and prosperity for both company and workers.

The above case highlights the use of Scientific principles and techniques by 'Coffee Bean'. Explain any one such principle and two techniques. [CBSE 2024]

Answers

If your answer matches with the answer given here then put (✓) in the box otherwise put (✗). In case you did not attempt the question leave the box blank.

Multiple Choice Questions

1. D ☐	2. B ☐
3. B ☐	4. D ☐
5. C ☐	6. A ☐
7. C ☐	8. D ☐
9. C ☐	10. B ☐
11. C ☐	12. D ☐
13. B ☐	14. B ☐
15. A ☐	16. C ☐
17. C ☐	18. B ☐
19. C ☐	20. A ☐
21. A ☐	22. C ☐
23. C ☐	24. C ☐
25. B ☐	26. C ☐
27. C ☐	28. C ☐
29. D ☐	30. D ☐
31. B ☐	32. C ☐
33. B ☐	34. C ☐
35. C ☐	36. A ☐

Assertion-Reason Questions

1. C ☐	2. C ☐
3. A ☐	4. A ☐
5. B ☐	6. C ☐
7. A ☐	8. A ☐
9. A ☐	10. D ☐

Your Score__________ *(No. of Correct Answers)*

Correct/Incorrect Statements

1. C ☐	2. C ☐
3. C ☐	4. A ☐
5. C ☐	6. A ☐
7. C ☐	8. C ☐
9. A ☐	10. C ☐

Your Score__________ *(No. of Correct Answers)*

Case Based Questions

1. (i) C ☐	(ii) D ☐
(iii) B ☐	(iv) B ☐
2. (i) B ☐	(ii) A ☐
(iii) A ☐	(iv) C ☐

Your Score__________ *(No. of Correct Answers)*

Explanations

Multiple Choice Questions

1. (D) Contingent
2. (B) The principle of "Optimum utilisation of resources and effective administration" in management emphasises efficiently using all available resources (human, financial, physical and informational) and managing operations effectively.
3. (B) Management principles are not rigid like principles of pure science; instead, they are broad guidelines for decision-making and behaviour.
4. (D) Management principles are not general rules for behaviour formed through common practice, they are instead broad guidelines derived from observation, experimentation and managerial experiences.
5. (C) By adopting improved management models and developing strategies for sustainable development, Coca-Cola aimed to adapt to the evolving business environment and meet the changing requirements imposed by external factors.

6. (A) This statement highlights the importance of principles of management in enabling managers to make decisions free from personal biases or prejudices, thus ensuring that their decisions are based on objective criteria rather than subjective influences.
7. (C) harmony, not discord
8. (D) Meeting changing environment requirements
9. (C) Unity of command states that an employee should receive orders from only one supervisor to avoid confusion and conflicting directives.
10. (B) The inability to enforce punctuality among employees indicates a lack of adherence to the principle of discipline, which emphasises the importance of orderly behaviour and adherence to rules and regulations within an organisation.
11. (C) Cellulose Ltd. adheres to the principle of unity of direction by ensuring that both the bike and car divisions operate towards a common goal or direction, which is likely the efficient manufacturing and distribution of vehicles.
12. (D) The principle of subordination of individual interest to general interest emphasises that individual interests should be subordinate to the general interest of the organisation.
13. (B) Esprit de corps
14. (B) The case illustrates the management principle of centralisation and decentralisation by contrasting a traditional banking system, which relies on a central authority, with a peer-to-peer file sharing network like BitTorrent, where users interact directly without a central server.
15. (A) Equity
16. (C) The principle of order, as articulated by Henri Fayol in his 14 principles of management, emphasises that there should be a place for everything and everyone and everything and everyone should be in their place.
17. (C) Unity of direction emphasises that all efforts within an organisation should be directed towards achieving the common goals of the organisation.
18. (B) Authority and responsibility emphasises that a manager should have the authority to issue orders and also the responsibility to ensure that these orders are carried out effectively.
19. (C) Discipline
20. (A) The principle of the scalar chain, proposed by Henri Fayol, refers to the clear and unbroken line of authority within an organisation.
21. (A) The principle of "subordination of individual interest to general interest" by Henri Fayol emphasises that the interests of the organisation should take precedence over the interests of individual employees.
22. (C) Every employee should be assigned one type of work to increase productivity.
23. (C) (iv) (iii) (i) (ii)
24. (C) (iv) (iii) (i) (ii)
25. (B) (ii) (i) (iii)
26. (C) The case exemplifies the principle of cooperation, not individualism, by fostering a culture of collaboration between labour and management, encouraging constructive suggestions from employees and involving them in important decision-making processes.
27. (C) Functional foremanship is a key concept in scientific management where specialised supervisors, known as foremen, oversee specific functions or areas of work.
28. (C) Taylor's principle of standardisation and simplification is aimed at streamlining complex processes to increase productivity and efficiency.
29. (D) The principle of "Development of personnel to their greatest efficiency and prosperity" emphasises the importance of investing in employees' growth and development to maximise their potential and well-being.
30. (D) Harmony, not discord emphasises the idea that there should be a harmonious relationship between employers and employees, where the interests of both parties are aligned for long-term prosperity.
31. (B) Motion

32. (C) Standardisation
33. (B) Method study, one of the techniques of scientific management proposed by Frederick Taylor, aims at improving the way tasks are performed to increase efficiency.
34. (C) Frederick Taylor's principles of scientific management were not based solely on personal experience but rather on systematic observation, experimentation and analysis of work processes.
35. (C) (ii) (iii) (i)
36. (A) (iv) (i) (ii) (iii)

Assertion-Reason Questions

1. (C) Real business situations are complex and dynamic and imperfect principles cannot give solutions to the problems.
2. (C) Division of work aims to improve efficiency by allowing employees to specialise in specific tasks. Job rotation, on the other hand, involves moving employees between different tasks to broaden their skills.
3. (A) Both Assertion (A) and Reason (R) are true and Reason (R) is the correct explanation of Assertion (A)
4. (A) Both Assertion (A) and Reason (R) are true and Reason (R) is the correct explanation of Assertion (A)
5. (B) While both statements are true, they describe different concepts. Centralisation focuses decision-making at the top, whereas decentralisation spreads it out.
6. (C) Equity aims to ensure fairness and justice in the workplace, leading to employee satisfaction, not dissatisfaction.
7. (A) Both Assertion (A) and Reason (R) are true and Reason (R) is the correct explanation of Assertion (A)
8. (A) Both Assertion (A) and Reason (R) are true and Reason (R) is the correct explanation of Assertion (A)
9. (A) Both Assertion (A) and Reason (R) are true and Reason (R) is the correct explanation of Assertion (A)
10. (D) If there is open communication system and goodwill, the workers desist from going on strikes and there will be no need of trade unions.

Correct/Incorrect Statements

1. (C) Both statements are correct
2. (C) Both statements are correct
3. (C) Both statements are correct
4. (A) Management principles indeed help managers anticipate the consequences of their decisions and actions, thereby reducing the need for a trial-and-error approach and minimising wastage.
5. (C) Both statements are correct
6. (A) Principle of division of work actually advocates for the specialisation of tasks to improve productivity, not merely dividing tasks into smaller components.
7. (C) Both statements are correct
8. (C) Both statements are correct
9. (A) Fayol focused on principles of management such as division of work, unity of command and unity of direction.
10. (C) Both statements are correct

Case Based Questions

1. (i) (C) This is evident from Mr. Biswajeet Dutt's continuous demonstration of enthusiasm and initiative in his work over the past ten years.
   (ii) (D) This is evident from his belief in employees' participation in the decision-making process, which fosters a collaborative work environment.
   (iii) (B) This is evident from Mr. Biswajeet Dutt's preference for a logical approach to business over a hit and trial method, emphasising the efficient use of resources and avoiding wastage.
   (iv) (B) Mr. Saurabh's belief in providing reasonable time to employees to show results indicates his understanding of the impor- tance of stability in the workforce to minimise recruitment, selection and training costs.

2. (i) (B) Aditi has divided the work into smaller units and ensured that each employee is well-trained to perform their tasks efficiently, aligning with the principle of division of work.
   (ii) (A) Aditi retains the authority to make final decisions regarding discounts, indicating centralisation of authority in this aspect of the business operations.
   (iii) (A) Aditi's commitment to honouring her promise of giving bonuses to her employees when the business was doing well reflects her adherence to the principle of discipline, which involves ensuring that rules and agreements are followed consistently.
   (iv) (C) Aditi's biasness towards her female employees in conflict resolution indicates a lack of equity or fairness in her managerial approach.

Subjective Questions

1. The principle of management violated here is 'unity of command.' This principle states that each employee should receive orders from only one superior to avoid confusion and conflict.
   In this case, the lack of a defined hierarchy and communication protocol led to multiple superiors and unclear reporting lines, resulting in communication breakdowns, delays and inefficiencies.

2. (i) The principle of 'discipline' positively impacts employee behaviour and performance in the manufacturing company by establishing clear expectations and guidelines for employee conduct.
   Through consistent enforcement of rules and policies, employees understand the consequences of their actions, leading to improved adherence to schedules, safety protocols and quality standards.
   By promoting a culture of accountability and professionalism, discipline fosters a productive work environment where employees are motivated to perform their best and contribute to the company's success.
   (ii) A performance based remuneration system aligns with the principle of 'remuneration' by linking employee compensation directly to their performance and contributions to the company's objectives.
   This system incentivises employees to enhance their discipline and productivity levels to earn higher rewards, such as bonuses, commissions, or profit-sharing opportunities.
   By rewarding merit and achievement, the remuneration system motivates employees to strive for excellence, driving overall organisational performance and competitiveness. Additionally, it helps in attracting and retaining top talent, as employees are incentivised to stay with the company and continuously improve their performance to maximise their financial rewards.

3. (i) The principle of 'division of work' improves store efficiency by
   (a) **Specialisation** Each team member focuses on specific tasks, boosting proficiency and reducing task switching.
   (b) **Time Management** Clear task allocation enhances resource allocation, minimising confusion and downtime.
   (c) **Coordination** Defined roles promote teamwork and prevent duplication, fostering smoother workflow.
   (ii) The manager ensures task delegation and authority balance by
   (a) **Clear Expectations** Communicating authority levels upfront prevents discontent.
   (b) **Training and Support** Providing resources and training builds confidence and competence.
   (c) **Feedback and Flexibility** Encouraging open communication resolves conflicts and ensures fairness.

4. (i) **Unity of Command** According to Fayol there should be one and only one boss for every individual employee. If an employee gets orders from two superiors at the same time the principle of unity of command is violated.
   The principle of unity of command states that each participant in a formal organisation should receive orders from and be responsible to only one superior. Fayol gave a lot of importance to this principle.

(ii) **Fatigue Study** A person is bound to feel tired physically and mentally if she/he does not rest while working.

The rest intervals will help one to regain stamina and work again with the same capacity. This will result in increased productivity. Fatigue study seeks to determine the amount and frequency of rest intervals in completing a task.

5. The principle of management which is violated here is the Fayol's principle of 'order'.

Fayol's principle of order says that everything has a place and everything should be at its place.

Essentially it means orderliness. If there is a fixed place for everything and it is present there, then there will be no hindrance in the activities of business/factory. This will lead to increased productivity and efficiency.

6. (i) The concept of management discussed here is 'mental revolution'. Taylor called for complete mental revolution on the part of both management and workers. It means that management and workers should transform their thinking.

(ii) The scientific principle which follows the concept identified is Harmony not discord.

(iii) Since the employee turnover ratio is low, the principle of management which must have been followed is 'stability of personnel'. Whenever there is violation of this principle of Fayol the employee turnover ratio increases. The increased employee turnover ratio is not good for an organisation and should be minimised.

7. Principles of scientific management highlighted are (any one)

(i) **Science, not Rule of Thumb** Taylor believed that there was only one best method to maximise efficiency which should be developed through study and analysis.

The method so developed should substitute "rule of thumb" throughout the organisation. This results in tremendous saving of human energy as well as wastage of time and material.

(ii) **Development of Each and Every Person to His or Her Greatest Efficiency and Prosperity** Taylor believed that each person should be scientifically selected. Then work assigned should suit his/her physical, mental and intellectual capabilities. To increase efficiency, they should be given the required training.

Techniques of scientific management highlighted here are

(i) **Method Study** The objective of method study is to find out one best way of doing the job. The objective of the whole exercise is to minimise the cost of production and maximise the quality and satisfaction of the customer. For this purpose, many techniques like process charts and operations research, etc are used.

(ii) **Standardisation and Simplification** Standardisation refers to the process of setting standards for every business activity. It can be standardisation of process, raw material, time, product, machinery methods or working conditions. Simplification involves streamlining processes or procedures to make them more straightforward and efficient. It aims to eliminate unnecessary complexities, redundancies, or steps that hinder productivity or clarity. This can include simplifying forms, reducing bureaucracy, or optimising workflows to achieve tasks with greater ease and effectiveness.

CHAPTER -3

Business Environment

Types & Nos. of Questions

Multiple Choice Questions	- 40
Assertion-Reason Questions	- 8
Correct/Incorrect Statements	- 8
Case Based Questions	- 3 Cases, each *with four Questions*
Subjective Questions	- 7

Trend Analysis

On the basis of analysis of last 2 years' papers, it is found that as an average 3 Multiple Choice Questions are asked from this chapter.

Focus Topics of the Chapter

- Concept of Business Environment
- Importance of Business Environment
- Dimensions of Business Environment
- Demonetisation

Multiple Choice Questions

No. of Questions : **40** Suggested Time : **60 Minutes**

Direction Each of the question given below is Multiple Choice Question (MCQ) i.e. there are Four Options/Choices for answer, out of which ONLY ONE is correct. You have to select the correct option. A response box is given with each option, mark (✓) in the box of the correct option. For each correct answer you will get 1 mark, while there is no penalty for incorrect answer or missed out questions.

1. These days consumers are making eco-friendly and healthy choices and are saying no to all things made of plastic and replacing it with stainless steel and ceramic containers, thus forcing business to change as well. Identify the feature of business environment highlighted above. *[CBSE 2023]*

   (A) Totality of external sources ☐
   (B) Specify and general forces ☐
   (C) Inter-relatedness ☐
   (D) Dynamic nature ☐

2. In some cases, new regulations can lead to increased uncertainty and volatility in the stock market, as investors may be unsure about how the regulations will impact the companies and industries will be affected. This can lead to short-term fluctuations in stock prices as investors adjust their positions.

   Identify characteristic of business environment reflected here.

   (A) Complexity ☐
   (B) Dynamic ☐
   (C) Uncertainty ☐
   (D) Relativity ☐

3. Godrej conducted a survey to understand why its brand was not resonating with the youth. The survey revealed that the average age of its customers was between 35 to 45 years, which posed a challenge in a country where 45 percent of the population is below 25. Additionally, the survey indicated that Godrej was not perceived as a technology brand by the youth, highlighting the dynamic nature of the business environment, where consumer preferences and perceptions evolve over time.

   Which characteristic of business environment is discussed above?

   (A) Complexity ☐ (B) Uncertainty ☐
   (C) Dynamic ☐ (D) Relativity ☐

4. In June 2013, Nabisco's Oreo, the most selling cookie brand globally, introduced a 'refreshing' new product extension. The new Oreo coming in watermelon flavour filling to create an association with its summer market launch.

   The internal flavour colouring aligned well with its Golden Oreo product. The filling of the snack was green and red to evoke the image of a slice of watermelon. Children were their target market because of their willingness to try new flavours.

   However, it was only available on shelves for under a year before being discontinued. The Watermelon Oreos case suggests that people's choices, even if popular in the moment, are not indicative of long-term success.

   Which characteristic of business environment is reflected here?

   (A) Complexity ☐ (B) Dynamic ☐
   (C) Uncertainty ☐ (D) Relativity ☐

5. 'Cartoony Planet' is a well-known indoor playground for organising parties for children in Noida. It has many play stations and it organises various activities for the kids to enjoy.

Looking at the increasing number of children visiting 'Cartoony Planet', a new indoor playground in the name of 'Tiny-Tots House' came up with advanced swings, play stations and entertainment activities near 'Cartoony Planet'.

To compare with the newly opened indoor playground, 'Cartoony Planet' also added some advanced swings and entertainment activities to attract more children. The above information highlights one of the features of 'business environment'. Identify the feature from the following. [CBSE 2023]

(A) Uncertainty ☐
(B) Dynamic nature ☐
(C) Relativity ☐
(D) Inter-relatedness ☐

6. Which of the following statements is incorrect?

(A) Understanding and analysis of business environment can be the basis for deciding the future course of action or training guidelines for decision-making ☐
(B) Management of every enterprise can benefit from being aware of these dimensions instead of being disinterested in them ☐
(C) Social trends present various opportunities and threats to business enterprises ☐
(D) Individual freedom, social justice, equality of opportunity and national integration are examples of social trends ☐

7. Which of the following statements is incorrect?

(A) Different elements or parts of business environment are closely inter-related ☐
(B) It becomes difficult to comprehend at once what exactly constitutes a given environment ☐
(C) A good understanding of environment by business managers enables them only to react to the forces external to their firms ☐
(D) Early identification of opportunities helps an enterprise to be the first to exploit them instead of losing them to competitors ☐

8. Match the Column I with Column II in the following information

	Column I		Column II
A.	It led to tax administration channelising savings into the formal financial system.	(i)	Environment
B.	It refers to the positive external trends or changes that will help a firm to improve its performance.	(ii)	Business environment
C.	It is a source of various resources for running a business.	(iii)	Demonetisation
D.	Just take the universe, subtract from it the subset that represents the organisation and the remainder is environment.	(iv)	Opportunities

Codes

	A	B	C	D	
(A)	(i)	(iv)	(iii)	(ii)	☐
(B)	(iii)	(iv)	(i)	(ii)	☐
(C)	(iv)	(ii)	(i)	(iii)	☐
(D)	(ii)	(i)	(iv)	(iii)	☐

9. Match the following

	Column I		Column II
A.	Uncertainty	(i)	Connected nature of different elements.
B.	First mover advantage	(ii)	Lack of predictability.
C.	Inter-relatedness	(iii)	Competitive benefit gained by a company.

Codes

	A	B	C			A	B	C	
(A)	(ii)	(iii)	(i)	☐	(B)	(iii)	(i)	(ii)	☐
(C)	(i)	(ii)	(iii)	☐	(D)	(ii)	(i)	(iii)	☐

10. Match the various characteristics of business environment given in Column I with their respective explanations in Column II [CBSE 2023]

Column I		Column II
A. Dynamic nature	(i)	Environment is a phenomenon that is relatively easier to understand in parts but difficult to grasp in its totality.
B. Complexity	(ii)	Business environment differs from country to country and even region to region.
C. Relativity	(iii)	Business environment keeps on changing, whether in terms of technological improvement or shifts in consumer preferences.

Codes

	A	B	C			A	B	C
(A)	(iii)	(ii)	(i)	☐	(B)	(ii)	(iii)	(i)
(C)	(iii)	(i)	(ii)	☐	(D)	(i)	(ii)	(iii)

11. KG Electrical Appliances, a company manufacturing bulbs incurred heavy expenditure on scientific research and development and invented a technology that made it possible to produce an energy efficient bulb that can last at least 15 times longer than a standard LED bulb.

This technology helped the company to increase its profitability and growth.

Identify the significance of the business environment highlighted above.

(A) It helps in assisting and policy formulation ☐
(B) It helps in tapping useful resources ☐
(C) It helps in improving performance ☐
(D) It helps the firm to identify threats and early warning signals ☐

12. Indian firms can prepare themselves to meet the threat by adapting such measures as improving the quality of the product, reducing cost of the production, engaging in aggressive advertising and so on.

Identify the advantage of business environment.

(A) It helps the firm to identify threats and early warning signals ☐
(B) It helps in improving performance ☐
(C) It helps in coping with rapid changes ☐
(D) It helps the firm to identify threats and early warning signals ☐

13. India has experienced a surge in start-ups and funding, with over 16,000 new tech companies added in 2020. Despite funding obstacles, investment firms have shown confidence in Indian start-ups, with a total funding of $ 8.4 billion in 2023.

India's start-up ecosystem soars with unprecedented growth and funding. The combination of a supportive regulatory environment, the availability of funding and the rise of digital technologies has created a range of opportunities for entrepreneurs to build and grow their businesses.

Investing in a start-up helped investors gain access to new technologies and ideas as start-ups are often at the forefront of innovation, working on cutting-edge projects that have the potential to change the world.

Identify the advantage of business environment.

(A) Business environment helps the firm to identify threats and early warning signals ☐
(B) Business environment helps in improving performance ☐
(C) Business environment helps in coping with rapid changes ☐
(D) Business environment helps planning and policy making ☐

14. The enterprise is an organisation that reconciles the workforce, real capital, techniques, information and knowledge to produce goods and services.

The enterprise cannot control or have any impact on the environment that it's surrounded by, only to adjust to it. Despite that, enterprises can be specialised in a special market segment, yet it will be subject to competitive pressure.

Furniture Manufacturing Tefik Canga Design has taken over the use of natural and unnatural resources to promote the development and growth or to solve financial and operational problems.

This research helped to prepare a growth model of a manufacturing enterprise in relation to the business environment. Implementation of the case is described and the profitability and productivity performance is analysed using five years of historical data product.

Therefore, by this study, it is expected to achieve results, that will improve the input-output relationship in order to increase the firm's productivity, increase the value of employees and create opportunities for development in order to cut production costs.

Which importance of business environment is related in the above case which helped Tefik Canga Design in developing an enterprise?

(A) Business environment helps the firm to identify threats and early warning signals ☐
(B) Business environment helps in improving performance ☐
(C) Business environment helps in tapping useful resources ☐
(D) Business environment helps in coping with rapid changes ☐

15. India is now prepping for cutting-edge technologies including 5G, AI, blockchain, augmented reality and virtual reality, machine learning and deep learning, robots, natural language processing, etc.

These will be critical in the government and industry, for planning or decision-making, expediting development or analysing deployment, issue solving or product creation, detecting new trends or drawing out linkages and associations.

Digitalisation opens doors to innovative products and services, expanding market reach and driving revenue growth.

In a rapidly evolving digital landscape, adopting cutting-edge technologies helps businesses stay ahead of the competition and maintain their market position.

Which point of importance is highlighted in the above case?

(A) Business environment helps the firm to identify threats and early warning signals ☐
(B) Business environment helps in improving performance ☐
(C) Business environment helps in coping with rapid changes ☐
(D) Business environment in planning and policy making ☐

16. Mr. Vivek is working as the General Manager of Oshin Hotels Ltd. Mr. Vivek observed that government was taking a special interest in the tourism industry as this sector is an important source of foreign exchange and employment promotion. On the basis of this news, the company decided to set-up hotels at several tourist places. Oshin Hotels Ltd. established 50 hotels before other companies considered this issue.

Very soon, this brand Oshin Hotels Ltd. became well known in the market. Identify the importance of business environment described here.

(A) It enables the firm to identify opportunities and getting the first mover advantage ☐
(B) It helps the firm to identify threats and early warning signals ☐
(C) It helps in tapping useful resources ☐
(D) It helps in improving performance ☐

17. 'Dolma' and 'Una' were gardeners with decades of hands on experience. They were the first ones to recognise the need of indoor gardens specially for plant lovers living in apartments.

They took advantage of this opportunity and decided to offer beautiful designing ideas for indoor gardening through their innovative venture 'My Space'.

'My Space' offered creative ideas like 'garden wall', 'hanging garden', 'window garden', 'book-shelf garden' and many more. Since there were no competitors they soon became the market leaders in the field.

From the following points, identify the importance of business environment highlighted above.

(A) Business environment helps the firm to identify threats and early warning signals ☐

(B) Business environment helps in tapping useful resources ☐

(C) Business environment enables the firm to identify opportunities and getting the first mover advantage ☐

(D) Business environment helps in assisting in planning and policy formulation ☐

18. Rajat was carrying a business of manufacturing plastic disposable like plastic plates, plastic cups and plastic straws. He heard about the upcoming ban on single use plastics. He was able to identify this external environmental trend which could hinder his firm's performance.

So, he took action and shifted to manufacturing the plates, cups and straws from bamboo and palm leaves. As a result, his business not only survived but was able to generate profit.

The point of importance of business environment highlighted above is *[CBSE 2024]*

(A) It enables the firm to identify opportunities and getting the first mover advantage ☐

(B) It helps the firm to identify threats and early warning signals ☐

(C) It helps in tapping useful resources ☐

(D) It helps in assisting planning and policy formulation ☐

19. 'SK Builders' became the market leader in the designer house segment as it was the first to recognise the need of using Aritificial Intelligence in designing houses in the changing environment of technological advancement. This highlights the following point of importance of business environment. *[CBSE 2024]*

(A) It helps to identify threats and early warning signals ☐

(B) It enables the firm to identify opportunities and getting the first mover advantage ☐

(C) It helps in tapping useful resources ☐

(D) It helps in improving performance ☐

20. In a recent ruling, the Supreme Court of India has ordered an immediate stop on commercial activities in a 500 metre radius of the Taj Mahal and asked Agra Development Authority to ensure compliance of its directive.

Which dimension of business environment is reflected here? *[CBSE 2023]*

(A) Social ☐

(B) Technological ☐

(C) Legal ☐

(D) Political ☐

21. The Government of India has recently come up with an amendment to Section 6 of the payment of Wages Act, 1936, to allow employees of certain industries to make payment through various electronic modes of payments.

The amendment will be applicable to all the public sector enterprises for wages disbursement using e-payment options. This is another milestone in the direction to further push to cashless economy.

Identify the dimension of business environment which relate to the above mentioned case.

(A) Political environment ☐
(B) Legal environment ☐
(C) Technological environment ☐
(D) All of the above ☐

22. Several initiatives have been undertaken by the Government of India to encourage domestic manufacturing and export of defence equipments. 'Make In India' in Defence, was one such scheme launched by the government to encourage companies across the world to manufacture defence products in India.

To which dimension of business environment does the above case relates to?

(A) Economic environment ☐
(B) Legal environment ☐
(C) Political environment ☐
(D) Social environment ☐

23. The advent of 'Talk GPT, in the information technology industry, companies have started investing in Artificial Intelligence in order to fulfill the expectations of the customers. Largely, the customers are showing a positive attitude to the new Artificial Intelligence based Talkbot. Identify the dimensions of the business environment being referred to here.

(A) Social and economic environment ☐
(B) Technological and social environment ☐
(C) Economic and technological environment ☐
(D) Legal and social environment ☐

24. Despite the remarkable progress, the Indian tech start-up ecosystem faces challenges such as funding accessibility, particularly for early-stage ventures and the need for a supportive regulatory environment.

However, the opportunities for growth are far outweigh these challenges. Government initiatives, such as the Start-up India Programme, provide crucial support to the sector.

Additionally, the increasing adoption of technology across industries is creating a fertile ground for start-ups to thrive.

The related elements of business environment being described in the above lines are

(A) political and technological ☐
(B) social and political ☐
(C) economic and political ☐
(D) technological and social ☐

25. The RBI Governor Shaktikanta Das announced the first monetary policy of FY25. One of the policy measures is repo rate kept unchanged at 6.5% along with the non-policy measure of introduction of a mobile app to access RBI's Retail Direct Scheme for participation in GSec market.

Identify the dimension of business environment discussed above.

(A) Legal and technological ☐
(B) Social and political ☐
(C) Economic and political ☐
(D) Technological and social ☐

26. Which of the following is an element of 'social environment'?

(A) Rates of saving and investment ☐
(B) Expectations from the workforce ☐
(C) The nature of relationship of our country with foreign countries ☐
(D) Planned outlay in public and private sectors ☐

27. Modi government is going to start Zero FIR for the first time after 75 years of the independence for the convenience of the citizens, with this initiative, the citizens will be able to lodge complaint even outside of their police station area.

Which dimension of business environment is discussed here?

(A) Technological environment ☐
(B) Economic environment ☐
(C) Political environment ☐
(D) Social environment ☐

28. With the presence of women in the work-force, there has been a shift towards formal wear, increased demand of electronic gadgets and increase in demand of cosmetics. The related dimension of business environment referred in the above lines is

(A) technological environment ☐
(B) social environment ☐
(C) political environment ☐
(D) economic environment ☐

29. Eating habits changed, skipping traditional meals has become a common eating habit of consumers worldwide. Already having a full plate with work, household, kids, fitness and other activities, many tend to invest less time in meal moments and the prepping that comes with it. Almost 1 in 2 consumers globally say they sometimes replace meals with a quick bite.

This presents an opportunity for products that act as a hybrid solution between meals. From breakfast to the late evening, consumers are looking for easy ways to satisfy their appetite in a healthful way, as they go through a hectic day.

Identify the dimension of business environment being reflected here.

(A) Technological environment ☐
(B) Social environment ☐
(C) Economic environment ☐
(D) Political environment ☐

30. No surrogate advertisement or indirect advertisement shall be made for goods or services whose advertising is otherwise prohibited or restricted by law, by circumventing such prohibition or restriction and portraying it to be an advertisement for other goods or services, the advertising of which is not prohibited.

Identify the dimension of business environment being reflected here.

(A) Technological environment ☐
(B) Social environment ☐
(C) Legal environment ☐
(D) Political environment ☐

31. Aiming to revive Jammu and Kashmir's attraction as a top location for film shooting the J & K film policy, 2021 offers a host of incentives to the filmmakers, such as subsidies and low long-term interest rates, for films with patriotic and certain other themes shot in J & K, for giving work opportunities to local artistes, etc. This will have an impact on business enterprises in the state.

Which component of business environment is highlighted above?

(A) Specific and general forces ☐
(B) Technological environment ☐
(C) Economic environment ☐
(D) Totality of external forces ☐

32. 'Pace' is a reputed chartered accountant firm which renders services to big MNC's. The chartered accountants of the firm are required to travel to Delhi and NCR for which they use company's cars. The firm decided to convert its petrol cars to electric cars in order to improve the quality of life of people.

Identify the dimensions of business environment.

(A) Political and legal environment ☐
(B) Legal and social environment ☐
(C) Technological and political environment ☐
(D) Social and technological environment ☐

33. Which dimension of business environment is shown in the below image?

(A) Legal ☐
(B) Political ☐
(C) Technological ☐
(D) Economic ☐

34. Which dimension of business environment is shown in the below image?

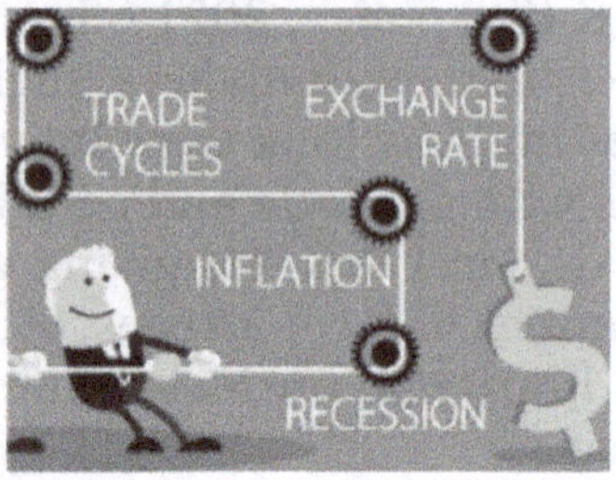

(A) Legal ☐ (B) Social ☐
(C) Technological ☐ (D) Economic ☐

35. Which dimension of business environment is shown in the below image?

(A) Legal ☐
(B) Social ☐
(C) Technological ☐
(D) Political ☐

36. The below symbol is depicting the .... environment.

(A) Legal ☐ (B) Social ☐
(C) Technological ☐ (D) Political ☐

37. Which of the following statements is incorrect?

(A) Political stability builds up confidence among business people to invest in the long-term projects for the growth of the economy ☐
(B) The attitudes of government officials towards business always have positive or negative impact upon business ☐
(C) Political uncertainty may create fear in the minds of investors ☐
(D) Technological improvements may render existing products obsolete ☐

38. Match the Column I with Column II in the following information

	Column I		Column II
A.	Planned outlay in private and public sectors.	(i)	Technological
B.	Composition of family.	(ii)	Economic
C.	The nature of relationship of our country with foreign countries.	(iii)	Social
D.	Shifts in demand from steam locomotives to diesel and electric engines.	(iv)	Political

Codes

	A	B	C	D	
(A)	(i)	(iii)	(iv)	(ii)	☐
(B)	(ii)	(iv)	(iii)	(i)	☐
(C)	(ii)	(iii)	(iv)	(i)	☐
(D)	(iv)	(ii)	(i)	(iii)	☐

39. The Government of India made an announcement regarding demonetisation of the Indian economy on 8th November, 2016 with profound implications for it. The process which put restrictions on convertibility of domestic money and bank deposits was meant to create a less-cash economy.

One argument against the cash-lite economy is that

(A) internet connectivity is a prerequisite ☐

(B) more people will be introduced into the formal economy ☐

(C) financial saving will increase ☐

(D) tax evasion will be reduced ☐

40. Which of the following concept is highlighted in the below image?

(A) Liberalisation ☐ (B) Globalisation ☐

(C) Demonetisation ☐ (D) None of these ☐

Assertion-Reason Questions

No. of Questions : **8** Suggested Time : **12 Minutes**

Direction Each of the question given below consist of the two statements; one labelled as **Assertion** (A) and other as **Reason** (R). List of common options applicable for each question is given below

(A) Both Assertion (A) and Reason (R) are true and Reason (R) is the correct explanation of Assertion (A)

(B) Both Assertion (A) and Reason (R) are true, but Reason (R) is not the correct explanation of Assertion (A)

(C) Assertion (A) is true, but Reason (R) is false

(D) Assertion (A) is false, but Reason (R) is true

You have to select the codes as *a, b, c* or *d* as your answer to the question by marking (✓) in the response box given against each option.

1. **Assertion** (A) Uncertainty is a feature of the business environment due to unpredictable external factors.

Reason (R) Businesses must navigate uncertain conditions arising from market fluctuations and regulatory changes.

(A) ☐ (B) ☐ (C) ☐ (D) ☐

2. **Assertion** (A) Inter-relatedness refers to the inter-connectedness of different elements within the business environment.

Reason (R) Understanding these inter-connections helps businesses anticipate changes and adapt their strategies accordingly.

(A) ☐ (B) ☐ (C) ☐ (D) ☐

3. **Assertion** (A) First mover advantage enables businesses to capture market share by introducing innovative products.

Reason (R) Being the first to market allows firms to establish brand loyalty and set industry standards.

(A) ☐ (B) ☐ (C) ☐ (D) ☐

4. **Assertion** (A) Economic environment consists of factors such as customs, traditions and social trends.

Reason (R) These economic indicators impact consumer purchasing power and business investment decisions.

(A) ☐ (B) ☐

(C) ☐ (D) ☐

5. **Assertion (A)** Social environment refers to the cultural norms, values and demographic trends prevailing in a society.

Reason (R) Businesses must adapt their strategies to align with societal expectations and consumer preferences.

(A) ☐ (B) ☐ (C) ☐ (D) ☐

6. **Assertion (A)** Political environment encompasses government policies, regulations and political stability.

Reason (R) Stable political conditions foster investor's confidence and encourage long-term investments.

(A) ☐ (B) ☐ (C) ☐ (D) ☐

7. **Assertion (A)** Legal environment includes laws and regulations that govern business operations and relationships.

Reason (R) Compliance with legal requirements is essential to avoid legal risks and protect stakeholders' interests.

(A) ☐ (B) ☐ (C) ☐ (D) ☐

8. **Assertion (A)** Technological environment comprises advancements in science and technology that drive innovation.

Reason (R) Businesses leverage technology to enhance productivity and gain competitive advantages in the market.

(A) ☐ (B) ☐ (C) ☐ (D) ☐

Correct/Incorrect Statements

No. of Questions : **8** Suggested Time : **12 Minutes**

Direction Each of the question given below consist of the two statements. List of common options applicable for each question is given below

(A) Statement I is correct and Statement II is incorrect
(B) Statement I is incorrect and Statement II is correct
(C) Both statements are correct
(D) Both statements are incorrect

You have to select the codes as *a, b, c* or *d* as your answer to the question by marking (✓) in the response box given against each option.

1. **Statement I** Besides opportunities, environment happens to be the source of many threats.

Statement II Environmental awareness can help managers to identify various threats on time and serve as an early warning signal.

(A) ☐ (B) ☐ (C) ☐ (D) ☐

2. **Statement I** Business environment is dynamic in nature.

Statement II Dynamic nature implies that the business environment is constantly changing and evolving.

(A) ☐ (B) ☐ (C) ☐ (D) ☐

3. **Statement I** First mover advantage is a key importance of the business environment.

Statement II First mover advantage allows businesses to have a competitive advantage.

(A) ☐ (B) ☐ (C) ☐ (D) ☐

4. **Statement I** Inter-relatedness implies that various elements of the business environment are closely connected.

Statement II Economic environment encompasses social trends and cultural values.

(A) ☐ (B) ☐
(C) ☐ (D) ☐

5. **Statement I** It is imperative for the management of every enterprise to obey the law of the land.

Statement II Government is discretionary for better business performance.

(A) ☐ (B) ☐ (C) ☐ (D) ☐

6. **Statement I** The significance of political conditions in business success lies in the predictability of business activities under stable political conditions.

Statement II There may be uncertainty of business activities due to political unrest and threats to law and order.

(A) ☐ (B) ☐ (C) ☐ (D) ☐

7. **Statement I** Technological environment includes factors such as GDP growth and inflation rates.

Statement II Inter-relatedness helps businesses identify opportunities and gain the first mover advantage.

(A) ☐ (B) ☐ (C) ☐ (D) ☐

8. **Statement I** Demonetisation involves the discontinuation of a currency unit's legal status.

Statement II Demonetisation is a process undertaken by governments to introduce new currency notes.

(A) ☐ (B) ☐ (C) ☐ (D) ☐

Case Based Questions

No. of Questions : **3** Suggested Time : **15 Minutes**

Direction This section contains 3 cases each having 4 questions of 1 mark each. You have to write the answer of each question based on the context of the related case.

Case 1 In 1868, Tata Gamsi found Tata group. It is the largest conglomerate in India and is owned by Tata Sons. Tata Motors is a leader in manufacturing of commercial, passenger, military and electric vehicles. It is also world's 4th largest truck and 2nd largest bus manufacturer by volume.

In January 2008, Tata Motors introduced Tata Nano, dubbed as the 'people's car' and also known as world's cheapest car. The car was launced in March 2009 which created a significant impact in the Indian automobile market. Tata Motors Ltd. is one of the few companies which has its own R&D centers. It has established an engineering research centre at Pune (with a strength of around 3,500 personnel).

The main target group of customers for Tata Nano are the lower and middle income families in India, many of whom resisted purchasing four wheelers mainly due to the price affordability and maintenance cost. Launching of Tata Nano gave an opportunity for those groups to purchase a car within their means.

During the initial launch, Tata Nano was priced at about ₹ 1 lakh. In December 2008, the cost of the car increased significantly due to higher raw material costs. Further in 2013, Tata Nano was rated as the most trusted four wheeler brand by Brand Trust Report India Study.

Tata Motors was so confident about Nano that they thought this is going to be a massive success.

But it failed and became one of the most disaster products in the history of marketing. So many Nano cars catch fire. This created a buzz in media.

Ratan Tata says, "It (Nano) became termed as the cheapest car by the public and I'm sorry to say, by ourselves, not by me, but the company when it was marketing it. I think that is unfortunate."

Questions

(i) Identify the related dimension of business environment which led to fall in demand for Nano.

(A) Political dimension ☐
(B) Legal dimension ☐
(C) Economic dimension ☐
(D) Social dimension ☐

(ii) After the announcement of Nano, the second hand market of cars faces a drop in price by 15% to 20%. Name the related feature of business environment which influenced the business of second hand cars.

(A) Dynamic nature ☐
(B) Inter-relatedness ☐
(C) Totality of external factors ☐
(D) Uncertainty ☐

(iii) The above case highlights one of the points related to the importance of business environment which led to failure of Nano cars. Identify.

(A) It helps in improving performance ☐
(B) It helps in coping with rapid changes ☐
(C) It helps the firm to identify threats and early warning signals ☐
(D) It helps in assisting in planning and policy formulation ☐

(iv) "It (Nano) became termed as the cheapest car by the public and I'm sorry to say, by ourselves, not by me, but the company when it was marketing it. I think that is unfortunate."

One of the major reasons for consumers being unable to accept 'people's car' (also known as world's cheapest car) was

(A) less powerful engine ☐
(B) weak presence in the global market ☐
(C) safety issues making consumers want to find a similar car with safer designs ☐
(D) better availability of cars ☐

Case 2 In 1992, Pepsi launched a new colourless soft drink called 'Crystal Pepsi.' At that time, it was a trend to launch drinks and products associated with purity and health. Pepsi concluded that a clear, colourless soft drink was the answer.

Pepsi marketed the new formula as a pure, caffeine-free alternative to the classic reddish-brown regular colas. At the time, sodas had a negative and unhealthy image and consumers were turning to healthier alternatives, such as natural juices.

There was a long list of colas, diet colas, caffeinated colas and other beverages on the shelves and Pepsi thought it was a good idea to launch another cola. After a positive response through focus groups testing and market research, the company launched Crystal Pepsi in April 1992. The marketing slogan for Crystal Pepsi was "You have never seen a taste like this."

But they didn't realise that its colourless look would be the main problem.

Although initial sales were promising, consumers were not satisfied with the taste. Sales (about $ 470 million in the first year) were probably more out of curiosity than anything else.

It tasted similar to the original Pepsi. Other colourless soft drinks like 7UP and Sprite had a citrus or lemon flavour, but consumers were not sure what Crystal Pepsi should taste like.

There was no similar product to compare it to, which is crucial for our brains to determine the value of something, in this case taste.

The colour of food and beverages has a strong influence on the perception of taste and flavours. It was toying with the idea of launching a coffee drink with a pink colour to make it more fun. But most people find it tastes like strawberry.

In conclusion, the launch of Crystal Pepsi was based on the assumption that consumers would prefer a 'clear' beverage over a traditional cola. Health conscious and less frequent cola drinkers were the target market of Crystal Pepsi.

But Crystal Pepsi didn't present an image of soft drink which is healthier to most consumers as it was supposed to be. However, it failed to provide the image of healthy and distinctive beverage, so Crystal Pepsi could not fully attract its target market.

Questions

(i) In the context of the above given case, identify one valid importance of business environment.

(A) Business environment helps in improving performance ☐

(B) Business environment helps in coping with rapid changes ☐

(C) Business environment helps in tapping resources ☐

(D) Business environment helps in assisting in planning and policy formulation ☐

(ii) "It failed to provide the image of healthy and distinctive beverage, so Crystal Pepsi could not fully attract its target market." Which dimension of business environment is reflected in the statement?

(A) Political dimension ☐

(B) Legal dimension ☐

(C) Social dimension ☐

(D) Economic dimension ☐

(iii) Which feature of the business environm-net is focused in the above paragraph?

(A) Relativity ☐

(B) Complexity ☐

(C) Dynamic ☐

(D) Uncertainty ☐

(iv) Identify the dimension of the business environment mentioned in the following statement.

"Consumers were turning to healthier alternatives, such as natural juices."

(A) Economic environment ☐

(B) Technological environment ☐

(C) Social environment ☐

(D) Legal environment ☐

Case 3 The name and taste of Coca-Cola is known to almost each and every individual in India as well as throughout the world. This carbonated soft drink holds the most market share in the soft drink market and got itself a special seat in each and every gathering.

The Coca-Cola Company has on occasion introduced other cola drinks under the Coke name. The most common of these are Diet Coke, along with others including Caffeine free Coca-Cola, Diet Coke Caffeine- free, Coca-Cola Zero Sugar, Coca-Cola Cherry, Coca-Cola Vanilla and the list goes on.

It has capitalised on each and every opportunity to market itself effectively and place itself in the middle of every gathering. The main reason for such an outstanding placement of product goes to the way they have established the connection between every occasion and the need for Coke to be present there, product design and creative advertising. *[CBSE QB]*

Questions

(i) In the context of the above given case, identify one valid importance of business environment.

(A) Enables a firm to identify opportunities and getting first mover advantage ☐

(B) Uncertainty ☐

(C) Delay in action ☐

(D) Pervasive function ☐

(ii) Identify the feature of business environment which the Coca-Cola Company managed to get in their favour.

(A) Complex ☐

(B) Specific and general forces ☐

(C) Futuristic ☐

(D) Mental exercise ☐

(iii) Which business environment did Coca-Cola majorly tap into?

(A) Technological environment ☐

(B) Social environment ☐

(C) Political environment ☐

(D) Economic environment ☐

(iv) Which of the following is not a product of Coca-Cola?

(A) Diet Coke Caffeine-free ☐

(B) Coca-Cola Zero Sugar ☐

(C) Coca-Cola Avocado ☐

(D) Coca-Cola Cherry ☐

Subjective Questions

Free Response Questions, Open-ended Questions etc.

No. of Questions : **7** Suggested Time : **56 Minutes**

1. Due to fast moving life of the corporates, the stress is a common problem amongst the working people. To beat the stress people are seeking yoga classes and counselling sessions.

(i) In the light of the above para, which dimension of the business environment is highlighted?

(ii) State any two features of business environment.

2. Kay Ltd. were planning to start a new project in Mumbai. Krishna, the CEO of the company wanted to understand the business environment of the area first. On analysis, he realised that it is very difficult to understand the business environment of Mumbai until it was divided into different business dimensions like legal, political, economic, social and technological conditions.

After comprehending the business scenarios, the company embarked on studying the intricate interconnections between various elements of the business environment. They gave a proper shape to their research and the business got started with full force.

Later they realised that the products they were selling in Mumbai were more fit for the American culture and decided to start a new branch in Columbia, where the demand of their products was very high from the first day.

By excelling in these areas, the company was able to establish itself as a renowned global brand, gaining recognition and market leadership in a relatively short period. The reason for its success in different countries was the adaptability it showed in meeting the changing environment.

The company kept track of all happenings and did a periodic survey of the choices of the customers. It recognised that there was no surety in the nature of market and it was very unpredictable.

Quoting lines from the above paragraph, identify and explain the features of business environment highlighted in the above case.

3. 'Konark Ltd.' is an electronic goods manufacturing enterprise situated in Shivpuri, Madhya Pradesh. It is earning a very low revenue in comparison to a competing electronic goods manufacturing enterprise, 'Nova Ltd.' situated in Mumbai.

Both Konark's and Nova's operations are affected directly by the investors, customers, competitors and suppliers, which are unique to their respective locations.

In addition to this, individuals firms of this field are affected indirectly by the factors like the money supply in the economy, composition of the families, the technological changes, etc.

(i) Identify and state the feature of the concept discussed in the above paragraph.

(ii) Also, state any four points of importance of this concept.

4. "Government of India banned Chinese apps due to face off between China and India on the Lure of Actual Control."

In its reasoning then, the ministry had said that these apps were "prejudicial to sovereignty and integrity of India, defence of India, security of State and public order." It created fear in the minds of Chinese investors.

Which component of business environment is responsible for the decision?

5. The Government of India has recently come up with an amendment to Section 6 of the Payment of Wages Act, 1936, to allow employers of certain industries to make payment through various electronics modes of payments.

The amendment will be applicable to all the public sector undertakings for wages disbursement using e-payment options. This is another milestone in the direction to further push to cashless economy.

ldentify and explain any two dimensions of business environment which relate to the above mentioned case.

6. In 5th September, the US Environmental Protection Agency charged AutoCorp with installing software in their diesel powered cars that allowed the vehicles to cheat on EPA emissions tests.

In a complaint filed in federal court, the FTC alleges that during this seven years period, AutoCorp deceived consumers by selling or leasing more than 5,50,000 diesel cars based on false claims that the cars were low emission, environmentally friendly, met emissions standards and would maintain a high resale value.

On the top of potential fines for false advertising, the company could have to pay up to $ 61 billion for violating the Clean Air Act.

(i) Identify the dimension of business environment highlighted above.

(ii) Also state any two importance of the business environment.

7. One of the decisions of government aimed to curb black money, corruption and counterfeit currency, leading to increased transparency and formalisation of the economy.

The push for digital transactions accelerated the adoption of digital payment platforms and financial inclusion.

This led to an increase in bank deposits, liquidity in the banking system and a push towards financial inclusion.

(i) Identify the concept reflected in the above para.

(ii) What was the impact of the above decision on various sectors of economy?

Answers

If your answer matches with the answer given here then put (✓) in the box otherwise put (✗). In case you did not attempt the question leave the box blank.

Multiple Choice Questions

1. C ☐	2. C ☐
3. C ☐	4. C ☐
5. B ☐	6. D ☐
7. C ☐	8. B ☐
9. A ☐	10. C ☐
11. C ☐	12. A ☐
13. B ☐	14. C ☐
15. B ☐	16. A ☐
17. C ☐	18. B ☐
19. B ☐	20. C ☐
21. C ☐	22. C ☐
23. B ☐	24. A ☐
25. A ☐	26. B ☐
27. C ☐	28. B ☐
29. B ☐	30. C ☐
31. C ☐	32. D ☐
33. C ☐	34. D ☐
35. B ☐	36. A ☐
37. B ☐	38. C ☐
39. A ☐	40. C ☐

Your Score_________ *(No. of Correct Answers)*

Assertion-Reason Questions

1. A ☐	2. A ☐
3. B ☐	4. C ☐
5. B ☐	6. C ☐
7. A ☐	8. A ☐

Your Score_________ *(No. of Correct Answers)*

Correct/Incorrect Statements

1. C ☐	2. A ☐
3. C ☐	4. A ☐
5. A ☐	6. C ☐
7. D ☐	8. C ☐

Your Score_________ *(No. of Correct Answers)*

Case Based Questions

1. (i) D ☐	(ii) B ☐
(iii) C ☐	(iv) C ☐
2. (i) C ☐	(ii) C ☐
(iii) B ☐	(iv) C ☐
3. (i) A ☐	(ii) B ☐
(iii) B ☐	(iv) C ☐

Your Score_________ *(No. of Correct Answers)*

Explanations

Multiple Choice Questions

1. (C) Inter-relatedness
2. (C) Uncertainty
3. (C) The fact that Godrej's brand was not resonating with the youth indicates that consumer preferences are evolving, reflecting the dynamic nature of the business environment.
4. (C) Despite Nabisco's Oreo introducing a new product extension, the Watermelon Oreos, which seemed popular initially, was discontinued within a year.
   This discontinuation indicates the uncertainty surrounding consumer preferences and the long-term success of new product offerings.
5. (B) The dynamic nature of the business environment refers to its constant and rapid change. This can be due to various factors such as technological advancements, shifts in consumer preferences, regulatory updates and competitive pressures.
6. (D) Individual freedom, social justice, equality of opportunity and national integration are not examples of social trends but rather fundamental principles or values underlying societal norms and behaviours.
7. (C) A good understanding of the business environment enables managers not only to react to external forces but also to proactively anticipate and shape them to their advantage.

8. (B) (iii) (iv) (i) (ii)
9. (A) (ii) (iii) (i)
10. (C) (iii) (i) (ii)
11. (C) The significance of the business environment highlighted is that it helps in improving performance by enabling the company to innovate and develop a technology that increases profitability and growth.
12. (A) It helps the firm to identify threats and early warning signals
13. (B) The supportive regulatory environment, availability of funding and advancements in digital technologies create opportunities for entrepreneurs to build and grow their businesses, ultimately contributing to the improvement of business performance.
14. (C) The business environment facilitated Tefik Canga Design in accessing and utilising valuable resources effectively. This could include factors such as market opportunities, technological advancements, financial resources and human capital, which contributed to the development and growth of the enterprise.
15. (B) The adoption of cutting-edge technologies such as 5G, AI, blockchain and others enables businesses to enhance their performance by streamlining processes, making data driven decisions and offering innovative products and services. This technological advancement helps them stay competitive, expand their market reach and drive revenue growth.
16. (A) The business environment can facilitate obtaining a first mover advantage by providing insights into market dynamics, emerging trends and consumer preferences. By closely monitoring the environment, businesses can identify untapped opportunities and act swiftly to capitalise on them before competitors do.
17. (C) Dolma and Una recognised a market need for indoor gardening solutions and leveraged this opportunity to become market leaders. This demonstrates how understanding the business environment can provide a first mover advantage by identifying opportunities before competitors.
18. (B) Rajat was able to foresee the upcoming ban on single-use plastics as a threat to his business. By identifying this early warning signal, he took proactive steps to adapt his business, ensuring its survival and profitability.
19. (B) SK Builders recognised the need for using artificial intelligence in designing houses, which was a new opportunity in the technologically advancing market. By acting on this insight first, they gained the first mover advantage and became the market leader in the designer house segment.
20. (C) The legal business environment encompasses the set of laws, regulations and legal frameworks within which businesses operate. It includes both national and international laws that govern various aspects of business activities.
21. (C) The dimension of the business environment related to the mentioned case is the technological environment because the amendment allowing electronic modes of payment reflects advancements in technology, facilitating a move towards a cashless economy.
22. (C) The political environment refers to the influence of government policies, regulations and political stability on businesses.
23. (B) The scenario involves both technological advancements, such as Artificial Intelligence (AI) and societal reactions, showcasing the intersection of technology and social attitudes.
24. (A) Challenges related to funding accessibility and the need for a supportive regulatory environment, are political factors. Additionally, it highlights the opportunities arising from increasing technology adoption, indicating the importance of technological aspects in the business environment.
25. (A) Legal policies are regarding monetary regulations and the technological advancements in digital access to financial markets are crucial factors shaping the business landscape.
26. (B) In the social environment of a business, expectations from the workforce refer to the societal norms, values and beliefs that influence how employees are perceived and treated within the organisation.
27. (C) Political environment
28. (B) social environment
29. (B) This case reflects the social environment dimension as it highlights changes in consumer eating habits and lifestyle choices, such as the trend towards skipping traditional meals in favour of quick and convenient food options.

30. (C) Regulations prohibiting surrogate or indirect advertising falls under the legal dimension of the business environment. This dimension encompasses laws and regulations that businesses must comply with.

31. (C) The economic environment encompasses the various economic factors that influence businesses' performance and decision-making. These include economic growth rates, interest rates, inflation, unemployment levels, fiscal and monetary policies, exchange rates and global economic trends.

32. (D) The firm's decision to convert its petrol cars to electric cars reflects a response to social concerns about improving the quality of life (social environment) and the adoption of new, sustainable technology (technological environment).

33. (C) Technological

34. (D) Economic environment pertains to factors like inflation, GDP growth and employment rates influencing business activities.

35. (B) Social

36. (A) Legal environment encompasses laws and regulations governing business operations, ensuring compliance and legal protection.

37. (B) While government attitudes can indeed influence business, they may not always have a direct positive or negative impact; their impact can vary depending on the specific policies and actions taken by officials.

38. (C) (ii) (iii) (iv) (i)

39. (A) This implies that without reliable internet access, individuals may face challenges in adopting digital payment methods, hindering the transition to a cashless economy.

40. (C) Demonetisation

Assertion-Reason Questions

1. (A) Both Assertion (A) and Reason (R) are true and Reason (R) is the correct explanation of Assertion (A)

2. (A) Both Assertion (A) and Reason (R) are true and Reason (R) is the correct explanation of Assertion (A)

3. (B) Both Assertion (A) and Reason (R) are true, but Reason (R) is not the correct explanation of Assertion (A)

4. (C) Economic environment includes GDP growth, inflation rates and monetary policies, which impact the overall economic conditions. These indicators influence consumer purchasing power and investment decisions, providing a logical connection between the assertion and reason.

5. (B) Both Assertion (A) and Reason (R) are true, but Reason (R) is not the correct explanation of Assertion (A)

6. (C) Stable political conditions may influence investor confidence, but they are not the only factor at play.

7. (A) Both Assertion (A) and Reason (R) are true and Reason (R) is the correct explanation of Assertion (A)

8. (A) Both Assertion (A) and Reason (R) are true and Reason (R) is the correct explanation of Assertion (A)

Correct/Incorrect Statements

1. (C) Both statements are correct

2. (A) The business environment indeed exhibits dynamic characteristics. Dynamic nature does not necessarily imply constant change. Instead, it refers to the complexity and unpredictability of the environment.

3. (C) Both statements are correct

4. (A) The inter-relatedness refers to the close connection between various elements of the business environment. The economic environment encompasses trends like GDP, inflation, etc. not social and cultural values.

5. (A) Statement I correctly highlight the necessity for enterprises to adhere to legal regulations for ethical conduct and legal compliance. However, Statement II erroneously suggests discretionary government involvement, overlooking the essential role of government regulations in maintaining law and order and fostering fair business practices.

6. (C) Both statements are correct

7. (D) The technological environment primarily encompasses factors related to technological advancements, innovation and adaption. While inter-relatedness is indeed valuable for identifying opportunities and gaining the first mover advantage, it is not the sole determinant of these outcomes.

8. (C) Both statements are correct

Case Based Questions

1. (i) (D) Many potential customers resisted purchasing Nano due to concerns about its safety and other social factors.
   (ii) (B) The failure of Nano affected the overall automobile market, including the second hand car market, demonstrating how different elements of the business environment are closely connected.
   (iii) (C) The importance of business environment highlighted in the case which led to the failure of Nano cars is it helps the firm to identify threats and early warning signals. The safety issues with Nano cars were potential threats that were not adequately identified and addressed.
   (iv) (C) The safety concerns, including instances of Nano cars catching fire, contributed to consumers' reluctance to accept Nano as a viable option, despite its affordability.
2. (i) (C) Pepsi's decision to launch Crystal Pepsi was influenced by market trends and consumer preferences, indicating how businesses need to utilise available resources effectively to capitalise on market opportunities.
   (ii) (C) Social dimension encompasses factors such as consumer perceptions, preferences and societal trends, which influence the acceptance and success of products in the market.
   (iii) (B) Complexity highlights how various factors such as consumer preferences, product perceptions, market dynamics and competitive landscapes interact in a complex manner, shaping the success or failure of a product like Crystal Pepsi.
   (iv) (C) The shift in consumer preference towards healthier alternatives like natural juices highlights the influence of social factors on business operations and market dynamics.
3. (i) (A) By effectively understanding and leveraging the business environment, companies like Coca-Cola can seize opportunities to innovate, market and position their products ahead of competitors.
   (ii) (B) The Coca-Cola Company managed to leverage both specific and general forces of the business environment in their favour. These forces include market dynamics, consumer preferences, competitive landscape, regulatory frameworks and socio-cultural trends.
   (iii) (B) Coca-Cola majorly tapped into the social environment, which includes factors such as consumer preferences, cultural trends, lifestyle choices and societal norms.
   (iv) (C) While Coca-Cola offers a variety of cola drinks and related products, 'Coca-Cola Avocado' is not a product of the company.

Subjective Questions

1. (i) Social environment
   (ii) Features of business environment are
      (a) **Dynamic Nature** Business environment is dynamic in that it keeps on changing whether in terms of technological improvement, shifts in consumer preferences or entry of new competition in the market.
      (b) **Uncertainty** Business environment is largely uncertain as it is very difficult to predict future happenings, especially when environment changes are taking place too frequently as in the case of information technology or fashion industries.
2. (i) **Dynamic Nature** "Krishna, the CEO of the company wanted to understand the business environment of the area first." This illustrates the dynamic nature of the business environment, where conditions are subject to change, prompting the CEO to seek understanding before proceeding with the project.
   (ii) **Complexity** "On analysis, he realised that it is very difficult to understand the business environment of Mumbai until it was divided into different business dimensions like legal, political, economic, social and technological conditions."
   This highlights the complexity within the business environment, indicating that it is difficult to comprehend at once what exactly constitutes a given environment, but it is easier to understand its components in parts.
   (iii) **Relativity** "Later they realised that the products they were selling in Mumbai were more fit for the American culture and decided to start a new branch in Columbia."

This suggests relativity within the business environment, as the suitability of products varied based on cultural contexts, prompting the decision to expand to Columbia where there was a better fit for their offerings.

(iv) **Inter-relatedness** "After comprehending the business scenarios, the company embarked on studying the intricate interconnections between various elements of the business environment."

This emphasises the inter- relatedness of factors within the business environment, as the company's actions, such as customer surveys, were influenced by and aimed to understand various aspects of the environment, including market trends and preferences.

3. (i) The concept discussed here is 'business environment' and the feature is 'specific and general forces'.

Specific and General Forces Their operations are directly affected by specific forces e.g. Investors, customers, competitors and suppliers. Besides this general forces e.g. Money supply in the economy, technological changes indirectly affect their business.

(ii) Four points of importance of this concept are

(a) **It enables the Firm to Identify Opportunities and get the First Mover Advantage** Opportunities are the positive trends that help firms to grow.

A good knowledge of business environment helps a manager to identify such opportunities earlier to take its benefit, rather than losing it to other competing enterprises. e.g. Maruti Udyog was the first automobile company in India to recognise the opportunity to develop small cars, due to which, it is still one of the market leaders in that segment.

(b) **It helps the Firm to Identify Threats and Early Warning Signals** Threats refer to the negative trends, which will hinder the performance of the enterprise. The businessmen, who are able to scan and understand the business environment on time get a warning signal to deal with such negative changes.

(c) **It helps in Tapping Useful Resources** Environment is a source of various resources for business like finance, machinery, raw materials, etc.

Contrary to this, business enterprise supplies goods and services to the society in the form of taxes, products, return on investment, etc.

A good understanding of environment helps the firm to convert such resources into output required by the environment and society.

(d) **It helps in Coping with Rapid Changes** Business environment is fast changing due to turbulent market conditions, more demanding customers, changing technology and increasing global competition.

In order to cope up with such changes and derive benefit from them, managers must examine their environment and develop suitable action.

4. The decision to ban Chinese apps by the Government of India is influenced by both the technological and political environment. The technological environment comes into play because these apps were deemed to pose threats to data security and privacy.

Meanwhile, the political environment, as evidenced by the tensions between China and India, also played a significant role in shaping this decision.

5. The various dimensions of business environment which relate to the above mentioned case are stated below (any two)

(i) **Political Environment** Political environment includes political conditions such as general stability and peace in the country and specific attitudes that elected government representatives hold towards business.

(ii) **Legal Environment** Legal environment includes various legislations passed by the government, administrative orders issued by government authorities, court judgments as well as the decisions rendered by various commissions and agencies at every level of the government centre, state or local. It is imperative for the management of every enterprise to obey the law of the land.

(iii) **Technological Environment** Technological environment includes forces relating to scientific improvements and innovations which provide new ways of producing goods and services and new methods and techniques of operating a business.

6. (i) Legal environment
(ii) The importance of business environment are
(a) **It helps the Firm to Identify Threats and Early Warning Signals** Threats refer to the external environment trends and changes that will hinder a firm's performance. Besides opportunities, environment happens to be the source of many threats. Environmental awareness can help managers to identify various threats on time and serve as an early warning signal.
(b) **It helps in Assisting in Planning and Policy Formulation** Since environment is a source of both opportunities and threats for a business enterprise, its understanding and analysis can be the basis for deciding the future course of action (planning) or training guidelines for decision-making (policy).

7. (i) Demonetisation
(ii) The impact of the given decision on various sectors of an economy is as follows
(a) **Money/Interest Rates** Decline in cash transactions, bank deposits increased, increase in financial savings.
(b) **Private Wealth** Declined since some high demonetised notes were not returned and real estate prices fell.
(c) **Public Sector Wealth** No effect.
(d) **Digitisation** Digital transactions amongst new users (RuPay/AEPS) increased.
(e) **Real Estate** Prices declined.
(f) **Tax Collection** Rise in income tax collection because of increased disclosure.

CHAPTER -4

Planning

Types & Nos. of Questions

Multiple Choice Questions	-	34
Assertion-Reason Questions	-	8
Correct/Incorrect Statements	-	8
Case Based Questions	-	2 Cases, each *with four Questions*
Subjective Questions	-	8

Trend Analysis

On the basis of analysis of last 2 years' papers, it is found that on an average 2 Multiple Choice Questions and 1 Long Question (Case Based) are asked from this chapter.

Focus Topics of the Chapter

- Concept of Planning
- Importance and Limitations of Planning
- Process of Planning
- Type of Plans

Multiple Choice Questions

No. of Questions : **34** Suggested Time : **51 Minutes**

Direction Each of the question given below is Multiple Choice Question (MCQ) i.e. there are Four Options/Choices for answer, out of which ONLY ONE is correct. You have to select the correct option. A response box is given with each option, mark (✓) in the box of the correct option. For each correct answer you will get 1 mark, while there is no penalty for incorrect answer or missed out questions.

1. "In actual practice, planning pre-supposes the existence of alternatives."

Which feature of planning is discussed here?

(A) Planning is futuristic ☐
(B) Planning focuses on achieving objectives ☐
(C) Planning is a mental exercise ☐
(D) Planning involves decision-making ☐

2. Plans are prepared for a specific period of time, may be for a month, a quarter or a year. At the end of that period, there is a need for a new plan to be drawn on the basis of new requirements and future conditions.

The feature of planning reflected in the above lines is *[CBSE 2024]*

(A) planning is futuristic ☐
(B) planning is continuous ☐
(C) planning is pervasive ☐
(D) planning is a mental exercise ☐

3. Which of the following statements is incorrect?

(A) Planning provides a rational approach for achieving pre-determined objectives ☐
(B) Planning will be a futile exercise if it is not acted upon or implemented ☐
(C) Planning is what managers at all levels do ☐
(D) Planning enables smooth interaction and clarity about each group's contribution towards the event ☐

4. The Vice-President of a company formulates specific goals along with the activities to be undertaken to achieve goals. It is not limited to top level of management, as planning is also done by departmental heads and supervisors by peeping into the future while analysing and predicting the future.

Identify a feature of planning referred to in the above paragraph.

(A) Planning is pervasive ☐
(B) Planning focuses on achieving objectives ☐
(C) Planning is continuous ☐
(D) Planning is mental exercise ☐

5. "The purpose of planning is to meet future events effectively to the best advantage of an organisation." This statement highlights which of the following features of planning? *[CBSE 2023]*

(A) Planning focuses on achieving objectives ☐
(B) Planning involves decision-making ☐
(C) Planning is the primary function of management ☐
(D) Planning is futuristic ☐

6. "Changes or events cannot be eliminated but they can be anticipated and managerial responses to them can be developed" is suggested by the following importance of planning.

(A) Planning facilitates decision-making ☐
(B) Planning promotes innovative ideas ☐
(C) Planning provides direction ☐
(D) Planning reduces the risks of uncertainty ☐

7. Saros Ltd. has given targets to its employees in advance. This has led to more focused approach resulting in saving of resources and all the employees are happy and satisfied. Which importance of planning is highlighted in the given case?
(A) Planning facilitates decision-making ☐
(B) Planning provides direction ☐
(C) Planning promotes innovative ideas ☐
(D) Planning reduces the risk of uncertainty ☐

8. "Competition in the market can also upset financial plans, sales targets may have to be revised and accordingly, cash budgets also need to be modified since they are based on sales figures."
From the above statement, which limitation of planning is reflected here?
(A) Planning does not guarantee success ☐
(B) Planning involves huge cost ☐
(C) Planning may not work in a dynamic environment ☐
(D) Planning is time consuming ☐

9. Sunil was working in a mobile assembling unit of a company. The standard unit of production was 12 units per day. During his working time, Sunil realised that by reorganising the sequence of tasks, more units can be assembled at a lower cost. He informed his discovery to the supervisor. But the supervisor instructed Sunil to continue the same method and techniques decided earlier.
Identify the limitation of the primary function of management.
(A) Planning focuses on achieving objectives ☐
(B) Planning reduces creativity ☐
(C) Planning involves huge cost ☐
(D) Planning is time consuming ☐

10. The first symptomatic infected individuals of coronavirus (Covid-19) was confirmed in December 2019 in the city of Wuhan, China. In India, the first reported case of Covid-19 was confirmed on 30th January, 2020. A lot of research was done to this area to find out the solution for this pandemic.
Identify the limitation of planning reflected in the above statement.
(A) Planning focuses on achieving objectives ☐
(B) Planning reduces creativity ☐
(C) Planning involves huge cost ☐
(D) Planning is time consuming ☐

11. 'Shrisha Motors' was in the business of manufacturing bicycles and had a monopoly in the market. The business was doing well and the company was consistently meeting its objective of 10% increase in sales every year.
Encouraged by the good track record, the managing director of the company kept an ambitious target of 20% increase in sales for the next year. The same year, two competitors also entered the market and because of this the company was not able to meet target.
Identify the limitation of one of the functions of management because of which the company was not able to achieve its target.
(A) Planning may not work in dynamic environment ☐
(B) Planning reduces creativity ☐
(C) Planning involves huge cost ☐
(D) Planning is time consuming ☐

12. 'Uttam Ayurvedic Ltd.' is an established Indian company manufacturing organic consumer goods like toothpastes and shampoos.
It has planned to increase its market share from 30% to 40% in the current financial year. With the expanding market of organic products, other companies in the consumer goods industry have also launched these products with organic components.
The competition in the market has increased and it was found that the sales of Uttam Ayurvedic Ltd. came down and its market share was reduced to 23%.

Identify the limitation of planning highlighted in the above case.

(A) Planning may not work in dynamic environment ☐
(B) Planning is time consuming ☐
(C) Planning involves huge costs ☐
(D) Planning reduces overlapping and wasteful activities ☐

13. Ritu Kapoor has set-up a bakery, 'Bakes and Cakes' in Pune. She receives online orders for cakes from within the city and supplies them on the same day. She set a target that she would earn a revenue of ₹ 5,00,000 in the first year. She informed her employees about the target and asked them to contribute ideas to achieve the same.

Ritu Kapoor has performed the first step in the process of one of the functions of management. The next step to be performed is

(A) identifying alternative courses of action ☐
(B) setting objective ☐
(C) developing premises ☐
(D) follow-up action ☐

14. "The manager will have to apply permutations, combinations and select the best possible course of action."

Identify the step of planning process mentioned here.

(A) Developing premises ☐
(B) Selecting an alternative ☐
(C) Identifying the alternative courses of action ☐
(D) Setting the objective ☐

15. Kautilya wants to start her own cafe. His goal is to get 60% of the market share. For this he collected information and made forecasts about the potential demand, purchasing power of the consumers as well as preferences of the consumers and government policy towards this business, etc.

By doing this, Kautilya had completed some steps in the process of planning.

Choose the step in the planning process that Kautilya has to follow.

(A) Setting objectives ☐
(B) Developing premises ☐
(C) Identifying alternative courses of action ☐
(D) Evaluating alternative courses ☐

16. If there is a plan to increase production then more labour, more machinery will be required. This step in the process of planning will involve organising for labour and purchase of machinery. Identify the step in the planning process being discussed above.

(A) Identifying alternative courses of action ☐
(B) Setting objectives ☐
(C) Selecting an alternative ☐
(D) Implementing the plan ☐

17. A sanitizer manufacturing company wants to become a market leader. For this purpose, the manager follows an activity with certain logical steps.

The first step suggested by him is to increase profits by at least 30% in the next quarter. What will be the last step of the activity being followed by the manager?

(A) Follow-up action ☐
(B) Identifying alternative courses of action ☐
(C) Setting objectives ☐
(D) Evaluating alternative courses of action ☐

18. Which step of the planning process is depicted in the below image?

(A) Developing premises ☐
(B) Setting objectives ☐
(C) Identifying alternative courses of action ☐
(D) None of the above ☐

19. Match the Column I with Column II in the following information

	Column I		Column II
A.	Most plans may not always be subjected to a mathematical analysis.	(i)	Implementing the plan
B.	This is the step where other managerial functions also come into the picture.	(ii)	Developing premises
C.	Every planner is using conjecture about what might happen in future.	(iii)	Selecting an alternative

Codes

	A	B	C	
(A)	(iii)	(i)	(ii)	☐
(B)	(i)	(ii)	(iii)	☐
(C)	(ii)	(i)	(iii)	☐
(D)	(iii)	(ii)	(i)	☐

20. Determining long-term objectives, adopting a particular course of action and allocating resources necessary to achieve the objectives are part of ....

(A) policy ☐ (B) programme ☐
(C) budget ☐ (D) strategy ☐

21. "When we prepare it, it is related to planning and when we use it as a tool to detect the deviation it becomes controlling." It is referred to one of the plan, identify.

(A) Policy ☐ (B) Programme ☐
(C) Budget ☐ (D) Strategy ☐

22. To meet the increased demand of internet due to online classes all over the world, the Indian Internet Companies decided to upgrade their plans to 5G network. This is an example of which type of plan?

(A) Policy ☐
(B) Strategy ☐
(C) Objective ☐
(D) Programme ☐

23. Which of the following statements is incorrect?

(A) Objectives may be set for the entire organisation and each department or unit within the organisation ☐
(B) Objectives should be stated clearly for all departments, units and employees ☐
(C) Objectives give direction to all departments ☐
(D) Objectives provide a basis for interpreting strategy which is usually stated in general terms ☐

24. Which plan is defined as the formalised or systematic way of doing routine and repetitive jobs?

(A) Objective ☐
(B) Strategy ☐
(C) Method ☐
(D) Budget ☐

25. It was only after 2001 Bhuj earthquake, when Mansukhbhai Prajapati realised that he wanted to create a clay refrigerator which can run without electricity.

It was the first concrete step in setting-up a house of innovation that Mitti Cool and its products are synonymous with today. Journalists photographed his broken matkas and referred to them with the caption "The Poor Man's Broken Fridge." An idea struck him to make a real fridge with the same cooling principle and after several tests of soil and fridge designs, he introduced the innovative 'Mitti Cool' fridge.

His company is growing at 20% annually and he seeks to achieve a target of ₹ 5 crore by the end of next fiscal year.

The company has stuck to its statement of keeping all the products price at a lower rate in order to be affordable.

Identify the plans referred to in the above case study.

(A) Objective and strategy ☐

(B) Strategy and policy ☐

(C) Policy and objective ☐

(D) Objective and rule ☐

26. Organising higher level management orientation programmes, lectures and seminars are example of which type of plan?

(A) Policy ☐

(B) Programme ☐

(C) Method ☐

(D) Strategy ☐

27. 'Best Electronics' is led by its visionary chief executive officer, Nikhil. It has a reputation for good quality products and customer service. Nikhil recognised the need to continually innovate and provide customers with the latest products. He wanted the company to be the market leader in electronics.

Nikhil knew that to realise his ambitious vision, he needed a clear and well-defined plan that would provide broad contours of the company's business. His team conducted extensive market research to uncover emerging trends, customer preferences and potential competitors.

On its basis, a plan was prepared defining the company's direction and scope in the long- run. On the implementation of the plan 'Best Electronics' became the market leader in two years.

The type of plan which helped 'Best Electronics' to become the market leader was

[CBSE 2024]

(A) policy ☐

(B) rule ☐

(C) strategy ☐

(D) procedure ☐

28. Green Innovations Pvt. Ltd. is a company dedicated to promoting sustainable practices. To launch their new product, a solar powered water purifier, they formulated a detailed plan for the launch event, which included grand unveiling, media interactions and a month long promotional campaign.

This plan was specific to this unique product launch and not intended to be used again in the future.

Simultaneously, Green Innovations Pvt. Ltd. has also established a set of guidelines and procedures for handling customer inquiries, maintaining quality standards and ensuring efficient production processes. These guidelines are meant to be followed consistently over time to ensure smooth operations within the company.

Based on the above case, identify which type of plan was formulated for the product launch event and which type of plan was established for handling ongoing operations?

(A) Single-use plan for the product launch event and standing plan for handling ongoing operations ☐

(B) Standing plan for the product launch event and single-use plan for handling ongoing operations ☐

(C) Both single-use plans for the product launch event and handling ongoing operations ☐

(D) Both standing plans for the product launch event and handling ongoing operations ☐

29. Which type of plan is illustrated in the following image?

(A) Policy ☐ (B) Method ☐
(C) Procedure ☐ (D) Rule ☐

30. Which type of plan is illustrated in the following image?

(A) Strategy ☐
(B) Single-use plan ☐
(C) Standing plan ☐
(D) Rule ☐

31. Which type of plan is illustrated in the following image?

(A) Policies ☐
(B) Rules ☐
(C) Strategy ☐
(D) Method ☐

32. Match the Column I with Column II in the following information

Column I		Column II
A. These are evaluated in the light of their feasibility and consequences.	(i)	Standing plan
B. These plans have a short-term horizon.	(ii)	Alternatives
C. Such a plan greatly enhances efficiency in routine decision-making.	(iii)	Single-use plans

Codes

	A	B	C	
(A)	(ii)	(iii)	(i)	☐
(B)	(ii)	(i)	(iii)	☐
(C)	(iii)	(i)	(ii)	☐
(D)	(i)	(ii)	(iii)	☐

33. Match the following

Column I		Column II
A. Methods	(i)	Market research and development for a new product.
B. Programmes	(ii)	Construction employees should compulsorily wear safety helmets.
C. Rules	(iii)	All customer complaints must be resolved within 24 hours.
D. Policies	(iv)	Procedure used by assembly line workers to assemble products.

Codes

	A	B	C	D	
(A)	(iv)	(i)	(ii)	(iii)	☐
(B)	(ii)	(i)	(iii)	(iv)	☐
(C)	(iii)	(iv)	(ii)	(i)	☐
(D)	(iv)	(iii)	(i)	(ii)	☐

34. Match the following

Column I		Column II
A. Pervasiveness	(i)	Provides a structured framework.
B. Continuous nature	(ii)	Required at all levels.
C. Helps in decision-making	(iii)	Plans are made again and again.
D. Goal-oriented	(iv)	Focused on achieving objectives.

Codes

	A	B	C	D	
(A)	(iv)	(i)	(ii)	(iii)	☐
(B)	(ii)	(i)	(iii)	(iv)	☐
(C)	(iii)	(iv)	(ii)	(i)	☐
(D)	(ii)	(iii)	(i)	(iv)	☐

Assertion-Reason Questions

No. of Questions : **8** Suggested Time : **12 Minutes**

Direction Each of the question given below consist of the two statements; one labelled as **Assertion** (A) and other as **Reason** (R). List of common options applicable for each question is given below

(A) Both Assertion (A) and Reason (R) are true and Reason (R) is the correct explanation of Assertion (A)

(B) Both Assertion (A) and Reason (R) are true, but Reason (R) is not the correct explanation of Assertion (A)

(C) Assertion (A) is true, but Reason (R) is false

(D) Assertion (A) is false, but Reason (R) is true

You have to select the codes as *a, b, c* or *d* as your answer to the question by marking (✓) in the response box given against each option.

1. **Assertion** (A) False sense of security and complacency lead to failure of planning instead of success.

   Reason (R) Planning if implemented properly, guarantee success.

   (A) ☐ (B) ☐ (C) ☐ (D) ☐

2. **Assertion** (A) Planning leads to rigidity, making it difficult to adapt to changing circumstances.

   Reason (R) Once plans are formulated, they often become inflexible, hindering the ability to respond effectively to dynamic environments.

   (A) ☐ (B) ☐
   (C) ☐ (D) ☐

3. **Assertion** (A) Planning reduces creativity by restricting autonomy among middle level management.

   Reason (R) Middle level managers are typically constrained to follow top down plans, limiting their ability to exercise initiative and creativity in problem solving and decision-making processes.

   (A) ☐ (B) ☐
   (C) ☐ (D) ☐

4. **Assertion** (A) Environmental changes, including social, economic, legal and technological shifts, may affect forecasting and planning.

   Reason (R) Unforeseen events such as natural calamities have little to no impact on organisational plans.

   (A) ☐ (B) ☐ (C) ☐ (D) ☐

5. **Assertion** (A) Setting objectives is the initial step in the planning process.

   Reason (R) Identifying alternative courses of action is the final step in the planning process.

   (A) ☐ (B) ☐ (C) ☐ (D) ☐

6. **Assertion** (A) Evaluating alternative courses is essential to make informed planning decisions.

   Reason (R) Without weighing the pros and cons of each alternative, managers cannot effectively prioritise actions to achieve objectives.

   (A) ☐ (B) ☐ (C) ☐ (D) ☐

7. **Assertion** (A) Single-use plans are formulated for one time events or projects and are not expected to be repeated in the future.

Reason (R) Standing plans, such as policies and procedures, are designed to facilitate the smooth operation of regular activities within an organisation.

(A) ☐ (B) ☐
(C) ☐ (D) ☐

8. Assertion (A) Policies provide general guidelines to facilitate the achievement of pre-determined objectives.

Reason (R) Objectives are the ends that management seeks to achieve through its operations.

(A) ☐ (B) ☐ (C) ☐ (D) ☐

Correct/Incorrect Statements

No. of Questions : **8** Suggested Time : **12 Minutes**

Direction Each of the question given below consist of the two statements. List of common options applicable for each question is given below

(A) Statement I is correct and Statement II is incorrect
(B) Statement I is incorrect and Statement II is correct
(C) Both statements are correct
(D) Both statements are incorrect

You have to select the codes as *a*, *b*, *c* or *d* as your answer to the question by marking ✓) in the response box given against each option.

1. Statement I Planning implies peeping into the future, analysing it and predicting it.

Statement II A critical issue in accomplishing the goals specified in the planning process is structuring the work of an organisation to adapt to the dynamic business environment.

(A) ☐ (B) ☐ (C) ☐ (D) ☐

2. Statement I The premises or assumptions must be the same for all and there should be total agreement on them.

Statement II Proper planning leads to the proper usage of all material, financial and human resources.

(A) ☐ (B) ☐ (C) ☐ (D) ☐

3. Statement I Setting objectives is the final step in the planning process.

Statement II Developing premises involves making assumptions about past events.

(A) ☐ (B) ☐ (C) ☐ (D) ☐

4. Statement I Policies define the broad parameters within which a manager may function.

Statement II The manager may use his/her discretion to interpret and apply a policy.

(A) ☐ (B) ☐ (C) ☐ (D) ☐

5. Statement I Programmes will include the entire gamut of activities as well as the organisation's policy and how it will contribute to the overall business plan.

Statement II Budget is a control device from which deviations can be taken care of.

(A) ☐ (B) ☐ (C) ☐ (D) ☐

6. Statement I Whenever a strategy is formulated, the business environment needs to be taken into consideration.

Statement II Rules are guidelines to managerial action and decisions in the implementation of strategy.

(A) ☐ (B) ☐ (C) ☐ (D) ☐

7. **Statement I** Single-use plans are designed to meet the needs of recurring events or projects.

Statement II Standing plans are formulated for one time events or projects.

(A) ☐ (B) ☐
(C) ☐ (D) ☐

8. **Statement I** Policies provide specific guidelines for handling activities within an organisation.

Statement II Procedures are general guidelines that facilitate the achievement of pre-determined objectives.

(A) ☐ (B) ☐ (C) ☐ (D) ☐

Case Based Questions

No. of Questions : **2** Suggested Time : **10 Minutes**

Direction This section contains 2 cases each having 4 questions of 1 mark each. You have to write the answer of each question based on the context of the related case.

Case 1 Simplex Limited had been taken over by Mundhra Group immediately following India's independence. Since then it enjoys a rich record of industry presence and experience. In 2005, with the aim to accelerate growth the company had gone through several rounds of meetings and discussions before launching ERP system to attract large projects.

The management had done effective forecast and critical thinking regarding allocation resources to reduce wastage. For this purpose the company had laid down multiple courses of action to meet the challenge of adverse situations. In 2008, the company suffered loss in many projects due to the great recession despite taking many cost cutting measures.

The management had taken utmost care regarding the possible outcome and timely review of the plans to achieve the set target during that hard time. In 2010 the system implemented successfully which subseque- ntly helped the company to execute numerous projects with precision and timeliness. *[CBSE QB]*

Questions

(i) "In 2005, with the aim to accelerate growth the company had gone through several rounds of meetings and discussions."

What is the objective mentioned here according to the process stated here?

(A) Developing premises ☐
(B) Growth and development ☐
(C) Launching IT enabled system ☐
(D) Cost cutting ☐

(ii) "In 2008, the company suffered loss in many projects due to the great recession despite taking many cost cutting measures."

Which limitation of the management process is indicated here?

(A) It fails to cope with sudden changes ☐
(B) It involves huge cost ☐
(C) It requires critical thinking ☐
(D) Economic environment ☐

(iii) State whether the given statement is true or false.

"The management had done effective forecast and critical thinking regarding allocation of resources to reduce wastage."

(iv) "The management had taken utmost care regarding the possible outcome and timely review of the plans to achieve the set target during that hard time."

Which is the last step of the process mentioned here?

(A) Implementation of plan ☐
(B) Timely execution of projects ☐
(C) Follow-up ☐
(D) To prepare alternative course of action ☐

Case 2 After completing a diploma in interior decoration, Shalu Sharma set-up a small office at Delhi to render services. Being new in the field of entrepreneurship, she put in logical and systematic thinking involving foresight, intelligent imagination and sound judgement rather than guess work.

She made certain assumptions as she knew that only accurate forecast will act as base material upon which the plans are to be drawn. Her friend, Ashu Bindal, who has done MBA, advised her to do planning effectively as a good planning will help develop managerial response to deal with the changes and uncertain events.

So, she acted in a conscious manner and made sub-plans for the juniors to follow.

Questions

(i) Which feature of planning is highlighted in the above case study?

(A) Planning is all pervasive ☐
(B) Planning is a mental exercise ☐
(C) Planning is a continuous process ☐
(D) Planning focuses on achieving objectives ☐

(ii) Which importance of planning did Ashu hint at while guiding Shalu?

(A) Planning facilities decision-making ☐
(B) Planning promotes innovative ideas ☐
(C) Planning reduces overlapping and wasteful activities ☐
(D) Planning reduces the risks of uncertainty ☐

(iii) Which step of planning process was taken by Shalu?

(A) Setting objectives ☐
(B) Developing premises ☐
(C) Selecting an alternative ☐
(D) Follow-up action ☐

(iv) Which limitation of planning is can you find in the above case study?

(A) Planning reduces creativity ☐
(B) Planning involves huge cost ☐
(C) Planning leads to rigidity ☐
(D) Planning does not guarantee success ☐

Subjective Questions

Free Response Questions, Open-ended Questions etc.

No. of Questions : **8** Suggested Time : **64 Minutes**

1. A firm wants to increase its sales by 25% in the coming year. Suggest two steps which should be examined critically by a manager.

2. The CEO of a fast growing tech company has asked the head of operations to lead a workshop for department heads on effective planning. The workshop will cover different types of plans, including strategies, policies, programme, objectives, rules and procedures.

   The goal is to enhance their understanding of these planning components and how they contribute to the company's success.

   Write six points to include in this workshop.

3. Company Z, a fashion start-up committed to sustainability, embarked on the journey of launching a new line of eco-friendly clothing. Based on the insights gained from market research, the company focuses on sales targets, sustainability goals (such as using organic materials and ethical manufacturing practices), brand positioning and desired market share. It involved allocating resources effectively to achieve the objectives set forth.

   This included budgeting for product development, sourcing sustainable materials, hiring skilled designers and manufacturers and investing in marketing and distribution channels.

   Company Z collaborated with designers, textile experts and manufacturers to develop a range of eco-friendly clothing items that aligned with their sustainability objectives and met consumer preferences. Company Z is at the real point of decision-making. It has arrived at this point after identifying various alternative courses of action.

   After identification he was thoroughly involved in the evaluation of each of these alternatives. It later got involved into making several permutations and combinations of these alternatives to arrive at this point.

   (i) Identify the function of management discussed above.

   (ii) Through which stage of the planning process is Company Z going?

   (iii) Also give the next two steps of the process of the function identified in (i).

4. A project manager working on a high profile construction project which involves constructing a state-of-the-art sports stadium with multiple facilities. As he starts the planning phase, he realises that there are several potential limitations associated with planning.

   Identify six limitations commonly associated with the planning phase.

5. Geeta Ltd. a leading tech firm, meticulously planned the launch of their latest product – a smartphone packed with innovative features. The tech market is highly volatile, with rapid advancements and changing consumer preferences. Despite thorough market research, unforeseen shifts in consumer trends and competitor strategies impacted the success of the launch. With the arrival of foreign firms it is feeling the pressure of improving its business strategy.

   Because of the firm's advance planning it could not suddenly bring changes in its plans as the whole organisation had started implementing the decided plan. But this year the organisation wants to ensure success.

   However, the firm knows that the external environment is changeable and continues to vary in a fast manner. In order to prepare for future the organisation wants to have full understanding of the budget planning and preparation system, not just to derive expenditure projections but to be able to advise policymakers on the feasibility and desirability of specific budget proposals.

   Which limitations of planning have been identified in the above case?

6. Atul Sharma was the chief executive officer of a footwear company, 'Stepone Footwear'. The company manufactured innovative and comfortable footwear for all age groups. Atul Sharma was known for meticulous planning. He ensured that the goals and objectives of the company are clearly stated so that they act as a guide for deciding what action should be taken and in which direction.

   Before each season, 'Stepone Footwear' carefully analysed market trends, customer preferences and production schedules. This analysis enabled the company to look ahead and anticipate changes and develop managerial responses, wherever necessary. As a result, they were able to consistently deliver innovative and comfortable shoes to the market.

   During one season, there was a sudden surge in demand for eco-friendly shoes. 'Stepone Footwear' had already planned their production for the year with specific goals to be achieved within a specific time frame. The managers of 'Stepone Footwear' did not have the flexibility to change the plan to cope with the changed circumstances. Another shoe company 'Eco Step' quickly adapted and started manufacturing comfortable eco-friendly shoes.

   By not being able to adjust to the rapidly changing market, 'Stepone Footwear' faced inventory surplus while 'Eco Step' emerged as a market leader in sustainable eco-friendly footwear.

   Quoting lines from the above paragraph, identify and explain two benefits and two limitations of 'planning' function of management discussed in the above case. *[CBSE 2024]*

7. Fireball Ltd. holds an Annual Management Programme every year in the month of March in which the top managerial personnel formulate plans for the next year by analysing and predicting the future to meet future events effectively.

   As they are responsible for providing direction to the organisation, facts are throughly checked through scientific calculations. Detailed plans are prepared after discussion with professional experts. Preliminary investigations are also undertaken to find out the viability of the plan. Since it is an intellectual activity requiring intelligent imagination and sound judgement, it is mainly done by the top management.

   Usually rest of the members just implement the plans, middle level managers are neither allowed to deviate from the plans nor are they permitted to act on their own.

   The top management ensures that the expenses incurred in formulating the plans justify the benefits derived from them.

   (i) State two limitations of planning discussed above.

   (ii) State two features of planning discussed above.

8. Company STEMED a dedicated education company, aimed to enhance its STEM (Science, Technology, Engineering and Mathematics) education programme for middle school students.

   Company STEMED conducted a comprehensive review of existing STEM curricula and pedagogical approaches. They collaborated with educators, curriculum specialists and industry experts to design a plan focused on integrating inquiry based learning methodologies, laboratory experiments, coding workshops and engineering design challenges into the curriculum.

   It estimated detailed project expenses for curriculum development, teacher training workshops, instructional materials, equipment and supplies, guest speakers, field trips and programme evaluation.

   It developed step-by-step process for rolling out the new curriculum in partner schools or districts. This plan included guidelines for conducting teacher training sessions, scheduling classroom activities, managing instructional materials, monitoring student progress and collecting feedback from stakeholders.

   (i) In the above case which types of plans have been highlighted?

   (ii) Which step of planning process is highlighted in the above case?

Answers

If your answer matches with the answer given here then put (✓) in the box otherwise put (✗). In case you did not attempt the question leave the box blank.

Multiple Choice Questions

1. D ☐	2. B ☐
3. D ☐	4. A ☐
5. D ☐	6. D ☐
7. B ☐	8. C ☐
9. B ☐	10. D ☐
11. A ☐	12. A ☐
13. C ☐	14. B ☐
15. C ☐	16. D ☐
17. A ☐	18. C ☐
19. A ☐	20. D ☐
21. C ☐	22. C ☐
23. D ☐	24. C ☐
25. A ☐	26. C ☐
27. C ☐	28. A ☐
29. D ☐	30. B ☐
31. A ☐	32. A ☐
33. A ☐	34. D ☐

Your Score__________ *(No. of Correct Answers)*

Assertion-Reason Questions

1. C ☐	2. A ☐
3. A ☐	4. C ☐
5. C ☐	6. A ☐
7. B ☐	8. A ☐

Your Score__________ *(No. of Correct Answers)*

Correct/Incorrect Statements

1. C ☐	2. A ☐
3. D ☐	4. C ☐
5. C ☐	6. A ☐
7. D ☐	8. A ☐

Your Score__________ *(No. of Correct Answers)*

Case Based Questions

1. (i) B ☐	(ii) A ☐
(iv) C ☐	
2. (i) B ☐	(ii) D ☐
(iii) B ☐	(iv) A ☐

Your Score__________ *(No. of Correct Answers)*

Explanations

Multiple Choice Questions

1. (D) Planning involves decision-making
2. (B) The statement describes the ongoing nature of planning, where plans are continuously revised and updated based on new requirements and future conditions, reflecting the feature of planning being continuous.
3. (D) While planning does facilitate coordination and clarity about contributions towards goals, it primarily focuses on achieving pre-determined objectives rather than specific events.
4. (A) Planning is not limited to the top level of management but is undertaken by departmental heads and supervisors across different levels of the organisation. This highlights the pervasiveness of planning.
5. (D) Planning is futuristic
6. (D) Planning helps anticipate changes or events, enabling managers to develop responses and thereby reduce the risks associated with uncertainty.
7. (B) In the given case, planning has provided clear targets and objectives to the employees in advance. This has enabled them to align their efforts and resources towards achieving those targets, leading to a more focused approach.
8. (C) Changes in market conditions, such as competition, can disrupt financial plans and sales targets, necessitating revisions to cash budgets and other plans. This reflects the limitation that planning may not be effective in a dynamic environment.
9. (B) The supervisor's decision to instruct Sunil to continue with the previously decided method and techniques despite Sunil's suggestion for a

more efficient approach, reflects a limitation in embracing creativity and innovation in the planning process.

10. (D) The emergence of the Covid-19 pandemic required swift responses and adaptability. However, the planning process, particularly in research and solution seeking, often takes time due to the need for thorough analysis, coordination and decision-making.

11. (A) Despite setting an ambitious sales target based on past performance, the unexpected entry of competitors altered the market dynamics. This change in the business environment rendered the initial planning ineffective, as it did not account for the dynamic nature of the market and the potential impact of new competitors.

12. (A) The case describes how Uttam Ayurvedic Ltd. planned to increase its market share, but due to the expanding market of organic products and increased competition, their market share actually decreased. This illustrates how planning can be ineffective in a dynamic and rapidly changing environment.

13. (C) Ritu Kapoor has set a revenue target of ₹ 5,00,000 for her bakery, which is the first step in the planning process. The next step, developing premises, involves making assumptions about future conditions to provide a framework for achieving this target.

14. (B) Selecting an alternative

15. (C) Kautilya has collected information and made forecasts to understand various aspects of starting a cafe business, such as potential demand, consumer preferences and government policies. This step involves identifying different options or courses of action based on the collected information.

16. (D) Implementing the plan involves putting the planned activities into action. In this case, the plan to increase production requires organising for labour and purchasing machinery, which are actions that need to be implemented to achieve the desired increase in production.

17. (A) Follow-up action is the final step in the process where the manager assesses the outcomes of the implemented plan, monitors progress and takes corrective actions if necessary to ensure that the objectives are being met.

18. (C) Identifying alternative courses of action

19. (A) (iii) (i) (ii)

20. (D) strategy

21. (C) Budget

22. (C) Objective

23. (D) Objectives provide direction and specific targets for departments and employees to work towards, while strategy typically outlines the broader approach or plan of action to achieve those objectives.

24. (C) Method

25. (A) The case study mentions Mansukhbhai Prajapati's goal of achieving a target of ₹ 5 crore by the end of the next fiscal year, which represents the objective.

Additionally, his strategy to achieve this goal involves sticking to the company's principle of keeping all product prices at a lower rate to ensure affordability.

26. (C) Organising higher level management orientation programmes, lectures and seminars could be considered methods employed within the broader framework of planning. These methods are specific actions taken to achieve certain objectives or goals within the organisation.

27. (C) A strategy is a broad plan of action designed to achieve a long-term or overall aim. In this case, Nikhil recognised the need for a clear and well-defined plan to achieve the company's vision of becoming the market leader in electronics.

28. (A) Green Innovations Pvt. Ltd. used a single-use plan for the product launch event, which was specific to this unique occurrence and not intended for future use.

For ongoing operations, they established standing plans, including guidelines and procedures, to ensure consistent and smooth operations over time.

29. (D) Rules are specific and definitive statements that guide or restrict behaviour in an organisation. They are precise directives that must be followed without any deviation.

30. (B) Budgets are actually a type of single-use plan. Once the budget period is over, a new budget is created for the next period based on new forecasts and objectives.

31. (A) Policies are general guidelines that provide a framework for decision-making and behaviour within an organisation. e.g. A company might have a policy that all customer complaints must be resolved within 24 hours to ensure customer satisfaction.

32. (A) (ii) (iii) (i) 33. (A) (iv) (i) (ii) (iii)

34. (D) (ii) (iii) (i) (iv)

Assertion-Reason Questions

1. (C) While effective planning significantly enhances the prospects of success by providing a structured approach and minimising uncertainties, it is not an absolute guarantee.
2. (A) Both Assertion (A) and Reason (R) are true and Reason (R) is the correct explanation of Assertion (A)
3. (A) Both Assertion (A) and Reason (R) are true and Reason (R) is the correct explanation of Assertion (A)
4. (C) Unforeseen events, including natural calamities, can indeed have a significant impact on planned activities.
5. (C) Identifying alternative courses of action is not the final step; instead, it is the third step in the planning process.
6. (A) Both Assertion (A) and Reason (R) are true and Reason (R) is the correct explanation of Assertion (A)
7. (B) Both Assertion (A) and Reason (R) are true, but Reason (R) is not the correct explanation of Assertion (A)
8. (A) Both Assertion (A) and Reason (R) are true and Reason (R) is the correct explanation of Assertion (A)

Correct/Incorrect Statements

1. (C) Both statements are correct
2. (A) Proper planning aims to optimise the utilisation of resources, but it does not guarantee their perfect usage.
3. (D) Setting objectives is typically the initial step in the planning process, not the final step. Developing premises involves making assumptions about the future, not past events.
4. (C) Both statements are correct
5. (C) Both statements are correct
6. (A) Rules may influence the implementation of strategy to some extent, but they are not inherently tied to strategy formulation.
7. (D) Single-use plans are specifically formulated for one time events or projects that are not expected to be repeated in the future. Standing plans are formulated for activities that occur regularly over time, not for one time events or projects.
8. (A) Procedures are not general guidelines but rather stipulated sequences of actions for handling specific activities within an organisation.

Case Based Questions

1. (i) (B) The statement indicates that the objective in 2005 was to accelerate growth, aligning with the process of setting objectives as part of the management process. This objective reflects the company's strategic focus on expanding its business and achieving developmental goals.

   (ii) (A) The statement suggests that despite taking cost cutting measures, the company suffered losses during the recession, indicating a limitation in coping with sudden changes. This limitation highlights the challenge of adapting to unforeseen economic downturns and the need for management processes that can effectively respond to such disruptions.

   (iii) True

   (iv) (C) The statement refers to the management's emphasis on reviewing plans and monitoring outcomes to achieve set targets, indicating the last step of the management process as follow-up. Follow-up involves assessing the effectiveness of implemented plans, identifying any deviations and making necessary adjustments to ensure goals are met.

2. (i) (B) Planning is a mental exercise

   (ii) (D) Planning reduces the risks of uncertainty

   (iii) (B) Developing premises

   (iv) (A) Planning reduces creativity

Subjective Questions

1. Two steps which should be examined critically by a manager are

   (i) Planning is concerned with future, which is uncertain. Thus, it is required that manager should make assumptions for the future.

   (ii) Manager should think twice before selecting an alternative, as it is the real point of decision-making.

2. Points to be included are
   (i) A strategic plan defines our company's long-term vision, mission and overarching objectives. It involves analysing market trends, identifying opportunities and understanding our strengths and weaknesses.
   (ii) Policies are broad guidelines and principles that guide decision-making and behaviour within the organisation. They define acceptable conduct, standards and rules for various activities and processes.
   (iii) Programmes are comprehensive plans that encompass multiple projects or activities with a common goal.
   (iv) Objectives are specific, measurable targets that support the achievement of the overall strategic plan.
   (v) Rules are specific and explicit guidelines that govern specific actions or conduct within the organisation. They define the do's and don'ts, ensuring clarity and uniformity in employee behaviour.
   (vi) Procedures are detailed step-by-step instructions on how to perform specific tasks or processes. They provide consistency and standardisation, ensuring tasks are executed accurately and efficiently.
3. (i) The function of management discussed is planning.
   (ii) The stage through which Company Z is going is 'Selecting an alternative'. The real point of decision-making is selecting an alternative.
   (iii) The next two steps in the process of planning are 'Implementing the plan' and 'Follow-up'.
4. Limitations associated with the planning phase are
   (i) One of the primary limitations of planning is the uncertainty of the future. No one can predict with absolute certainty how the external environment or internal conditions will change over time.
   Changes in market trends, technological advancements, economic conditions or political factors can disrupt even the most well-thought-out plans.
   (ii) Planning can be a time consuming process, especially for complex organisations and projects. Gathering data, analysing information, setting goals and formulating strategies require considerable time and effort, which may delay the actual implementation of actions.
   (iii) Strict adherence to plans may lead to rigidity in decision-making. If managers are unwilling to adapt or deviate from the original plan when unforeseen circumstances arise, it can hinder the organisation's ability to respond effectively to changing conditions.
   (iv) Planning can be costly, particularly when it involves extensive research, market surveys or hiring specialised consultants. Smaller organisations or those with limited resources might find it challenging to afford comprehensive planning processes.
   (v) Planning often relies on forecasts and assumptions about the future. Over reliance on predictions can lead to unrealistic expectations and misalignments between actual outcomes and planned goals.
   (vi) Some employees or stakeholders may resist the implementation of new plans, especially if they perceive the changes as threatening or disruptive to their current roles or ways of doing things. This resistance can undermine the successful execution of the plan.
5. The limitations of planning highlighted in the given case are
   (i) **Planning leads to Rigidity** Geeta Ltd.'s advance planning for the launch of their latest product resulted in inflexibility when unforeseen shifts in consumer trends and competitor strategies occurred. The organisation found it challenging to make sudden changes to their plans as the entire organisation had already started implementing the decided plan.
   (ii) **Planning may not Work in a Dynamic Environment** Despite thorough market research, Geeta Ltd. faced challenges in adapting to the rapidly changing external environment, characterised by unpredictable shifts in consumer preferences and competitor actions. The company recognised the need to prepare for future uncertainties as the external environment continued to vary rapidly.
   (iii) **Planning involves Huge Costs** Geeta Ltd. acknowledged the importance of understanding the budget planning and preparation system to advise policymakers effectively. This indicates that planning efforts, particularly in budgeting, require investment in resources, time and expertise, highlighting the significant costs associated with comprehensive planning initiatives.

6. By quoting lines from the paragraph, the benefits of 'planning' function of management are

(i) He ensured that the goals .... in which direction.

Planning provides Directions By stating in advance how work is to be done, planning provides direction for action. It clearly defines what the employees have to do, when to do, how to do and for whom to do.

When employees are aware of what they have to do, departments and individuals are able to work in coordination.

(ii) This analysis enabled ... shoes to the market.

Planning promotes Innovative Ideas Planning is an intellectual process, which involves generation of new ideas through creativity, innovation and foresightedness.

These new ideas can take the shape of concrete plans. Planning is the most challenging activity for the management as it guides all future actions leading to growth and prosperity of the business.

By quoting lines from the paragraph, the limitations of planning function of management are

(i) The manager of 'Stepone Footwear' .... circumstances.

Planning leads to Rigidity A specific plan is made in an organisation which clearly indicates the objective to be achieved within a specific time frame. These plans decide the future course of action, which the manager may not be in a position to change. This kind of rigidity in plans may create difficulty.

Following a pre-decided plan in case of change in circumstances may not turn out to be in the organisation's interest.

(ii) Another shoe company .... eco-friendly footwear.

Planning may not Work in a Dynamic Environment Business environment is dynamic. It consists of number of dimensions like economic, political, physical, legal and social dimensions.

The organisation has to constantly adapt itself to changes. Changes in economic policy, instability of political conditions or natural calamity makes it difficult to accurately assess future trends in the environment.

Further, market competition can also upset the financial plan, sale targets as well as cash budgets. Planning cannot foresee everything and there may be obstacles to effective planning.

7. (i) Two limitations of planning discussed in case are as follows

(a) **Planning reduces Creativity** The members of the organisation are not allowed to deviate from plans and are not permitted to act on their own.

(b) **Planning involves Huge Cost** It usually involves a lot of time, money and effort and cost of the mangers. Sometimes the cost incurred may not justify the benefit derived from the plans.

(ii) Two features of planning discussed are as follows

(a) **Planning is Futuristic** It is essentially looking ahead, as it is based on forecasting and is prepared for the future.

(b) **Planning is a Mental Exercise** It is a mental exercise as it requires creativity, imagination and higher thinking skills with sound judgement.

8. (i) The types of plans which have been highlighted above are

(a) **Method** They collaborated with educators, curriculum specialists and industry experts to design a plan focused on integrating inquiry based learning methodologies, laboratory experiments, coding workshops and engineering design challenges into the curriculum.

(b) **Budget** It estimated detailed project expenses for curriculum development, teacher training workshops, instructional materials, equipment and supplies, guest speakers, field trips and programme evaluation.

(c) **Procedure** It developed step-by-step process for rolling out the new curriculum in partner schools or districts.

This plan included guidelines for conducting teacher training sessions, scheduling classroom activities, managing instructional materials, monitoring student progress and collecting feedback from stakeholders.

(ii) The step of planning process highlighted in the above case is 'Setting objectives'.

Company STEMED, a dedicated education company, aimed to enhance its STEM (Science, Technology, Engineering and Mathematics) education programme for middle school students.

CHAPTER -5

Organising

Types & Nos. of Questions

Multiple Choice Questions	– 25
Assertion-Reason Questions	– 8
Correct/Incorrect Statements	– 9
Case Based Questions	– 2 Cases, *each with four Questions*
Subjective Questions	– 7

Trend Analysis

On the basis of analysis of last 2 years' papers, it is found that on an average 3 Multiple Choice Questions and 1 Short Answer Type Question (Case Based) are asked from this chapter.

Focus Topics of the Chapter

- Concept of Organising
- Organisation Structure
- Concept of Delegation
- Decentralisation

Multiple Choice Questions

No. of Questions : **25** Suggested Time : **38 Minutes**

Direction Each of the question given below is Multiple Choice Question (MCQ) i.e. there are Four Options/Choices for answer, out of which ONLY ONE is correct. You have to select the correct option.

A response box is given with each option, mark (✓) in the box of the correct option. For each correct answer you will get 1 mark, while there is no penalty for incorrect answer or missed out questions.

1. ……… is the process of defining and grouping activities of the enterprise and establishing authority relationships among them.

(A) Decentralisation ☐
(B) Planning ☐
(C) Staffing ☐
(D) Organising ☐

2. 'Compro Solutions' offer IT services to clients across the country. During Covid-19, to accommodate changes taking place in the business environment, it suitably modified its organisation structure in a way that work from home became the new way of working for all employees bringing cost benefits and flexibility in the organisation.

The point of importance of organising discussed above is *[CBSE 2023]*

(A) benefits of specialisation ☐
(B) adaptation to change ☐
(C) development of personnel ☐
(D) clarity in working relationships ☐

3. Successful management lies in responding to internal and external change. This involves

(A) the clarification of objectives ☐
(B) the specification of problems ☐
(C) the search for and implementation of solutions ☐
(D) All of the above ☐

4. Identify the incorrect statement.

(A) The informal organisation does not provide a complete picture of how an organisation works. ☐
(B) When an informal organisation spreads rumours, it becomes a destructive force and goes against the interest of the formal organisation. ☐
(C) The management may not be successful in implementing changes if the informal organisation opposes them. ☐
(D) Poor organisation practices may not provide adequate recognition to creative talent, since it does not allow any deviations from rigidly laid down polices. ☐

5. Rishabh joined an entertainment company Avtaar, as a creative head. As a manager looking after the creative unit of the company, one of the functions he has to perform is the process of organising. Which step of the process will he need to perform after identifying and dividing the work that has to be done in accordance with previously determined plans?

(A) Identification and division of work ☐
(B) Departmentalisation ☐
(C) Assignment of duties ☐
(D) Establishing reporting relationships ☐

6. "Merely allocating work is not enough. Each individual should also know who has to take orders from and to whom he is accountable."

The above statement is related to one of the steps of organising process. Identify the step from the following. [CBSE 2024]

(A) Identification and division of work ☐
(B) Departmentalisation ☐
(C) Assignment of duties ☐
(D) Establishing authority and reporting relationship ☐

7. Which step of the organising process involves stating the job description, a document that clearly defines the contents and responsibilities related to a job?
(A) Departmentalisation ☐
(B) Assignment of duties ☐
(C) Establishing reporting relationships ☐
(D) Identification and division of work ☐

8. Amazon's CEO Jeff Bezos makes strategic decisions and has control over the entire organisation. All senior executives have to report directly to the CEO, which allows Jeff Bezos to be in direct control of all the organisation in terms of its functions, product lines, divisions, and service.

Identify the type of structure adopted by Jeff Bezos.
(A) Centralisation ☐
(B) Decentralisation ☐
(C) Formal ☐
(D) Informal ☐

9. Which of the following is an advantage of informal organisation? [CBSE 2024]
(A) It provides stability to the organisation because behaviour of employees can be fairly predicted since there are specific rules to guide them. ☐
(B) It leads to effective accomplishment of goals by providing a framework for the operations to be performed. ☐
(C) It enhances the employee's job satisfaction since it gives them a sense of belongingness in the organisation and allows them to find like minded people. ☐
(D) It helps in avoiding duplication of efforts as there is no ambiguity in the role that each member has to play. ☐

10. Which type of organisation is depicted in the following image?

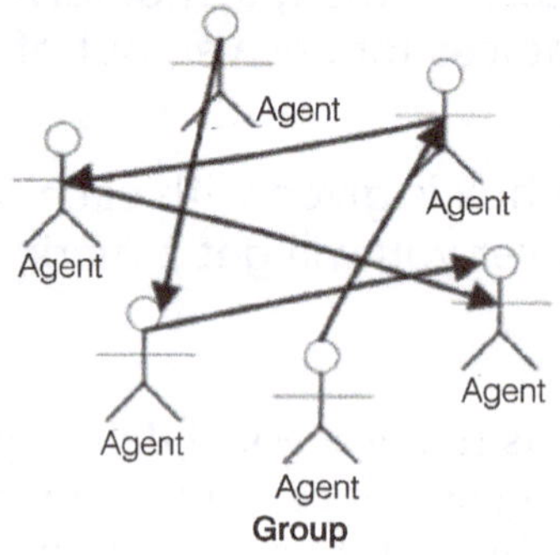

(A) Informal ☐
(B) Formal ☐
(C) Centralised ☐
(D) None of the above ☐

11. From the given picture identify the advantage of informal organisation illustrated.

(A) Fills inadequacies of formal structure ☐
(B) Spreads rumors ☐
(C) Fulfills social needs ☐
(D) Faster spread of information ☐

12. This organisational structure follows the principle of forming the company's structure with regard to the workforce's skills and knowledge. Identify the structure.
(A) Functional ☐
(B) Divisional ☐
(C) Formal ☐
(D) Informal ☐

13. The Netflix organisational structure has divisions responsible for different outputs including original programming and other content. The 'other content' division manages content by working with other content producers and distributors to license their content and make it available on the Netflix platform. The 'original programming' division is responsible for distributing and managing Netflix's original content.

Identify the type of structure adopted by Netflix.

(A) Functional ☐
(B) Divisional ☐
(C) Formal ☐
(D) Informal ☐

14. Flatter structures can be achieved by

(A) increasing the span of control ☐
(B) reducing layers from the top or removing layers of middle management ☐
(C) Both (A) and (B) ☐
(D) None of the above ☐

15. Aarohan Ltd. is a company manufacturing automobiles where division of work into key areas includes production, purchase, marketing, accounts and personnel. Which of the following is a disadvantage of the organisation structure of Aarohan Ltd.?

(A) It may lead to increase in cost ☐
(B) Managers may gain power and assert independence and ignore organisation interests ☐
(C) It ensures that different functions get due attention ☐
(D) Heads do not get training for top management positions ☐

16. Online retailer 'Bizen' has grown to be the biggest provider worldwide in the field of e-commerce. Its revenues are growing steadily year after year. It owes its success to the rapid rate of digitisation and its organisational structure.

'Bizen's managing director, Mohit makes strategic decisions and has control over the entire organisation. In 'Bizen', jobs of similar nature are grouped together into human resource department, marketing department, purchase department and research and development department.

These departments are further divided into sections and all departmental heads report to Mohit who is the coordinating head. This ensures efficiency in the utilisation of manpower and minimises duplication of efforts. The type of organisational structure of 'Bizen' is *[CBSE 2024]*

(A) informal organisational structure ☐
(B) divisional organisational structure ☐
(C) functional organisational structure ☐
(D) Both (B) and (C) ☐

17. Identify the incorrect statement.

(A) A functional structure helps in increasing managerial and operational efficiency and this results in increased profit. ☐
(B) A functional structure leads to minimal duplication of effort which results in economies of scale and this lowers cost. ☐
(C) A functional structure places less emphasis on overall enterprise objectives than the objectives pursued by a functional head. ☐
(D) Functional structure makes training of employees easier as the focus is only on a limited range of skills. ☐

18. Match the following

Column I		Column II
A. Authority	(i)	Increases the role of subordinates in the organisation by giving them more autonomy.
B. Functional structure	(ii)	Flows downwards from superior to subordinate.
C. Decentralisation	(iii)	Cannot be entirely delegated.
D. Responsibility	(iv)	Minimum duplication of efforts and hence economical.

Codes

	A	B	C	D
(A)	(i)	(iii)	(ii)	(iv)
(B)	(ii)	(iv)	(i)	(iii)
(C)	(iii)	(iv)	(i)	(ii)
(D)	(iii)	(i)	(iv)	(ii)

19. Match the following

Column I	Column II
A. It promotes control and coordination within a department.	(i) Divisional structure
B. It keeps employees in a state wherein they are constantly challenged and have to develop solutions for the various problems they encounter.	(ii) Functional structure
C. It promotes flexibility and initiative	(iii) Decentralisation

Codes

	A	B	C
(A)	(ii)	(iii)	(i)
(B)	(i)	(iii)	(ii)
(C)	(ii)	(i)	(iii)
(D)	(iii)	(ii)	(i)

20. Match the following

Column I	Column II
A. Difficult for a multiproduct company.	(i) Divisional
B. Easy to fix responsibility for performance.	(ii) Formal organisation
C. Managers are leaders.	(iii) Functional

Codes

	A	B	C
(A)	(iii)	(i)	(ii)
(B)	(i)	(iii)	(ii)
(C)	(ii)	(i)	(iii)
(D)	(iii)	(ii)	(i)

21. What is the significance of delegation in the scenario where Sara, as a superior, entrusts her authority to Tiara, her subordinate, to enable her learning, skill development and better chances of promotion?

(A) Facilitation of growth
(B) Effective management
(C) Employees' development
(D) Motivation of employees

22. Analyse the given picture below and identify the concept of management neglected by the manager.

(A) Delegation
(B) Decentralisation
(C) Authority
(D) Accountability

23. Many leaders are reflecting on how small, nimble teams built in a hurry to deal with the Covid-19 emergency made important decisions faster and better. The fact companies have learned cannot be unlearned–namely, which a flatter organisation that delegates decision-making down to a dynamic network of teams is more effective.

Identify the concept discussed in the above lines.

(A) Decentralisation
(B) Accountability
(C) Responsibility
(D) Delegation

24. .... refers to retention of decision-making authority by higher management levels. *[CBSE 2023]*

(A) Decentralisation
(B) Departmentalisation
(C) Span of control
(D) Centralisation

25. Name the concept which explains the manner in which decision-making responsibilities are divided among hierarchical levels.

(A) Organisational structure
(B) Span of management
(C) Delegation
(D) Decentralisation

Assertion-Reason Questions

No. of Questions : **8** Suggested Time : **12 Minutes**

Direction Each of the question given below consist of the two statements; one labelled as **Assertion** (A) and other as **Reason** (R). List of common options applicable for each question is given below

(A) Both Assertion (A) and Reason (R) are true and Reason (R) is the correct explanation of Assertion (A)
(B) Both Assertion (A) and Reason (R) are true, but Reason (R) is not the correct explanation of Assertion (A)
(C) Assertion (A) is true, but Reason (R) is false
(D) Assertion (A) is false, but Reason (R) is true

You have to select the codes as *a, b, c* or *d* as your answer to the question by marking (✓) in the response box given against each option.

1. **Assertion (A)** Pursuing departmental interests at the cost of organisational interests can hinder the interaction between two or more departments.

Reason (R) A manager may gain power and in a bid to assert independence may ignore organisational interest.

(A) ☐ (B) ☐ (C) ☐ (D) ☐

2. **Assertion (A)** Organisation structure is an indispensable means, and the wrong structure will seriously impair business performance and even destroy it.

Reason (R) A proper organisation structure is essential to ensure a smooth flow of communication and better control over the operations of a business enterprise.

(A) ☐ (B) ☐ (C) ☐ (D) ☐

3. **Assertion (A)** Formal organisation provides stability to the organisation.

Reason (R) Behaviour of employees can be fairly predicted since there are specific rules to guide them.

(A) ☐ (B) ☐ (C) ☐ (D) ☐

4. **Assertion (A)** Formal organisation pressurises members to conform to group expectations.

Reason (R) This can be harmful to the organisation if the norms set by the group are against organisational interests.

(A) ☐ (B) ☐ (C) ☐ (D) ☐

5. **Assertion (A)** Delegation is a pre-requisite to the efficient functioning of an organisation.

Reason (R) It enables a manager to use his time on high priority activities.

(A) ☐ (B) ☐ (C) ☐ (D) ☐

6. **Assertion (A)** Delegation allows employees to develop those skills which will enable them to perform complex tasks and assume those responsibilities which will improve their career prospects.

Reason (R) It helps to avoid overlapping of duties and duplication of effort.

(A) ☐ (B) ☐ (C) ☐ (D) ☐

7. **Assertion (A)** Decentralisation is a philosophy that implies selective dispersal of authority as it propagates the belief that people are competent, capable and resourceful.

Reason (R) It recognises the decision maker's need for autonomy.

(A) ☐ (B) ☐ (C) ☐ (D) ☐

8. **Assertion (A)** Complete centralisation would imply concentration of all decision-making functions at the apex of the management hierarchy.

Reason (R) Such a scenario would obviate the need for a management hierarchy.

(A) ☐ (B) ☐
(C) ☐ (D) ☐

Correct/Incorrect Statements

No. of Questions : **9** Suggested Time : **14 Minutes**

Direction Each of the question given below consist of the two statements. List of common options applicable for each question is given below

(A) Statement I is correct and Statement II is incorrect
(B) Statement I is incorrect and Statement II is correct
(C) Both statements are correct
(D) Both statements are incorrect

You have to select the codes as *a, b, c* or *d* as your answer to the question by marking (✓) in the response box given against each option.

1. **Statement I** Organising can be defined as a process that initiates implementation of plans by clarifying jobs and working relationships and effectively deploying resources for attainment of identified and desired results (goals).

   Statement II It is essential for effective performance that a proper match is made between the nature of a job and the ability of an individual.

   (A) ☐ (B) ☐ (C) ☐ (D) ☐

2. **Statement I** Accountability can be delegated.

   Statement II Responsibility can be delegated completely.

   (A) ☐ (B) ☐ (C) ☐ (D) ☐

3. **Statement I** Departmentalisation assigns work to individuals based on their skills and capabilities.

   Statement II Organising enhances clarity in working relationships.

   (A) ☐ (B) ☐ (C) ☐ (D) ☐

4. **Statement I** An organisation structure, at all times should contribute towards the achievement of the enterprise's objectives and should provide scope for initiative so that contribution of personnel can be maximum and effective.

   Statement II Efforts of various departments are coordinated, interlinked and integrated through the informal organisation.

   (A) ☐ (B) ☐
   (C) ☐ (D) ☐

5. **Statement I** Functional structure promotes control and coordination.

   Statement II Functional structure has diversified activities.

   (A) ☐ (B) ☐
   (C) ☐ (D) ☐

6. **Statement I** Growth prospects are high in divisional structure.

   Statement II It leads to specialisation of physical facilities.

   (A) ☐ (B) ☐
   (C) ☐ (D) ☐

7. **Statement I** Functional heads get the training for top management positions because they are able to gather experience in diverse areas.

   Statement II Complete centralisation would obviate the need for higher managerial position.

   (A) ☐ (B) ☐ (C) ☐ (D) ☐

8. **Statement I** Delegation allows them to develop those skills which will enable them to perform complex tasks and assume those responsibilities which will improve their career prospects.

Statement II It helps to avoid overlapping of duties and duplication of effort.

(A) ☐ (B) ☐
(C) ☐ (D) ☐

9. **Statement I** Delegation is the entrustment of responsibility and authority to another and the creation of accountability for performance.

Statement II Irrespective of the extent of delegated authority, the manager shall still be accountable to the same extent as before delegation. *[CBSE 2024]*

(A) ☐ (B) ☐ (C) ☐ (D) ☐

Case Based Questions

No. of Questions : **2** Suggested Time : **10 Minutes**

Direction This section contains 2 cases having 4 Questions of 1 mark each. You have to write the answer of each question based on the context of the related case.

Case 1 Started in 1965, ChemCo is a leading manufacturer of car batteries in the UK market. Since then, it has been under the charge of Mr. Jones, the founder-owner of the firm. In 1999, the company decided to go for a diversification by expanding the product line. The new product was batteries for fork-lift trucks.

At the same time, Mr. Marek was appointed as the Senior Vice-President of marketing in the company. However, soon after its successful diversification into fork-lift batteries, the sales in this segment began dropping steadily.

Mr. Marek wanted to introduce some radical changes in the advertising and branding of the new business but the proposal was turned down by the old-fashioned Mr. Jones. At this juncture in 2002, the firm is losing heavily in the fork-lift batteries business and its market share in car batteries is also on a decline. Mr. Jones has asked Mr. Marek to show a turnaround in the company within a year.

Questions

(i) "However, soon after its successful diversification into fork-lift batteries, the sales in this segment began dropping steadily".
What could be the reason of failure?
(A) Inefficient software systems ☐
(B) Misleading advertisement ☐
(C) Mismanaged product diversification in a price sensitive market ☐
(D) Poor dealer and service network ☐

(ii) "The company decided to go for a diversification by expanding the product line".
Identify the organisational structure reflected in the above line.
(A) Formal ☐
(B) Functional ☐
(C) Divisional ☐
(D) Informal ☐

(iii) "In 1999, the company decided to go for a diversification by expanding the product line". Adopting the structure provides which of the following benefits?
(A) Product specialisation ☐
(B) It promotes flexibility and initiative ☐
(C) It facilitates expansion and growth ☐
(D) All of the above ☐

(iv) What could be a potential consequence of Mr. Jones' refusal to entertain radical changes proposed by Mr. Marek?
(A) Improved market position ☐
(B) Increased profitability ☐
(C) Continued decline in sales ☐
(D) Enhanced brand reputation ☐

Case 2 In 2013-14 PTC Food division decided to enter the fast growing (20-30% annually) snacks segment, an altogether new to it. It had only one national competitor-Trepsico's Trito. After a year its wafer snack brand- Ringo, fetched 20% market share across the country. Ringo's introduction was coincided with the cricket world cup. The wafer snacks market is estimated to be around ₹ 250 crores.

The company could take the advantage of its existing distribution network and also source potatoes from farmers easily. Before the PTC could enter the market a cross-functional team made a customer survey through a marketing research group in 14 cities of the country to know about the snacks of eating habits of people.

The result showed that the customers within the age-group of 15-24 years were the most promising for the product as they were quite enthusiastic about experimenting new snack taste.

The company reported to its chefs and the chefs came out with 16 flavours with varying tastes suiting to the targeted age-group. The company decided to target the youngsters as primary target on the assumption that once they are lured in, it was easier to reach the whole family. Advertising in this category was extremely crowded.

Every week two-three local products in new names were launched, sometimes with similar names. To break through this clutter the company decided to bank upon humour appeal. The industry sources reveal that PTC spent about ₹ 50 crores on advertisement and used all possible media-print and electronic, both including the creation of its own website, Ringoringoyoungo.com with offers of online games, contests, etc. Mobile phone tone downloading was also planned which proved very effective among teenagers.

The site was advertised on all dotcom networks. Em TV, Shine TV, Bee TV and other important channels were also used for its advertisement along with FM radio channels in about 60 cities with large hoardings at strategic places.

Analysts believes that Ringo's success story owes a lot to PTC's widespread distribution channels and aggressive advertisements. Humour appeal was a big success.

The 'Ringo' was made visible by painting the railway bogies passing across the States. It has also been successful to induce Lovely Brothers' Future Group to replace Trito in their Big-Bazaar and chain of food Bazaars. PTC is paying 4% higher margin than Trepsico to Future group and other retailers.

Ringo to giving Trepsico a run for its money. Trito's share has already been reduced considerably. Retail tie-ups, regional flavours, regional humour appeals have helped PTC. But PTC still wants a bigger share in the market and in foreign markets also, if possible.

Questions

(i) Identify the function of management highlighted above.

(A) Staffing ☐ (B) Planning ☐

(C) Organising ☐ (D) Controlling ☐

(ii) Which organisation structure changes should the company bring about in order to retain its market share?

(A) It should adopt functional structure ☐

(B) It should adopt divisional structure ☐

(C) It should adopt decentralisation ☐

(D) It should adopt centralisation ☐

(iii) How will the changes suggested by you help the firm?

(A) It will help in increasing managerial and operational efficiency, resulting in increased profit. ☐

(B) It will facilitate expansion and growth as new divisions can be added without interrupting the existing operations by merely adding another divisional head and staff for the new product line. ☐

(C) It will help in quick decision-making since decisions will be taken at levels which are nearest to the point of action. ☐

(D) It will facilitate effective management. ☐

(iv) "The company reported to its chefs and the chefs came out with 16 flavours with varying tastes suiting to the targeted age-group."

Identify the step of the function identified in (i) highlighted in the above lines.

(A) Identification and division of work ☐

(B) Departmentalisation ☐

(C) Assignment of duties ☐

(D) Establishing reporting relationships ☐

Subjective Questions

Free Response Questions, Open-ended Questions etc.

No. of Questions : **7** Suggested Time : **55 Minutes**

1. SLM management institute believes in proper organising. It places more emphasis on work to be performed than interpersonal relationships among the employees. It believes that through proper organising, they can move away from present norms and accept new challenges with success.

Through this, they will be able to add more activities and projects in their yearly plan.

(i) Which importance of organising has been indicated in the above paragraph?

(ii) Define organisation structure.

(iii) Identify the type of organisation discussed above.

2. Surja runs a company in Bombay. The company is known for its product specialisation and has a lot of reputation in the market. There is flexibility and initiative in departments.

Identify the organisational structure and state any three advantages of it.

3. A tech start-up with a flat organisational structure encourages open communication and collaboration, leading to the emergence of leaders who wield influence beyond their official roles.
Employees grab lunch together and attend after-work events. As a result, employees develop trust and camaraderie, which can lead to smoother collaboration and problem solving during work hours.

When facing a complex problem, employees often turn to their trusted network for insights and guidance.

(i) Identify the type of organisational structure followed in the organisation.

(ii) State any three advantages of the organisation identified in (i) discussed in the para.

4. XYZ Retail Chain operates 50 stores across the country. The CEO delegates responsibility to regional managers, empowering them to oversee a cluster of stores. Regional managers are tasked with setting performance goals, providing support and ensuring compliance with company policies.

Departments are organised based on their functions, allowing for focused expertise and streamlined communication.

(i) Identify the function of management discussed above.

(ii) Identify and state the concept followed by the company.

(iii) Which organisational structure is adopted by the company?

5. Preeti started her own cooking channel on Youtube 'Mood Art'. As her subscribers increased, she was not in a position to manage everything on her own. She hired Rahul and Riya to help her with filming, editing, lighting and content research. She granted authority to them to operate within prescribed limits. She was thus, able to use her time on high priority activities like developing new recipes and content development etc.

As a result, Rahul and Riya were given opportunities to develop and exercise initiative. Preeti was now able to focus on objectives and meet the target of achieving a subscriber base of one million in six months.

(i) Identify the concept of management used by Preeti to focus on objectives of her business and meet her targets.

(ii) Explain any five points of importance of the concept identified in (i) above. *[CBSE 2024]*

6. Lakshmibai School, a prestigious institution, offers the CBSE curriculum for Class XII students. The school aims to provide a well-organised and comprehensive learning experience to prepare students for their board examinations and future endeavours.

The school leadership team thoroughly studied the CBSE Class XII curriculum guidelines, including the syllabus, marking scheme and examination pattern. This provided a clear understanding of the academic requirements and learning objectives for each subject.

A structured time table was created, balancing the workload across subjects and ensuring adequate time for teaching, practice, revision and duplication can be avoided and the burden of work can be shared among the teachers.

The time table incorporated regular breaks to prevent student burnout and optimise learning effectiveness. Qualified and experienced teachers were assigned to teach specific subjects based on their expertise and qualifications.

Each teacher was responsible for planning and delivering lessons in their respective subjects, adhering to the curriculum guidelines and instructional standards set by the school.

It is essential for effective performance that a proper match is made between the nature of a job and the ability of an individual.

Further departments such as science department, commerce and humanities departments were made to facilitate specialisation. Adequate resources, including textbooks, reference materials, laboratory equipment and digital resources, were allocated to support teaching and learning activities.

The school invested in modern facilities and technology infrastructure to enhance the learning experience and facilitate interactive and experiential learning opportunities.

A comprehensive assessment and evaluation system was implemented to monitor student progress and performance. This included regular unit tests, mid-term examinations, mock board exams and practical assessments, aligned with the CBSE examination pattern.

Detailed feedback and constructive criticism were provided to students to help them identify areas for improvement and take corrective actions. While academic excellence was prioritised, the school also emphasised the importance of extra-curricular and co-curricular activities for holistic development.

Students were encouraged to participate in sports, cultural events, community service projects, and competitions to nurture their talents and leadership skills. Open communication channels were established with parents to keep them informed about their child's academic progress, attendance and behaviour.

Parent-teacher meetings, progress reports and digital communication platforms were utilised to facilitate regular interaction and collaboration between parents and teachers.

(i) Identify the function highlighted in the above case.

(ii) Identify and state the steps of the function identified in (i) with the help of quoting the lines.

7. Jojo and Jojo is a company known for its consumer business of baby oil and bandages, but many people do not know that the company also runs a medical device and diagnostics business, as well as a pharmaceutical company.

With more than 1,80,000 employees worldwide the company has chosen to share decision-making authority with lower levels and place it nearest to the point of action. Therefore the response does not take time. This propagates the belief that people are competent, capable and resourceful who can get a chance to prove their abilities. And enables the company in identifying those executives who have the necessary potential to become dynamic leaders, so that the checking required on decisions taken by lower levels of management is the least.

This makes it possible to evaluate performance at each level and each department can be individually held accountable for their results. By quoting the lines given above identify and briefly explain the benefits of the concept discussed above.

Answers

If your answer matches with the answer given here then put (✓). In the box otherwise put (✗). In case you did not attempt the question leave the box blank.

Multiple Choice Questions

1. D	☐	2. B	☐
3. D	☐	4. D	☐
5. B	☐	6. D	☐
7. B	☐	8. A	☐
9. C	☐	10. A	☐
11. C	☐	12. A	☐
13. B	☐	14. C	☐
15. D	☐	16. C	☐
17. C	☐	18. D	☐
19. A	☐	20. A	☐
21. C	☐	22. A	☐
23. A	☐	24. D	☐
25. D	☐		

Your Score__________ *(No. of Correct Answers)*

Assertion-Reason Questions

1. A	☐	2. A	☐
3. A	☐	4. D	☐
5. A	☐	6. B	☐
7. A	☐	8. A	☐

Your Score__________ *(No. of Correct Answers)*

Correct/Incorrect Statements

1. C	☐	2. D	☐
3. B	☐	4. A	☐
5. C	☐	6. C	☐
7. D	☐	8. C	☐
9. C	☐		

Your Score__________ *(No. of Correct Answers)*

Case Based Questions

1. (i) C ☐
   (ii) C ☐
   (iii) D ☐
   (iv) C ☐

2. (i) C ☐
   (ii) B ☐
   (iii) C ☐
   (iv) C ☐

Your Score__________ *(No. of Correct Answers)*

Explanations

Multiple Choice Questions

1. (D) Organising
2. (B) The adaptation allowed the company to effectively respond to the changing business environment brought about by the pandemic, showcasing flexibility and resilience in its operations.
3. (D) Successful management involves not only clarifying objectives and specifying problems but also searching for and implementing solutions to both internal and external changes.
4. (D) In practical sense, poor organisational practices may indeed hinder recognition of creative talent due to bureaucratic hurdles and resistance to change, but this does not necessarily mean that it completely disallows any deviations from policies.
5. (B) Departmentalisation
6. (D) Establishing authority and reporting relationship
7. (B) Assignment of duties
8. (A) Centralisation
9. (C) It enhances the employee's job satisfaction since it gives them a sense of belongingness in the organisation and allows them to find like minded people.
10. (A) Informal organisation refers to the network of social relationships, interactions and connections that emerge spontaneously among employees within a formal organisational structure.
11. (C) Fulfills social needs
12. (A) The organisational structure described follows the principle of forming the company's structure with regard to the workforce's skills and knowledge. This structure is known as functional structure.
13. (B) Divisional
14. (C) Both (A) and (B)
15. (D) Heads do not get training for top management positions is a disadvantage because in a functional organisational structure like Aarohan Ltd., managers often become highly specialised in their respective functions.
16. (C) A functional organisational structure groups employees based on their specialised skills and functions, such as marketing, finance or operations. Each department operates independently under its respective functional head, facilitating efficient coordination and expertise focused decision-making within the organisation.
17. (C) In a functional structure, while each functional head may prioritise their departmental objectives, the ultimate goal is to align these objectives with the overall enterprise objectives to ensure organisational success.
18. (D) (iii) (i) (iv) (ii)
19. (A) (ii) (iii) (i)
20. (A) (iii) (i) (ii)
21. (C) Delegation involves entrusting authority and responsibility to subordinates, which not only facilitates the accomplishment of tasks but also contributes to the development of employees.
22. (A) Delegation
23. (A) Decentralisation
24. (D) Centralisation
25. (D) Decentralisation

Assertion-Reason Questions

1. (A) Both Assertion (A) and Reason (R) are true and Reason (R) is the correct explanation of Assertion (A)
2. (A) Both Assertion (A) and Reason (R) are true and Reason (R) is the correct explanation of Assertion (A)
3. (A) Both Assertion (A) and Reason (R) are true and Reason (R) is the correct explanation of Assertion (A)
4. (D) Informal organisation pressurises members to conform to group expectations.
5. (A) Both Assertion (A) and Reason (R) are true and Reason (R) is the correct explanation of Assertion (A)
6. (B) Both Assertion (A) and Reason (R) are true, but Reason (R) is not the correct explanation of Assertion (A)
7. (A) Both Assertion (A) and Reason (R) are true and Reason (R) is the correct explanation of Assertion (A)
8. (A) Both Assertion (A) and Reason (R) are true and Reason (R) is the correct explanation of Assertion (A)

Correct/Incorrect Statements

1. (C) Both statements are correct
2. (D) Accountability cannot be fully delegated as individuals ultimately remain responsible for the outcomes of tasks they delegate. Responsibility can be partially delegated, but it cannot be completely transferred as individuals retain some level of accountability for the tasks they delegate.
3. (B) Departmentalisation groups similar activities together. Organising clarifies working relationships within an organisation, ensuring that employees understand their roles and responsibilities clearly.
4. (A) Efforts of various departments are coordinated, interlinked and integrated through the formal organisation.
5. (C) Both statements are correct
6. (C) Both statement are correct
7. (D) Divisional heads get the training for top management positions because they are able to gather experience in diverse areas.
   Complete decentralisation would obviate the need for higher managerial position.
8. (C) Both statement are correct
9. (C) Both statements are correct

Case Based Questions

1. (i) (C) Despite successful diversification, the company may have failed to understand the unique demands and dynamics of the fork-lift batteries market, leading to a decline in sales.
   (ii) (C) Divisional structure involves organising the company into separate divisions based on product lines or services, which allows for focused management and accountability within each division.
   (iii) (D) All of the above
   (iv) (C) In a dynamic business environment, failure to embrace necessary changes can lead to a loss of competitiveness and declining sales.
2. (i) (C) Organising
   (ii) (B) Adopting a divisional structure would allow the company to create separate divisions for different product lines, such as Ringo snacks, facilitating better focus, coordination and accountability for each product line.
   (iii) (C) The changes suggested by adopting a divisional structure would indeed facilitate quick decision-making since decisions will be taken at levels closest to the point of action.
   (iv) (C) The chefs are assigned the duty of developing flavours for the Ringo snack brand, indicating the assignment of duties within the organisation's structure.

Subjective Questions

1. (i) The importance of organising which is indicated above is 'Expansion and Growth'.
   (ii) Organisation structure is the framework within which managerial and operational tasks are performed within an organisation. It explains the relationship between people, the work to be done by them and the resources to be utilised by them.
   (iii) Formal organisation
2. Organisational structure followed is divisional structure. The divisional structure offers many advantages
   (i) Product specialisation helps in the development of varied skills in a divisional head and this prepares him for higher positions.

(ii) Divisional heads are accountable for profits, as revenues and costs related to different departments can be easily identified and assigned to them. This provides a proper basis for performance measurement. It also helps in fixation of responsibility in cases of poor performance of the division and appropriate remedial action can be taken.

(iii) It promotes flexibility and initiative because each division functions as an autonomous unit which leads to faster decision-making.

3. (i) Informal organisation

(ii) The advantages are as follows

(a) It helps to fulfill the social needs of the members and allows them to find like minded people.

(b) It encourages open communication and collaboration among employees, leading to the emergence of informal leaders who can positively influence their peers.

(c) Informal interactions such as having lunch together and attending after work events foster trust and camaraderie among employees. This trust and camaraderie contribute to smoother collaboration and problem solving during work hours.

4. (i) The function of management discussed above is 'organising'.

(ii) The concept followed by the company is 'delegation of authority'. It refers to the process of assigning decision-making authority and responsibility from higher levels of management to lower levels.
In this scenario, the CEO empowers regional managers to set performance goals, provide support and ensure compliance with company policies, thereby delegating authority to them.

(iii) The organisational structure adopted by the company is a 'functional structure'. A functional structure organises departments based on their functions or areas of specialisation.
In this case, departments are organised based on their functions, allowing for focused expertise and streamlined communication.

5. (i) Delegation

(ii) The importance of delegation is as follows

(a) **Effective Management** Delegation is crucial for effective management as it allows managers to focus on high-priority tasks while empowering subordinates to handle routine tasks, leading to increased efficiency and productivity.

(b) **Employee Development** Delegation provides opportunities for employees to take on new responsibilities, develop new skills and grow professionally, contributing to their career advancement and job satisfaction.

(c) **Motivation of Employees** Delegation can motivate employees by showing trust in their abilities, fostering a sense of ownership and responsibility, and providing opportunities for autonomy and recognition.

(d) **Facilitation of Growth** Delegation facilitates organisational growth by empowering employees to make decisions and take actions that contribute to achieving organisational goals, thereby enabling the organisation to expand and evolve.

(e) **Basis of Management Hierarchy** Delegation forms the basis of management hierarchy by establishing clear lines of authority and responsibility, ensuring efficient decision-making and coordination within the organisation's structure.

6. (i) Organising

(ii) Steps of organising identified are

(a) **Identification and Division of Work** "A structured time table was created, balancing the workload across subjects and ensuring adequate time for teaching, practice, revision and duplication can be avoided and the burden of work can be shared among the teachers."
This step involves analysing the workload and breaking it down into manageable tasks. In the provided context, a structured timetable was created to allocate time for various activities such as teaching, practice and revision, ensuring that the workload is balanced and shared among teachers.

(b) **Assignment of Duties** "Each teacher was responsible for planning and delivering lessons in their respective subjects, adhering to the curriculum guidelines and instructional standards set by the school. It is essential for effective performance that a proper match is made between the nature of a job and the ability of an individual."

After identifying the tasks, the next step is to assign specific responsibilities to individuals based on their skills and abilities.

In this case, each teacher was assigned the responsibility of planning and delivering lessons in their respective subjects, ensuring adherence to curriculum guidelines and instructional standards set by the school.

(c) **Departmentalisation** "Further departments such as science department, commerce and humanities departments were made to facilitate specialisation."

This step involves grouping similar tasks or functions into departments to facilitate specialisation and coordination.

In the given context, departments such as science, commerce and humanities were established to facilitate specialisation in different subject areas, allowing for more focused expertise and efficient coordination within each department.

7. Decentralisation is highlighted in the given lines. Importance of decentralisation are

(i) **Quick Decision-making** "Response does not take time". In a decentralised organisation, since decisions are taken at levels which are nearest to the point of action and there is no requirement for approvals from many levels, the process is much faster.

(ii) **Develops Managerial Talent for the Future** "Who can get a chance to prove their abilities". Decentralisation gives managers a chance to prove their abilities and creates a reservoir of qualified manpower that can be considered to fill up more challenging positions through promotion.

(iii) **Develops Initiative among Subordinates** "Identifying those executives who have the necessary potential to become dynamic lenders".

Decentralisation helps to promote self-reliance and confidence amongst the subordinates.

It also keeps them in a state wherein they are constantly challenged and have to develop solutions for the various problems they encounter.

(iv) **Better Control** "This makes it possible to evaluate performance at each level and each department can be individually held accountable for their results". Feedback from levels helps to analyse variances and improve operations.

CHAPTER -6

Staffing

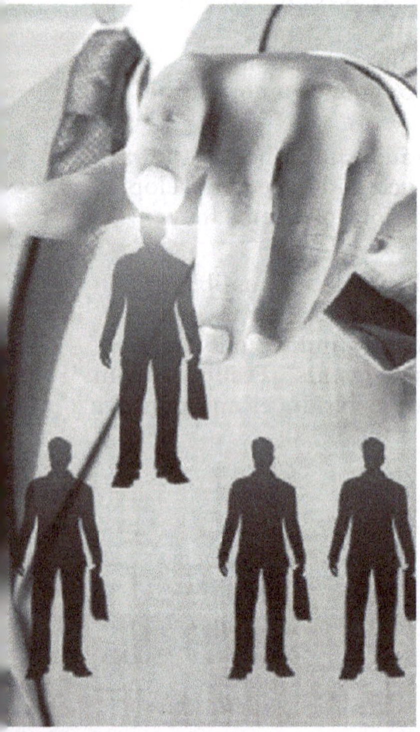

Types & Nos. of Questions

Multiple Choice Questions	-	29
Assertion-Reason Questions	-	8
Correct/Incorrect Statements	-	8
Case Based Questions	-	2 Cases, *each with four Questions*
Subjective Questions	-	7

Trend Analysis

On the basis of analysis of last 2 years' papers, it is found that on an average 2 Multiple Choice Questions and 2 Short Answer Type Questions (Case Based) are asked from this chapter.

Focus Topics of the Chapter

- Staffing and its Process
- Recruitment and its Sources
- Process of Selection
- Training and Development

Multiple Choice Questions

No. of Questions : **29** Suggested Time : **45 Minutes**

Direction Each of the question given below is Multiple Choice Question (MCQ) i.e. there are Four Options/ Choices for answer, out of which ONLY ONE is correct. You have to select the correct option.
A response box is given with each option, mark (✓) in the box of the correct option. For each correct answer you will get 1 mark, while there is no penalty for incorrect answer or missed out questions.

1. "It is a well-executed process , essential for building and maintaining a skilled and motivated workforce that contributes to an organisation's long-term success. It's a continuous, people-centric and strategic endeavour that aligns with ethical and legal standards while adapting to changing circumstances."

Identify the concept of management highlighted above.

(A) Planning ☐ (B) Organising ☐
(C) Staffing ☐ (D) Directing ☐

2. "It is a separate and specialised function and there are many aspects of human relations to be considered." Identify the concept.

(A) Selection ☐
(B) Staffing ☐
(C) Human resource ☐
(D) Directing ☐

3. These programmes are essential for organisations seeking an upskilled and knowledgeable workforce whereas some programmes make it easy to showcase that your organisation cares about employees' professional growth.

Identify the step of staffing process highlighted in the above statement.

(A) Placement and orientation ☐
(B) Training and development ☐
(C) Performance appraisal ☐
(D) Promotion and career planning ☐

4. The CEO of Rajnath Services, Mr. Ashwini Ponnappa believes, to build engagement among the employees to encourage teamwork, boost morale and motivation.It provides various benefits to employee like insurance coverage (medical, dental, life) cellphone plans, health and wellness reimbursements, etc.

Identify the incentive provided by the company.

(A) Salary ☐ (B) Commision ☐
(C) Perquisites ☐ (D) Bonus ☐

5. SCT Services CEO Rajan Gopinath's compensation includes salary, commission and other allowances. The company also pays for his insurance and vacations. Identify one indirect payment being made by the company to the CEO.

(A) Employer paid insurance ☐
(B) Salary ☐
(C) Commission ☐
(D) Allowances ☐

6. "The ratings aroused to influence promotions and salary adjustments of the employees and also as a criterion for assigning further rating for them". One of the step of the function of management is highlighted in the above para.

Identify the step.

(A) Performance appraisal ☐
(B) Promotion and career planning ☐
(C) Compensation ☐
(D) Training and development ☐

7. Identify the step of staffing process shown in the picture below

(A) Training and development ☐
(B) Placement and orientation ☐
(C) Performance appraisal ☐
(D) Estimating manpower requirement ☐

8. Identify the external source of recruitment illustrated by the picture given below *[CBSE 2023]*

(A) Direct recruitment ☐
(B) Casual callers ☐
(C) Advertisement ☐
(D) Labour contractor ☐

9. RP Infotech Ltd. decided to approach Patel Engineering College to recruit qualified personnel for various technical jobs in its newly opened branch in Surat.

Which source of recruitment from the following has been used by RP Infortech Ltd. in the above case? *[CBSE 2023]*

(A) Direct recruitment ☐
(B) Placement agencies and management consultants ☐
(C) Campus recruitment ☐
(D) Recommendation of employees ☐

10. "These agencies are run by the government and help to match personnel demand and supply by serving as a link between job seekers and employers." Name the source of the recruitment.

(A) Promotion ☐
(B) Direct recruitment ☐
(C) Campus recruitment ☐
(D) Employment exchange ☐

11. An organisation maintains a list of probable applicants along with their contact information. As and when vacancies arise; it contacts them and persuades them to apply for the jobs available. This is referred to as

(A) casual callers ☐
(B) campus recruitment ☐
(C) direct recruitment ☐
(D) placement agencies ☐

12. Identify the method of recruitment suitable to recruit technical, professional and managerial personnel.

(A) Web publishing ☐
(B) Campus recruitment ☐
(C) Both (A) and (B) ☐
(D) Management consultants ☐

13. Ashok Leyland is a leading automotive manufacturer in the global market with roots based in India. Founded in 1948, the organisation has since then revolutionised the Indian vehicle market with innovative solutions and now has a presence across the globe.

Ashok Leyland has always promoted an engaging work culture with the correct balance and as a result, it was awarded the AON Best Employers for India award.

With offices spreading throughout the nation, the organisation is constantly looking to hire talent with strong analytical thinking and communication skills who possess the drive to build a robust and long-lasting career with them.

It decided to conduct interviews universities, vocational schools and management institutes to recruit qualified personnel for various jobs.

The source of recruitment used by Ashok Leyland to recruit the employees is

(A) employment exchange ☐
(B) adertisement ☐
(C) casual callers ☐
(D) campus recruitment ☐

14. Astra Builders has to deliver the flats to its buyers on time. Due to this there is a sudden rush of work.

Therefore, the company needs to arrange workers to work at the sites at a short notice. The source of recruitment which may be used by the company to tap the casual vacancy is

(A) direct recruitment ☐
(B) advertisement ☐
(C) recommendation of employees ☐
(D) employment exchange ☐

15. Carlson companies running a family business, did not have any successor to take over the reins. The senior management tried to look both internally and externally for a potential successor. They ultimately decided to give advertisement in a website Indeed.com.

According to Beverly Behan of Hay's Group; Carlson should commend for not only making the right decision in not hiring the heir apparent but for handling the job search in a calm and effective way.

Identify the source of recruitment adopted by Carlson companies.

(A) Web publishing ☐
(B) Advertising ☐
(C) Campus recruitment ☐
(D) Placement agencies ☐

16. The various activities involved with the process of recruitment are

(A) identification of the different sources of labour supply ☐
(B) choosing the most suitable source or sources ☐
(C) Both (A) and (B) ☐
(D) Only (B) ☐

17. Choose the incorrect statement.

(A) Complete reliance on internal recruitment involves danger of 'inbreeding' by stopping 'infusion of new blood' into the organisation ☐
(B) Selection process may continue even after the offer of employment, acceptance and joining of the candidate ☐
(C) The effectiveness of the staffing process would ultimately be tested in terms of on-the-job of the chosen person ☐
(D) Attestation form contains certain vital details about the candidate, which are authenticated and attested by him or her ☐

18. Match the terms given in Column I with their meanings in Column II *[CBSE 2024]*

	Column I		Column II
A.	Placement	(i)	Introducing the selected employee to other employees and familiarising him with the rules and policies of the organisation.
B.	Recruitment	(ii)	It refers to the employee occupying the position or post for which he/she has been selected.
C.	Orientation	(iii)	Evaluating an employee's current and/or past performance as against certain predetermined standards.
D.	Performance appraisal	(iv)	The process of searching for prospective employees and stimulating them to apply for jobs in the organisation.

Codes

	A	B	C	D
(A)	(i)	(ii)	(iii)	(iv)
(B)	(ii)	(iii)	(i)	(iv)
(C)	(ii)	(iv)	(i)	(iii)
(D)	(ii)	(i)	(iv)	(iii)

19. After the job offer has been made and candidate accepts the offer, certain documents need to be executed by the employer and the candidate. One such document is the

(A) Attestation form ☐
(B) Job offer ☐
(C) Contract of employment ☐
(D) None of the above ☐

20. Choose the incorrect statement.

(A) Education does not provide definite answers, but rather develops a logical and rational mind that can determine relationships among pertinent variables and thereby understand a phenomenon ☐
(B) Trade test indicates the person's capacity to develop ☐
(C) The selection process ends after the offer of employment through a contract of employment ☐
(D) Staffing is that part of the process of management which is concerned with obtaining, utilising and maintaining a satisfactory and satisfied work force ☐

21. Identify the type of test illustrated in the picture.

(A) Trade test ☐
(B) Aptitude test ☐
(C) Intelligence test ☐
(D) Personality test ☐

22. Match the Column I with Column II in the following information

Column I	Column II
A. The trainees work under the guidance of master worker.	(i) Vestibule training
B. Trainees learn on the equipment they will be using, but training is conducted away from the actual workfloor.	(ii) Internship training
C. Trainees work in some factory or office to acquire practical knowledge and skills along with regular studies.	(iii) Apprenticeship training

Codes

	A	B	C
(A)	(iii)	(i)	(ii)
(B)	(ii)	(iii)	(i)
(C)	(i)	(ii)	(iii)
(D)	(iii)	(ii)	(i)

23. "Such tests are good indices of a person's future success score." Identify the type of test.

(A) Aptitude test ☐ (B) Intelligent test ☐
(C) Personality ☐ (D) Trade ☐

24. "Arec Ltd. wants to train the employees to meet the demand for generative AI and quantum computing solution."

The method of training by which the company can prepare the employees is

(A) apprenticeship training ☐
(B) internship training ☐
(C) vestibule training ☐
(D) induction training ☐

25. A 26 years old construction labourer was electrocuted when he tripped and came into contact with a crane. The crane had become energised through accidental contact with a high voltage line overhead. The labourer was carrying a wire rope over to be used to attach a pile of plywood to the crane's hook.

The labourer tripped and brushed against the corner of the energised crane.

Cardiopulmonary resuscitation was immediately administered by co-workers until paramedics arrived. The labourer was pronounced dead.

Which type of training would have helped to save the worker?

(A) Apprenticeship programme ☐
(B) Internship training ☐
(C) Vestibule training ☐
(D) Induction training ☐

26. "It is a career-oriented process designed to help the employees in the progress towards maturity and acutalisation of their potential capabilities."

Identify the process. *[CBSE 2024]*

(A) Staffing ☐
(B) Selection ☐
(C) Development ☐
(D) Training ☐

27. The method of training which can be adopted to train the workers shown in the picture below is

(A) Apprenticeship training ☐
(B) Internship training ☐
(C) Vestibule training ☐
(D) Induction training ☐

28. Match the Column I with Column II in the following information

Column I	Column II
A. It is commonly part of the recruitment process.	(i) Promotion
B. It is practically a horizontal movement of employees.	(ii) Job description
C. It is a vertical shifting of employees.	(iii) Advertising
D. Analysing jobs, collecting information about the jobs.	(iv) Transfer

Codes

	A	B	C	D	
(A)	(iii)	(iv)	(i)	(ii)	☐
(B)	(iv)	(ii)	(i)	(iii)	☐
(C)	(iv)	(i)	(ii)	(iii)	☐
(D)	(iii)	(i)	(ii)	(iv)	☐

29. Match the Column I with Column II in the following information

Column I	Column II
A. It is an indicator of a person's learning ability or the ability to make decisions and judgments.	(i) Personality test
B. It indicates the person's capacity to develop.	(ii) Trade test
C. These are difficult to design and implement.	(iii) Aptitude test
D. These tests measure the existing skills of the individual.	(iv) Intelligent test

Codes

	A	B	C	D	
(A)	(iv)	(ii)	(i)	(iii)	☐
(B)	(iv)	(ii)	(iii)	(i)	☐
(C)	(iv)	(i)	(ii)	(iii)	☐
(D)	(iii)	(i)	(ii)	(iv)	☐

Assertion-Reason Questions

No. of Questions : **8** Suggested Time : **12 Minutes**

Direction Each of the question given below consist of the two statements; one labelled as **Assertion** (A) and other as **Reason** (R). List of common options applicable for each question is given below

(A) Both Assertion (A) and Reason (R) are true and Reason (R) is the correct explanation of Assertion (A)

(B) Both Assertion (A) and Reason (R) are true, but Reason (R) is not the correct explanation of Assertion (A)

(C) Assertion (A) is true, but Reason (R) is false

(D) Assertion (A) is false, but Reason (R) is true

You have to select the codes as *a, b, c* or *d* as your answer to the question by marking (✓) in the response box given against each option.

1. **Assertion** (A) The ability of an organisation to achieve its goal depends upon the quality of its human resources.

   Reason (R) Staffing is not a managerial function.

   (A) ☐ (B) ☐ (C) ☐ (D) ☐

2. **Assertion** (A) Employees need to be trained and motivated to work in harmony with the goals of the organisation.

   Reason (R) Staffing is seen as a generic function of management.

   (A) ☐ (B) ☐ (C) ☐ (D) ☐

3. **Assertion** (A) Staffing is referred to as both a line as well as a staff activity.

   Reason (R) Staffing enhances the self-esteem and prestige of those selected and conveys to them the seriousness with which the things are done in the organisation.

   (A) ☐ (B) ☐ (C) ☐ (D) ☐

4. **Assertion** (A) Neither over-staffing nor under-staffing is a desirable situation.

   Reason (R) It is important to translate the manpower requirements into specific job description and the desirable profile of its occupant.

   (A) ☐ (B) ☐ (C) ☐ (D) ☐

5. **Assertion** (A) Certain pay plans can be created which are a combination of time based pay plus incentives for higher performance.

   Reason (R) Staffing includes acquisition, retention, development, performance appraisal, promotion and compensation of the most important resource of an organisation, that is, its human capital.

   (A) ☐ (B) ☐ (C) ☐ (D) ☐

6. **Assertion** (A) Job transfers are helpful in avoiding termination and in removing individual problems and grievances.

   Reason (R) Transfer is a tool of training the employees to prepare them for higher jobs.

   (A) ☐ (B) ☐ (C) ☐ (D) ☐

7. **Assertion** (A) Promotion refer to being placed in positions of increased responsibility.

   Reason (R) Promotions are an integral part of people's career.

   (A) ☐ (B) ☐ (C) ☐ (D) ☐

8. **Assertion** (A) In internship training, a master worker is appointed as the trainer.

   Reason (R) In job rotation, a trainee is systematically transferred from one job to another.

   (A) ☐ (B) ☐ (C) ☐ (D) ☐

Correct/Incorrect Statements

No. of Questions : **8** Suggested Time : **12 Minutes**

Direction Each of the question given below consist of the two statements. List of common options applicable for each question is given below

(A) Statement I is correct and Statement II is incorrect
(B) Statement II is correct and Statement I is incorrect
(C) Both statements are correct
(D) Both statements are incorrect

You have to select the codes as *a, b, c* or *d* as your answer to the question by marking (✓) in the response box given against each option.

1. **Statement I** Growth of an organisation requires the continual infusion of quality staff.

   Statement II An organisation can achieve its objectives only when it has the right persons in the right positions.

   (A) ☐ (B) ☐ (C) ☐ (D) ☐

2. **Statement I** By avoiding overmanning, staffing prevents under-utilisation of personnel and high labour costs.

   Statement II Staffing avoids compliance of work by indicating in advance the shortages of personnel.

   (A) ☐ (B) ☐ (C) ☐ (D) ☐

3. **Statement I** It is the responsibility of top level managers to directly deal with and select people to work for the organisation.

   Statement II Human relations approach recognises human factor as the most important instrument of success in an organisation.

   (A) ☐ (B) ☐ (C) ☐ (D) ☐

4. **Statement I** Directing is seen as a generic function of management.

   Statement II Managing the human component of an organisation is the most important task.

   (A) ☐ (B) ☐ (C) ☐ (D) ☐

5. **Statement I** Human resource management is the practice of finding, evaluating and establishing a working relationship with people, for a purpose.

   Statement II Directing is a distinct functional area of management just as marketing management and financial management.

   (A) ☐ (B) ☐ (C) ☐ (D) ☐

6. **Statement I** Joining a job marks the beginning of socialisation of the employee at the workplace.

   Statement II Promotions are an integral part of people's career.

   (A) ☐ (B) ☐ (C) ☐ (D) ☐

7. **Statement I** Selection is the most fundamental and critical drive of organisational performance.

   Statement II The ability of an organisation to achieve its goal depends upon the quality of its human resources.

   (A) ☐ (B) ☐ (C) ☐ (D) ☐

8. **Statement I** Transfers can also be used for training of employees for learning different jobs.

   Statement II External recruitment also simplifies the process of selection and placement.

   (A) ☐ (B) ☐ (C) ☐ (D) ☐

Case Based Questions

No. of Questions : **2** Suggested Time : **10 Minutes**

Direction This section contains 2 cases each having 4 Questions of 1 mark each. You have to write the answer of each question based on the context of the related case.

Case 1 Mr. Vikas Goel is an HR Manager of "Sanduja Furniture Private Limited." At the beginning of the new year, he anticipated that the company will need 30 new additional persons to fill up different vacancies. He gave an advertisement in the newspaper inviting applications for filling up different vacant posts. As many as 120 applications were received.

The same were scrutinised. Out of these, conditions of 15 applicants were not acceptable to the company. Letters of regret, giving reasons, were sent to them. Remaining candidates were called for preliminary interview. The candidates called for were asked to fill up blank application forms. Thereafter, they were given four tests.

The objective of the first test was to find out how much interest the applicant takes in his work. The objective of the second test was to find out 'specialisation' of the applicant in any particular area. Third test aimed at making sure whether the applicant was capable of learning through training or not.

The purpose of the fourth test was to find out how much capability a person has to mix-up with other persons and whether he can influence other persons and get influenced by them. *[CBSE QB]*

Questions

(i) The purpose of the fourth test was to find out how much capability a person has to mix-up with other persons and whether he can influence other persons and get influenced by them. Which tests is indicated in this situation?

(A) Personality test ☐
(B) Intelligent test ☐
(C) Aptitude test ☐
(D) Trade test ☐

(ii) At the beginning of the new year, he anticipated that the company will need 30 new additional persons to fill up different vacancies. Identify the first step of staffing.

(A) Placement and orientation ☐
(B) Training and development ☐
(C) Recruitment ☐
(D) Estimating manpower requirement ☐

(iii) From the given lines, "Out of these, conditions of 15 applicants were not acceptable to the company. Letters of regret, giving reasons, were sent to them." Which aspect of staffing is highlighted in the statement?

(A) Recruitment ☐
(B) Selection ☐
(C) Training ☐
(D) Education ☐

(iv) The applicants were given four tests like intelligent test to interest test after filling up blank application form. Identify which step of selection process was followed by the management.

(A) Selection decision ☐
(B) Selection test ☐
(C) Job offer ☐
(D) Medical examination ☐

Case 2 Kanta Ltd. is a company that specialises in manufacturing electronic items. They have recently got extra orders from a major retail chain. In addition, the company entertains four day rush orders, which require rework at one or two operations, thus, delaying the process of delivering work modifications of a client.

This is because the company's workers are shifted from one work operation to another depending on the demand of the operation. In this sense, some workstations are left vacant, while some workstations are overloaded. Moreover, disturbance in the operations of the company is may be attributed to telephone calls from the customer's engineers who had encountered a design problem.

This leads to the realisation that operations and productivity method improvements are not being implemented due to the pressure for output, the constant shifting of workers from one job to the next and in inhibiting experimentation with new ideas.

Furthermore, the introduction and implementation of new ideas and methods has led to further confusion, as the increase in the production of a particular station resulted to the piling up of work in another, thus, rescheduling orders and reassigning workers. This further impeded the productivity of the company.

Moreover, due to the delay of production and the increase in the reworking of products, the company has fewer shipments, with actual deliveries delayed with an average of 9 days.

This forced the company to hire an addition of eight employees assigned in the production force. The company decided to call the employees from the database of applications. Further it was also decided to advertise in the newspapers.

Questions

(i) Identify the function of management discussed above.

(A) Directing ☐
(B) Planning ☐
(C) Organising ☐
(D) Staffing ☐

(ii) "This forced the company to hire an addition of eight employees assigned in the production force." Identify the concept which will help the company to find out the number and type of personnel available.

(A) Recruitment ☐
(B) Workload analysis ☐
(C) Workforce analysis ☐
(D) All of the above ☐

(iii) "Company's workers are shifted from one work operation to another depending on the demand of the operation."

The method of recruitment used by the company was

(A) transfer ☐
(B) promotion ☐
(C) casual callers ☐
(D) management consultant ☐

(iv) "The company decided to call the employees from the database of applications." Identify the external source of recruitment used by the company to hire new employees.

(A) Direct recruitment ☐
(B) Campus recruitment ☐
(C) Management consultants ☐
(D) Casual callers ☐

Subjective Questions

Free Response Questions, Open-ended Questions etc.

No. of Questions : **7** Suggested Time : **56 Minutes**

1. Human resources are the most important asset of an organisation. The ability of an organisation to achieve its goal depends upon the quality of its human resources. The General Manager of 'Allied and Sons' appointed an IIM graduate, Pawan Rai, specialised in finance as Marketing Manager.

   On montly evaluation, it was found that Pawan Rai's performance was not up to expectations and he was not able to meet the monthly targets of the organisation. The Chief Executive Officer (CEO) of the company asked for investigation into the matter.

   The CEO was told that Pawan Rai has a specialisation in finance but was appointed as a Marketing Manager. The CEO discussed this matter with the General Manager and explained to him the importance of putting the right person at the right job. He further explained that it would not only lead to higher performance but would also provide many other benefits.

   Besides the benefits of putting the right man at the right job, state the three other benefits which the CEO might have explained to the General Manager that are not given in the above para. *[CBSE 2023]*

2. Atlantic Pharma Incorporation, a distributor of durable medical equipment and sports medicine is currently facing problems in managing company's infrastructure and IT projects.

   To effectively cope with the situation, the company has created a new position of 'Senior Systems Administrator', who will be able to understand the volatile health care industry, as well as its IT environment. Since the position requires more than just technical expertise, the company has taken the following decisions, for timely fulfilment of the manpower requirement

   - Assessing the new role's requirements through job description, in order to ensure the appointment of a person with the required specific set of educational qualifications, experience, personality and characteristics.
   - Hiring 'Unifold Consultants', a renowned consultancy firm which maintains a database of candidates and which will advertise the job on behalf of Atlantic Pharma Limited.
   - Adopting a deeper screening process of the candidate possessing the technical and business process knowledge.

   Identify and state the steps which Atlantic Pharma Incorporation has decided to carry out in order to fill the new job position introduced by the company.

3. Palak, the Sales Head, Kanta, the Assistant Manager and Subodh, the Human Resource Manager of Calibri Ltd. decided to leave the company.

   The Chief Executive Officer of the company called Sarah, the Human Resource Manager and requested her to fill up the vacancies before leaving the organisation.

   Sarah informed that her subordinate Miss Taruna was very competent and trustworthy and can be vertically shifted. The company wants to rapidly fill vacant positions, minimising disruptions to operations during peak periods. The company decided to check the list of job-seekers and screen to fill the vacancies.

   While the approach offers speed and flexibility, ongoing efforts to improve quality control and optimise the recruitment process are essential to ensure the continued success of this strategy.

   Sarah suggested 'Creators Agency' who provide a nationwide service in matching personnel demand and supply.

(i) Name the internal/external sources of recruitment used by 'Calibri Ltd.' to fill up the above stated vacancies.

(ii) Also state any one merit of each of the above identified source of recruitment.

4. Zenith Corporation is a leading automotive parts manufacturer with facilities located in several regions. The company specialises in producing components for major automotive brands and operates in a highly competitive market.

As Zenith Corporation continues to grow and expand its operations, it seeks to assess the cognitive abilities and problem solving skills of its employees to ensure they are well suited for their roles and can contribute effectively to the company's success.

For this it conducts test which will help to check the skills, such as numerical reasoning, verbal comprehension, logical reasoning and problem solving exercises. And standardised assessments such as IQ tests or customised evaluations tailored to specific job roles and functions.

The company wants to ensure proper testing of the recruited candidates. After this the candidates will be judged on the basis of in-depth formal conversation.

After the conduction of tests the company believes employees have to be trained on the equipment they will be using but this training will take place away from the workplace.

(i) Which type of recruitment should the company depend upon?

(ii) Which type of test was conducted by the organisation to suit their need? Explain.

(iii) Which stage in the selection process is highlighted after the written test?

(iv) What type of training is given to the candidates?

5. 'Verfab' was a garment manufacturing company known for its high quality fashionable clothing. They had been in the fashionable clothing business for the last 23 years.

The company was earning enough profit and the demand for their fashionable clothing was rising tremendously.

The company was expanding and needed to hire new talent to meet the growing demand. They followed a comprehensive process to ensure that they brought in the best candidates.

The process began with a first round evaluation of applications. The human resources team carefully reviewed each candidate's qualifications, experience and suitability for the available positions.

It eliminated unqualified or unfit job seekers based on the information supplied in the application forms and shortlisted 21 candidates who met the basic requirements.

The shortlisted candidates were then asked to take a series of tests that attempted to measure certain characteristics of individuals, ranging from manual dexterity to intelligence to personality.

These tests included assessments of their sewing skills, attention to detail and knowledge of garment manufacturing processes.

15 candidates who performed well in the tests were invited for a formal in-depth conversation with the senior staff from the design team. Thereafter, 10 candidates were found suitable for the job position available.

Since these 10 candidates had cleared all the above steps, 'Verfab' conducted verification by contacting their previous employers to confirm the details the candidates had provided.

Thereafter, a decision was made to choose 8 candidates who were best fitted for the roles.

Explain the steps of the comprehensive process discussed above till the verification stage, to ensure that the company brought in the best candidates to meet the growing demand for fashionable clothing. *[CBSE 2024]*

6. The rapid changes having taken place in the society have created pressure on organisations to readapt its products, type of jobs required and type of skills necessary to complete these jobs.

To keep up pace with the rapid changes in the business environment, Suzon cars, a company manufacturing automobiles for the last thirty years decided to start manufacturing electric cars with Artificial Intelligence technology.

With the introduction of Artificial Intelligence, the company had to improve the knowledge and skills of its employees. They wanted that all their employees improve their performance on the current job and are prepared for any intended job in future. This way they would not only be able to increase their knowledge and skills but would also improve their performance. By doing this, the organisation too would get various benefits.

(i) Identify the concept discussed above which would help the employees to do the job in a better way using Artificial Intelligence Technology.

(ii) State any five benefits of the concept identified in (i) above to the organisation.

7. A renowned car company named 'BB Motors' was known for producing high performance cars. They were committed to ensure that its employees had the skills and knowledge to build these innovative high performance cars.

To achieve this, they implemented a unique approach for training. The company transformed a section of its factory into what they called the 'learning floor'. Actual work environment was created by allotting a specialised space.

The space was equipped with a range of car components, tools and sophisticated car equipment identical to those used on the factory floor, where the company's employees would undergo their training.

Identify and explain the method of training used by 'BB Motors' to ensure that its employees had the skills and knowledge to build innovative high performance cars.

[CBSE 2024]

Answers

If your answer matches with the answer given here then put (✓) in the box otherwise put (✗). In case you did not attempt the question leave the box blank.

Multiple Choice Questions

1. C ☐ 2. B ☐ 3. B ☐
4. C ☐ 5. A ☐ 6. A ☐
7. B ☐ 8. A ☐ 9. C ☐
10. D ☐ 11. A ☐ 12. C ☐
13. D ☐ 14. B ☐ 15. A ☐
16. C ☐ 17. C ☐ 18. C ☐
19. C ☐ 20. B ☐ 21. C ☐
22. A ☐ 23. A ☐ 24. C ☐
25. C ☐ 26. C ☐ 27. A ☐
28. A ☐ 29. A ☐

Your Score__________ *(No. of Correct Answers)*

Assertion-Reason Questions

1. C ☐ 2. A ☐ 3. C ☐
4. B ☐ 5. B ☐ 6. B ☐
7. A ☐ 8. D ☐

Your Score__________ *(No. of Correct Answers)*

Correct/Incorrect Statements

1. C ☐ 2. A ☐ 3. B ☐
4. B ☐ 5. D ☐ 6. C ☐
7. B ☐ 8. A ☐

Your Score__________ *(No. of Correct Answers)*

Case Based Questions

1. (i) A ☐ (ii) D ☐
(iii) B ☐ (iv) B ☐
2. (i) D ☐ (ii) C ☐
(iii) A ☐ (iv) D ☐

Your Score__________ *(No. of Correct Answers)*

Explanations

Multiple Choice Questions

1. (C) Staffing
2. (B) Staffing
3. (B) Training and development programmes are designed to improve employees' skills and knowledge, ensuring they are well-equipped to perform their jobs effectively and progress in their careers.
4. (C) Perquisites, often called 'perks', are benefits that companies provide to their employees in addition to their regular salary and wages.
5. (A) Employer paid insurance is considered an indirect payment because it is a benefit provided by the employer that is not directly part of the CEO's salary or cash compensation.
6. (A) Performance appraisals involve evaluating employees' performance against predetermined criteria, such as ratings, which can then influence decisions regarding promotions, salary adjustments and further development opportunities.
7. (B) Placement and orientation
8. (A) Direct recruitment
9. (C) Campus recruitment
10. (D) Employment exchange
11. (A) casual callers
12. (C) Both (A) and (B)
13. (D) campus recruitment
14. (B) In a situation where there's a sudden rush of work and the need to arrange workers at short notice, advertising would be the appropriate source of recruitment.
15. (A) Carlson companies adopted web publishing as their source of recruitment by advertising the job opportunity on the website Indeed.com.
16. (C) Both (A) and (B)
17. (C) While on-the-job performance is an important factor, the effectiveness of the staffing process is also evaluated based on various other factors such as the fit between the candidate and the job, employee turnover rates, organisational culture, and overall productivity.
18. (C) (ii) (iv) (i) (iii)
19. (C) Contract of employment
20. (B) Trade tests typically evaluate a person's skills and proficiency in a specific trade or occupation, rather than their capacity to develop.
21. (C) It is a psychological assessment designed to measure an individual's cognitive abilities and intellectual potential. It aims to evaluate various aspects of human intelligence, such as problem solving skills, logical reasoning, etc.
22. (A) (iii) (i) (ii)
23. (A) Aptitude test
24. (C) Vestibule training involves creating a simulated work environment where employees can learn and practice new skills without the pressure of real work.

    This method is particularly useful for complex and technical skills, such as those required for generative AI and quantum computing solutions.
25. (C) Vestibule training involves simulating actual working conditions in a controlled environment, which could include training on safety protocols, handling equipment and recognising hazards like high voltage lines.
26. (C) Development
27. (A) Apprenticeship training is a form of vocational education that combines on-the-job training with classroom instruction. It is a structured training programme designed to prepare individuals for skilled occupations in various industries.
28. (A) (iii) (iv) (i) (ii)
29. (A) (iv) (ii) (i) (iii)

Assertion-Reason Questions

1. (C) Staffing is a very important managerial function.
2. (A) Both Assertion (A) and Reason (R) are true and Reason (R) is the correct explanation of Assertion (A)
3. (C) Selection enhances the self-esteem and prestige of those selected and conveys to them the seriousness with which the things are done in the organisation.

4. (B) Both Assertion (A) and Reason (R) are true, but Reason (R) is not the correct explanation of Assertion (A)
5. (B) Both Assertion (A) and Reason (R) are true, but Reason (R) is not the correct explanation of Assertion (A)
6. (B) Both Assertion (A) and Reason (R) are true, but Reason (R) is not the correct explanation of Assertion (A)
7. (A) Both Assertion (A) and Reason (R) are true and Reason (R) is the correct explanation of Assertion (A)
8. (D) A master worker is appointed as a trainer in apprenticeship training.

Correct/Incorrect Statements

1. (C) Both statements are correct.
2. (A) Staffing avoids disruption of work by indicating in advance the shortages of personnel.
3. (B) It is the responsibility of all managers to directly deal with and select people to work for the organisation.
4. (B) Staffing is seen as a generic function of management.
5. (D) Staffing is the practice of finding, evaluating and establishing a working relationship with people, for a purpose.
   Staffing is a distinct functional area of management just as marketing management and financial management.
6. (C) Both statements are correct.
7. (B) Staffing is the most fundamental and critical drive of organisational performance.
8. (A) Internal recruitment also simplifies the process of selection and placement.

Case Based Questions

1. (i) (A) Personality test
   (ii) (D) Estimating manpower requirement
   (iii) (B) Selection
   (iv) (B) Selection test
2. (i) (D) Staffing
   (ii) (C) Workforce analysis
   (iii) (A) transfer
   (iv) (D) Casual callers refer to individuals who are contacted informally or on an ad-hoc basis, often from a database of previous applicants or potential candidates.

Subjective Questions

1. Staffing benefits to the organisation are
   (i) It helps in discovering and obtaining competent personnel for various jobs.
   (ii) It ensures the continuous survival and growth of an enterprise through the succession planning by managers.
   (iii) Improves job satisfaction and morale of employees through objective assessment and fair reward for their contribution.
2. Steps which Atlantic Pharma Ltd. has decided to carry out in order to fill in the new job position are
   (i) **Estimating the Manpower Requirements** It is important to translate the manpower requirements into specific job description and the desirable profile of its occupant i.e. the desired qualifications, experience, personality characteristics and so on.
   (ii) **Recruitment** It may be defined as the process of searching for prospective employees and stimulating them to apply for jobs in the organisation.
   (iii) **Selection** It is the process of choosing from among the pool of prospective job candidates developed at the stage of recruitment.
3. (i) Sources of recruitment used are
   (a) Promotion—for the post of Human Resource Manager
   (b) Placement Agencies and Management Consultants—for the post of Marketing Head
   (c) Casual Callers—for the post of Assistant Manager
   (d) Recommendation from present employees
   (ii) One merit of each source of recruitment
   (a) **Promotion** Promotion of employees helps in improving their motivation, loyalty and satisfaction level.
   (b) **Management Consultants** Management Consultancy firms help the organisation to recruit technical, professional and managerial personnel. They recommend suitable names to their clients.
   (c) **Casual Callers** Maintaining a database of unsolicited applicants in their offices helps the organisation in reducing the cost of recruiting workforce. It is the cheapest source of recruitment.

(d) **Recommendation from Present Employees** Such applications are likely to be good employees because their background is sufficiently known.

4. (i) Based on the scenario described, the company seeks to assess the cognitive abilities and problem solving skills of its employees through various tests and assessments.

Therefore, the type of recruitment that the company should depend upon is internal recruitment.

(ii) The type of test needed by the organisation to suit their need is aptitude test and intelligence test

(a) **Aptitude Test** For this it conducts test which will help to check the skills, such as numerical reasoning, verbal comprehension, logical reasoning and problem solving exercises.

(b) **Intelligence Test** And standardised assessments such as IQ tests or customised evaluations tailored to specific job roles and functions.

(iii) The stage in the selection process which is highlighted after the written test is employee interview.

After this a stage in the selection process will come when the candidates will be judged on the basis of in-depth formal conversation.

(iv) The type of training given to the candidates is vestibule training. Employees have to be trained on the equipment they will be using but this training will take place away from the workplace.

5. The steps of selection are as follows

(i) **Preliminary Screening** It helps the manager to eliminate unqualified or unfit job seekers, based on the information supplied in the application forms.

Suitable applicants are called for preliminary interviews which help to reject misfits for reasons, which did not appear in the application forms.

(ii) **Selection Tests** An employment test is a mechanism (either a paper and pencil test or an exercise) that attempts to measure certain characteristics of individuals. These characteristics range from aptitudes, such as manual dexterity, to intelligence, to personality, etc.

(iii) **Employment Interview** Interview is a formal, in-depth conversation, conducted to evaluate the applicant's suitability for the job.

Through an interview, an interviewer seeks to obtain maximum information about the interviewee and the interviewee seeks information about the job and the company.

(iv) **Reference and Background Checks** Many employers request names, addresses and telephone numbers of references for the purpose of verifying information and gaining additional information of an applicant.

6. (i) Training

(ii) Benefits of training to an organisation

(a) It is a systematic learning, always better than hit and trial methods which lead to wastage of efforts and money.

(b) It enhances employee productivity both in terms of quantity and quality, leading to higher profits.

(c) It equips the future manager who can take over in case of emergency.

(d) It increases employees' morale and reduces absenteeism and employee turnover.

(e) It helps in obtaining effective response to fast changing environment.

7. The method of training used by 'BB Motors' to ensure that its employees had the skills and knowledge to build innovative high performance cars is 'vestibule training'.

Vestibule Training Employees learn their jobs on the equipment they will be using, but the training is conducted away from the actual work floor. Actual work environments are created in a class room and employees use the same materials, files and equipment. This is usually done when employees are required to handle sophisticated machinery and equipment.

CHAPTER -7

Directing

Types & Nos. of Questions

Multiple Choice Questions	–	30
Assertion-Reason Questions	–	9
Correct/Incorrect Statements	–	9
Case Based Questions	–	2 Cases, *each with four Questions*
Subjective Questions	–	7

Trend Analysis

On the basis of analysis of last 2 years' papers, it is found that on an average 2 Multiple Choice Questions and 1 Short Answer Type Question (Case Based) are asked from this Chapter.

Focus Topics of the Chapter

- Concept of Directing
- Motivation
- Leadership
- Communication

Multiple Choice Questions

No. of Questions : **30** Suggested Time : **45 Minutes**

Direction Each of the question given below is Multiple Choice Question (MCQ) i.e. there are Four Options/ Choices for answer, out of which ONLY ONE is correct. You have to select the correct option.
A response box is given with each option, mark (✓) in the box of the correct option. For each correct answer you will get 1 mark, while there is no penalty for incorrect answer or missed out questions.

1. "A mining engineer explains about safety precautions to be followed while working in a coal mine." Identify the function of management reflected in the line.

   (A) Directing ☐ (B) Staffing ☐
   (C) Organising ☐ (D) Controlling ☐

2. Indra Nooyi served as the CEO of PepsiCo from 2006 to 2018, during which she implemented several strategic initiatives that reshaped the company and solidified its position as a global leader in the food and beverage industry.

   She recognised early on the shifting consumer preferences towards healthier food and beverages and diversified PepsiCo's product portfolio to include more nutritious options.

   Identify the element of directing implemented in the above para.

   (A) Motivation ☐ (B) Communication ☐
   (C) Leadership ☐ (D) Supervision ☐

3. Google famously implemented the '20% time' policy, allowing employees to dedicate 20% of their work hours to pursuing projects or learning new skills outside of their main responsibilities.

   Identify the non-financial incentive practised by Google.

   (A) Employee recognition ☐
   (B) Organisational climate ☐
   (C) Employee empowerment ☐
   (D) Employee participation ☐

4. Tata Consultancy Services (TCS) has rolled out the 'Quick Joiner Incentive Plan' under which the company offers candidates an additional ₹40,000 for senior roles with the concern that they join within a month.

   Identify the incentive referred in the above statement.

   (A) Status ☐
   (B) Bonus ☐
   (C) Perquisite ☐
   (D) Employee recognition programme ☐

5. XYZ Corp is a tech start-up specialised in artificial intelligence solutions. Founded in 2018, it has rapidly grown its customer base and revenue streams.

   To attract and retain top talent in a competitive market, XYZ Corp decides to offer its employees company's shares at a set price which is lower than market price as part of their compensation package.

   The incentive offered to the employees by the company is

   (A) productivity linked with wage incentive ☐
   (B) co-partnership ☐
   (C) profit sharing ☐
   (D) bonus ☐

6. Amazon recognises the importance of social connections in the workplace and fosters a sense of camaraderie among employees. Teamwork is encouraged through collaborative projects, team-building

activities and recognition programmes that celebrate individual and group achievements.

Additionally, Amazon provides opportunities for employees to connect outside of work through social events and community engagement initiatives.

Identify the need which is fulfilled by Amazon towards its employees.

(A) Esteem need ☐
(B) Social need ☐
(C) Security need ☐
(D) Self–actualisation need ☐

7. Jimmy is, by all accounts a hardworking, accomplished manager used to being in command, having positioned himself as Mr. Dependable and enjoying his boss's unstinted support and confidence.

Jimmy's idea of self as the most admired, respected manager is threatened by the arrival of a new incumbent, Varun, whose charming ways and effervescence make him equally, if not more popular with the whole office.

Jimmy and Varun are both high-achievers enjoying dominance in their area of work. Both also want to win on a daily basis, regardless of everything else. If they spent more time together, listened to each other and demonstrated mutual regard, the situation would not come to such a pess. The inflated ego also stops people from seeing things as they are, distorts attitudes and judgements, and hinders personal growth and learning.

Which element of directing is being discussed above?

(A) Motivation ☐
(B) Communication ☐
(C) Leadership ☐
(D) Supervision ☐

8. Cat Shelter Paws Need Families believe that happy employees make good organisations. Della, a cleaner in Cat Shelter Paws Need Families became an assistant manager and was soon promoted to be a manager. Surprisingly, after promotion she started arriving late, letting applicants sit and slipped on inoculations, all serious offenses.

Instead of confronting Della directly, meetings were held and an assistant manager was hired to compensate for Della's shortcomings. Ultimately, Della never cleaned up her act and fires.

Ken Blanchard, co-author of 'The One Minute Manager' believes this situation may want to have been avoided with short meetings, time to time interaction and a review or feedback system. With the help of these, we can become aware of troubles earlier than they become actual problems.

Identify the element of directing reflected in the above statement.

(A) Supervision ☐ (B) Motivation ☐
(C) Leadership ☐ (D) Communication ☐

9. Ahmedabad-based Tridhya Tech, a leading provider of digital transformation services has facilitated 13 employees with 13 cars for appreciation of their hardwork and dedication towards the company's mission over the years.

The company has gifted Toyota Glanza cars to employees who performed the best and contributed the most. The CEO said, "I strongly believe in sharing the wealth we have created with our employees."

Identify the non-financial incentive practised by Tridhya Tech.

(A) Employee recognition ☐
(B) Organisational climate ☐
(C) Employee empowerment ☐
(D) Employee participation ☐

10. TATA motors has a recognition and reward programme called 'Udaan' that recognises and rewards employees for their exeptional performance. The TATA Group's HR practices are a reflection of its commitment to employee welfare development and engagement.

Identify the incentive mentioned in the above case.

(A) Employee recognition programme ☐
(B) Employee empowerment ☐
(C) Employee participation ☐
(D) Organisational climate ☐

11. Microsoft organises hackathons and innovation challenges where employees can collaborate and work on innovative projects.

Identify the incentive referred in the above statement.

(A) Job enrichment ☐
(B) Job security ☐
(C) Employee empowerment ☐
(D) Employee recognition programme ☐

12. Gitanjali Makan is a successful business leader. She believes that if jobs are made interesting by including greater variety of work content and providing a meaningful experience the jobs themselves become a source of motivation to individuals.

The non-financial incentive that has been discussed in the above case is *[CBSE 2023]*

(A) employees participation ☐
(B) job enrichment ☐
(C) career advancement opportunity ☐
(D) job security ☐

13. Identify the incorrect statement.

(A) Incentive means that all measures which are used to motivate people to improve performance ☐
(B) The authority, responsibility, rewards, recognition, perquisites and prestige of job indicate the status given to a person holding a managerial position ☐
(C) Promotion works as a tonic and encourages employees to exhibit improved performance ☐
(D) Formal communications are written only and generally recorded and filed in the office ☐

14. Which type of incentive is highlighted in the given image?

(A) Non-monetary ☐
(B) Status ☐
(C) Job security ☐
(D) Monetary ☐

15. Match the various communications barriers given in Column II with their respective categories given in Column I *[CBSE 2023]*

Column I	Column II
A. Semantic barriers	(i) Distrust
B. Psychological barriers	(ii) Lack of proper incentives
C. Organisational barriers	(iii) Symbols with different meanings
D. Personal barriers	(iv) Status

Codes

	A	B	C	D	
(A)	(i)	(ii)	(iii)	(iv)	☐
(B)	(iv)	(iii)	(i)	(ii)	☐
(C)	(iii)	(i)	(iv)	(ii)	☐
(D)	(iii)	(ii)	(iv)	(i)	☐

16. For taking the company out of losses, Ravi Kumar took over as the Managing Director of the struggling 'Vova Watch Company' in January 2020. As soon as he joined, he tried to find out the reason for the company not doing well.

He found that the employees were not involved in decision-making and they had to just follow orders, resulting in low morale of employees. Recognising the need for change, Ravi Kumar started on a journey to bring back the enthusiasm and motivation of the employees.

He initiated open dialogues and encouraged them to actively participate in decision-making. Together, they developed action plans to address the company's challenges regarding outdated designs and inefficient production processes, etc.

As time passed, 'Vova Watch Company' transformed from a struggling enterprise to a profit making enterprise. Identify the leadership style of Ravi Kumar. *[CBSE 2024]*

(A) Autocratic leadership style ☐
(B) Democratic leadership style ☐
(C) Free-rein leadership style ☐
(D) Both (a) and (b) ☐

17. "The supervisor recognises and rewards employees who exceed their performance targets to encourage high productivity."

Identify the element of directing reflected in the line statement.

(A) Staffing ☐
(B) Motivation ☐
(C) Organising ☐
(D) Controlling ☐

18. Saurabh values group discussion and input from his team and can be seen as drawing from a pool of his team members' strong points in order to obtain the best performance from his team.

Which style of leadership is followed by Saurabh?

(A) Autocrative ☐
(B) Democratic style ☐
(C) Free-rein ☐
(D) None of the above ☐

19. Mr. Sarthi, the ex-chairman of Swadesh Ltd. built up his successor before retiring. Following the norms set up by himself, he handed over the reins of the company to the co-founder Mr. Shravan, who had the potential to bring about change in the behaviour of others.

Name the concept of management which was the reason why Mr. Sarthi chose Mr. Shravan to be his successor.

(A) Motivation ☐ (B) Leadership ☐
(C) Communication ☐ (D) Staffing ☐

20. In an organisation, employees always feel that they are under enormous unnecessary stress, as the manager does not provide any information about future plans but simply instructs them what to do. He also not listen to any of the suggestions given by the subordinate.

Identify the type of leadership style followed by the manager in the above situation.

(A) Autocratic ☐ (B) Democratic ☐
(C) Free-rein ☐ (D) None of these ☐

21. During the negotiation process, the American team uses idiomatic expressions and colloquialisms that are common in English but may not translate well into Japanese. For example, they use phrases like "let's hit the ground running" or "let's get the ball rolling" to convey a sense of urgency and enthusiasm.

Identify the type of semantic barrier referred in the above statement.

(A) Technical jargon ☐
(B) Badly expressed message ☐
(C) Symbols with different meanings ☐
(D) Unclarified assumptions ☐

22. Communication occurring organically through interactions such as brainstorming sessions, impromptu meetings and casual conversation is an example of which type of communication?

(A) Formal ☐ (B) Informal ☐

(C) Oral ☐ (D) Written ☐

23. IBM has a clearly defined hierarchical structure with distinct levels of authority and responsibility. Each employee at IBM has a clearly defined job role and set of responsibilities.

It places a strong emphasis on rules and regulations to maintain order and control within the organisation.

Which communication style is been adopted by IBM?

(A) Formal ☐ (B) Informal ☐

(C) Oral ☐ (D) Written ☐

24. At support.com, there is no reward or appreciation for a good suggestion. Thus, the subordinates are not willing to offer any useful suggestions to their superiors. Identify the type of barrier to communication that has been created in the firm due to this.

(A) Semantic barrier ☐

(B) Personal barrier ☐

(C) Organisational barrier ☐

(D) Psychological barrier ☐

25. "The manager conducts regular team meetings to discuss ongoing projects and address any concerns employees might have."

Identify the element of directing reflected in the statement.

(A) Controlling ☐

(B) Planning ☐

(C) Communication ☐

(D) Organising ☐

26. Identify the incorrect statement.

(A) Encoding is the content of ideas, feelings, suggestions, order, etc. intended to be communicated ☐

(B) Grapevine channels carry information rapidly ☐

(C) Communication act as a basis of decision-making ☐

(D) Semantic barrier are related with the problems in the process of encoding and decoding of message into words or impressions ☐

27. Which semantic barrier is shown in the picture below?

(A) Badly expressed message ☐

(B) Symbols with different meanings ☐

(C) Technical jargon ☐

(D) Unclarified assumptions ☐

28. Match the Column I with Column II in the following information

	Column I		Column II
A.	It is the process of converting the message into communication symbols such as words, pictures, gestures.	(i)	Feedback
B.	It is the process of converting encoded symbols of the sender.	(ii)	Encoding
C.	It includes all those actions of receiver indicating that he has received and understood message of sender.	(iii)	Decoding

Codes

	A	B	C	
(A)	(ii)	(iii)	(i)	☐
(B)	(iii)	(ii)	(i)	☐
(C)	(i)	(iii)	(ii)	☐
(D)	(ii)	(i)	(iii)	☐

29. Match the Column I with Column II in the following information

Column I	Column II
A. A person communicates with all on non-selective basis.	(i) Horizontal/ Lateral
B. A person communicates randomly with others.	(ii) Free flow network
C. Communication takes place between one department/ division and another to coordinate different activities or to resolve inter-related problems.	(iii) Gossip network
D. Each person can communicate with others freely.	(iv) Probability network

Codes

	A	B	C	D	
(A)	(iii)	(i)	(ii)	(iv)	☐
(B)	(iv)	(ii)	(i)	(iii)	☐
(C)	(iv)	(i)	(ii)	(iii)	☐
(D)	(iii)	(i)	(iv)	(ii)	☐

30. Match the Column I with Column II in the following information

Column I	Column II
A. Submission of progress report.	(i) Horizontal communication
B. Ordering subordinates to complete an assigned task.	(ii) Downward communication
C. A production manager may contact marketing manager to discuss about product design, quality, etc.	(iii) Upward communication

Codes

	A	B	C	
(A)	(iii)	(ii)	(i)	☐
(B)	(i)	(ii)	(iii)	☐
(C)	(ii)	(i)	(iii)	☐
(D)	(iii)	(i)	(ii)	☐

Assertion-Reason Questions

No. of Questions : **9** Suggested Time : **14 Minutes**

Direction Each of the question given below consist of the two statements; one labelled as **Assertion** (A) and other as **Reason** (R). List of common options applicable for each question is given below

(A) Both Assertion (A) and Reason (R) are true and Reason (R) is the correct explanation of Assertion (A)

(B) Both Assertion (A) and Reason (R) are true, but Reason (R) is not the correct explanation of Assertion (A)

(C) Assertion (A) is true, but Reason (R) is false

(D) Assertion (A) is false, but Reason (R) is true

You have to select the codes as *a*, *b*, *c* or *d* as your answer to the question by marking (✓) in the response box given against each option.

1. Assertion (A) People have a tendency to resist changes in the organisation.

Reason (R) Staffing facilitates introduction of needed changes in the organisation.

(A) ☐ (B) ☐ (C) ☐ (D) ☐

2. **Assertion** (A) Directing ensures integration of employees efforts towards attainment of organisational goals.

Reason (R) Directing coordinates and integrates the efforts of employees working at different levels and in different job position through supervision.

(A) ☐ (B) ☐
(C) ☐ (D) ☐

3. **Assertion** (A) Supervisors maintain day-to-day contact and relationships with the workers.

Reason (R) Supervision does not include providing feedback to the workers.

(A) ☐ (B) ☐ (C) ☐ (D) ☐

4. **Assertion** (A) Directing is an ongoing process.

Reason (R) Without direction, organisational activities cannot continue further.

(A) ☐ (B) ☐ (C) ☐ (D) ☐

5. **Assertion** (A) Communication is basic to an organisation's existence right from its birth through its continuing life.

Reason (R) When communication stops, organised activity ceases to exist.

(A) ☐ (B) ☐ (C) ☐ (D) ☐

6. **Assertion** (A) Communication lubricates the entire organisation and keeps the organisation at work with efficiency.

Reason (R) Followers make a person, a good leader by acceptance of leadership.

(A) ☐ (B) ☐ (C) ☐ (D) ☐

7. **Assertion** (A) Managers and leaders need to identify effective communication channels to reach the appropriate stakeholders.

Reason (R) Effectiveness of a manager depends significantly on his ability to communicate effectively with his superiors, subordinates and external agencies such as bankers, suppliers, union and government.

(A) ☐ (B) ☐ (C) ☐ (D) ☐

8. **Assertion** (A) People's behaviour is affected by rumours and informal discussions and sometimes may hamper work environment.

Reason (R) Informal channels are used by the managers to transmit information so as to know the reactions of his/her subordinates.

(A) ☐ (B) ☐ (C) ☐ (D) ☐

9. **Assertion** (A) The person who conveys the message is the receiver.

Reason (R) Noise is the obstruction or hindrance in the communication process.

(A) ☐ (B) ☐ (C) ☐ (D) ☐

Correct/Incorrect Statements

No. of Questions : **9** Suggested Time : **15 Minutes**

Direction Each of the question given below consist of the two statements. List of common options applicable for each question is given below

(A) Statement I is correct and Statement II is incorrect
(B) Statement II is correct and Statement I is incorrect
(C) Both statements are correct
(D) Both statements are incorrect

You have to select the codes as *a, b, c* or *d* as your answer to the question by marking ✓ in the response box given against each option.

1. **Statement I** Directing is first initiated at top level and flows to the bottom through organisational hierarchy.

   Statement II Staffing guides employees to fully realise their potential and capabilities by motivating and providing effective leadership.

   (A) ☐ (B) ☐ (C) ☐ (D) ☐

2. **Statement I** The directing function is not a continuous process.

   Statement II Directing is a persuasive function of management.

   (A) ☐ (B) ☐ (C) ☐ (D) ☐

3. **Statement I** Supervision is not an element of the directing function of management.

   Statement II Supervisor sorts out differences among workers placed under his control.

   (A) ☐ (B) ☐ (C) ☐ (D) ☐

4. **Statement I** Motivation arises out of the needs of individuals.

   Statement II Realisation of a motive causes restlessness in the individual which prompts some action to reduce such restlessness.

   (A) ☐ (B) ☐
   (C) ☐ (D) ☐

5. **Statement I** Motivation depends upon satisfying needs of people.

   Statement II Motivator is the technique used to motivate people in an organisation.

   (A) ☐ (B) ☐
   (C) ☐ (D) ☐

6. **Statement I** Motivation produces goal-directed behaviour.

   Statement II Motivation is a complex process as the individuals are homogeneous in their expectations, perceptions and reactions.

   (A) ☐ (B) ☐ (C) ☐ (D) ☐

7. **Statement I** Any type of motivation may not have uniform effect on all the members.

   Statement II High rate of turnover compels management to go for new recruitment and training which involve additional investment of money, time and effort.

   (A) ☐ (B) ☐
   (C) ☐ (D) ☐

8. **Statement I** If jobs are enriched and made interesting, the job itself becomes a source of motivation to the individual.

   Statement II Leadership is exercised to achieve common goals of the organisation.

   (A) ☐ (B) ☐
   (C) ☐ (D) ☐

9. **Statement I** A good leader always allows his followers to ventilate their feelings and disagreement but persuades them by giving suitable clarifications.

   Statement II Leadership is the sum of all things one person does when he wants to create understanding in the mind of another.

   (A) ☐ (B) ☐
   (C) ☐ (D) ☐

Case Based Questions

No. of Questions : **2** Suggested Time : **10 Minutes**

Direction This section contains 2 cases each having 4 questions of 1 mark each. You have to write the answer of each question based on the context of the related case.

Case 1 Sarah is the director of a marketing firm, tasked with leading a team of ten employees. The team is responsible for developing and executing marketing campaigns for various clients.

Recently, there has been a decline in productivity and morale within the team, leading to missed deadlines and decreased client satisfaction.

Due to lack of clear directions, the team members feel uncertain about their roles and responsibilities within projects, leading to confusion and inefficiency. Communication breakdown was also seen due to which there is a lack of effective communication channels within the team, resulting in misunderstandings and missed opportunities for collaboration.

Team morale is low, as employees feel undervalued and disconnected from the company's goals and vision. Sarah conducts individual meetings with each team member to discuss their strengths, interests and career goals.

Sarah introduces a performance recognition programme, where outstanding achievements are publically acknowledged and rewarded. She also provides opportunities for professional development and growth, such as training workshops and mentorship programmes, to keep employees engaged and motivated.

With clear direction and defined roles, team members feel more confident and focused, leading to improved productivity and efficiency within projects.

Questions

(i) Identify the function of management discussed in the above case.

(A) Planning ☐ (B) Organising ☐
(C) Staffing ☐ (D) Directing ☐

(ii) Identify the incentive given by the company to its employees.

(A) Job enrichment ☐
(B) Career advancement opportunity ☐
(C) Job security ☐
(D) Employee recognition programme ☐

(iii) Which need of the employees will be satisfied through the incentive identified in part (ii)?

(A) Esteem need ☐
(B) Social need ☐
(C) Safety need ☐
(D) Self-actualisation need ☐

(iv) "Sarah conducts individual meetings with each team member to discuss their strengths, interests and career goals."

Which element of directing is referred in the above statement?

(A) Motivation ☐
(B) Leadership ☐
(C) Communication ☐
(D) Supervision ☐

Case 2 Mr. Sunil Diali is a safety officer in a reputed PSU sector ECL. He supervises the workers towards the predetermined goals of the organisation and directs how to eradicate unsafe practices of inundation, fire breakouts, existence of inflammable gases, etc. On one such instances there was huge fire breakout in the underground mines and the workers morale was down and demotivated because of several risk hazards.

Mr. Diali observed the whole situation and consulted with all his workers and constantly monitored, guided and inspired them to integrate their efforts and accept the situation as a challenge and take adequate safety measures for fire extinguish and subsidising its effects. There by, production turnover was outstanding and out performed other subsidiaries. Mr. Diali was recognised with Bravery Award from CIL. *[CBSE QB]*

Questions

(i) Mr. Diali worked towards predetermined goals of the organisation. Which important function of directing is addressed here?

(A) Means of motivation ☐
(B) Initiate action ☐
(C) Facilitate change ☐
(D) Bring stability ☐

(ii) Mr. Diali consulted with all his workers, he listened to their opinions. Which form of leadership is identified here?

(A) Laissez-faire ☐
(B) Autocratic ☐
(C) Democratic ☐
(D) Free-rein ☐

(iii) Bravery award is .... form of non-financial incentive.

(A) status ☐
(B) job security ☐
(C) career advancement ☐
(D) employee recognition ☐

(iv) Under Maslow's hierarchy need theory, which need of Mr. Diali has been met through respect and recognition among other employees?

(A) Self-actualisation need ☐
(B) Safety and security needs ☐
(C) Esteem needs ☐
(D) Physiological needs ☐

Subjective Questions

Free Response Questions, Open-ended Questions etc.

No. of Questions : **7** Suggested Time : **50 Minutes**

1. Lilly and Milly are working as marketing manager and finance manager respectively in an insurance company. In consultation with the human resource manager, Lilly formulates a plan which links the salaries of the insurance agents of the company with the volume of sales, in order to provide incentive to make them achieve beyond the assigned monthly targets.

Identify and briefly explain the incentive provided to the employees by Lilly.

2. The manager of a team in a fast-paced IT company, notices a decline in employee motivation and productivity. Outline how he can use Maslow's theory to identify and address the various needs of his employees.

3. Shanta Enterprises was in the business of manufacturing solar panels for the last fifteen years. With their expertise, now they were able to manufacture good quality solar panels at lower cost.

As a result 'Shanta Enterprises' was flooded with orders and was able to generate a good profit margin. To motivate the employees, the company decided to compensate some of them for their hardwork.

Arvind and Yogesh, who were working on contract basis, were absorbed permanently in the company. Both were happy as now there was stability about their future income. Ekta, a regular employee of the company, working as research and development head, was awarded the 'Best Employee of the Year Award'. *[CBSE 2024]*

(i) Identify and explain the incentives given by Shanta Enterprises to its employees.

(ii) State the needs of the employees being met by such incentives as per Maslow's Need Hierarchy Theory.

4. Sandhya is a successful manager at Manisons Enterprises. She has a team of twelve people working under her. She encouraged them to set their own objectives and take decisions. She respects their opinions and supports them, so that they can perform their duties and accomplish organisational objectives. To manage and exercise effective control she uses forces within the group.

As an intelligent manager, at times, she also makes use of positive aspects of informal communication. This way, she is able to unify diverse interests and ensure that targets are met.

(i) There are many theories and styles of influencing people's behaviour. Identify the style used by Sandhya which is based on the use of authority.

(ii) State two positive aspects of the communication discussed above, which Sandhya is using as an intelligent manager.

5. Despite having a skilled workforce, Khajuraho company has been experiencing a decline in productivity and higher turnover rates.

Employees feel that their hardwork and achievements are not adequately recognised or rewarded. Many employees feel stagnant in their roles and see little room for career advancement within the company.

The company soon realised and took certain steps to overcome the problems. This included offering training and upskilling opportunities, mentorship programmes and regular performance evaluations to identify areas for growth.

Significantly, it was seen, employee satisfaction scores increased by 20% within the first six months.

Employee turnover rates decreased by 15% as employees felt more valued and fulfilled in their roles. Productivity and innovation levels rose as motivated employees became more proactive and invested in the company's success.

The company was able to create a more positive and conducive work environment, leading to improved employee retention and organisational success.

(i) Which element of directing has been applied by the management?

(ii) Identify and explain the reasons for decline in productivity and higher turnover rates.

(iii) In the above case, which type of incentive has been used by the company to improve employee performance?

6. Analyse the following scenarios and identify the specific barriers to effective communication in each case.

Scenario 1 During a team meeting, two team members from different status have different interpretations of a project's deadline. As a result, they end up working on different timelines, causing confusion and delays.

Scenario 2 In an email exchange between team members, one team member uses technical jargon and industry specific terms that others may not fully understand. As a result, some team members misinterpret the message, leading to misunderstandings and misaligned tasks.

Scenario 3 A team member consistently interrupts others during team discussions, not allowing them to express their ideas fully. This behaviour leads to frustration among team members and limits open and constructive communication.

Scenario 4 During a virtual team meeting, poor internet connectivity causes frequent disruptions and audio glitches.

As a result, some team members miss crucial information and the overall meeting efficiency is reduced.

7. Consider a scenario in a multinational corporation where a project manager, Sarah is responsible for leading a team of diverse professionals located across different continents.

Sarah communicates project updates, deadlines and expectations through e-mails, video conferences, and project management software. However, despite her efforts, she notices a lack of clarity and understanding among team members, resulting in delays and misunderstandings.

(i) Identify and analyse potential elements of communication breakdown in Sarah's scenario based on the elements of communication.

(ii) How can Sarah improve communication to ensure effective collaboration and project success?

Answers

If your answer matches with the answer given here then put (✓) in the box otherwise put (✗). In case you did not attempt the question leave the box blank.

Multiple Choice Questions

1. A ☐	2. C ☐
3. C ☐	4. B ☐
5. B ☐	6. B ☐
7. B ☐	8. D ☐
9. A ☐	10. A ☐
11. A ☐	12. B ☐
13. D ☐	14. D ☐
15. C ☐	16. B ☐
17. B ☐	18. B ☐
19. B ☐	20. A ☐
21. A ☐	22. B ☐
23. A ☐	24. A ☐
25. C ☐	26. A ☐
27. C ☐	28. A ☐
29. A ☐	30. A ☐

Your Score__________ *(No. of Correct Answers)*

Assertion-Reason Questions

1. C ☐	2. A ☐	3. C ☐
4. A ☐	5. A ☐	6. B ☐
7. A ☐	8. A ☐	9. D ☐

Your Score__________ *(No. of Correct Answers*

Correct/Incorrect Statements

1. A ☐	2. B ☐	3. B ☐
4. B ☐	5. C ☐	6. A ☐
7. C ☐	8. C ☐	9. A ☐

Your Score__________ *(No. of Correct Answers)*

Case Based Questions

1.	(i) D ☐	(ii) D ☐
	(iii) B ☐	(iv) C ☐
2.	(i) B ☐	(ii) C ☐
	(iii) D ☐	(iv) C ☐

Your Score__________ *(No. of Correct Answers)*

Explanations

Multiple Choice Questions

1. (A) Directing involves guiding, leading and supervising employees to ensure that they are working effectively and safely.
2. (C) Indra Nooyi implemented strategic initiatives that reshaped PepsiCo and diversified its product portfolio. This involves making decisions, providing guidance and influencing the company's direction, which aligns with the element of leadership.
3. (C) Google's '20% time' policy empowers employees by giving them the autonomy to dedicate a portion of their work hours to pursue projects or learning activities of their choice. This fosters creativity, innovation and personal development among employees.
4. (B) The incentive offered by TCS acts as a bonus for candidates joining quickly, motivating them to expedite the joining process and fill critical roles within the organisation.
5. (B) co-partnership
6. (B) Social need
7. (B) In the scenario provided, the interaction between Jimmy and Varun highlights communication dynamics within a team or organisational context.
8. (D) In this scenario, communication breakdowns seem to have contributed to the issues with Della's performance.

   Instead of directly addressing her behaviour and performance concerns, meetings were held and an assistant manager was hired to compensate for her shortcomings.
9. (A) Employee recognition
10. (A) Employee recognition programme
11. (A) Job enrichment
12. (B) job enrichment
13. (D) Formal communications can be both written and verbal. They are typically structured and follow official channels within an organisation.
14. (D) Monetary
15. (C) (iii) (i) (iv) (ii)
16. (B) Democratic leadership style
17. (B) Motivation involves encouraging and inspiring employees to perform at their best by meeting their needs and providing incentives.
18. (B) Democratic style
19. (B) Leadership
20. (A) In an autocratic leadership style, the manager makes decisions unilaterally without involving subordinates, provides little to no information about future plans and does not solicit or consider employees' suggestions.
21. (A) Technical jargon
22. (B) Informal
23. (A) Formal
24. (A) Semantic barrier
25. (C) Communication
26. (A) Message is the content of ideas, feelings, suggestions, order, etc. intended to be communicated.
27. (C) Technical jargon refers to specialised language used by professionals within a particular field or industry. This language includes terms, phrases and abbreviations that have specific meanings in a technical context but may not be easily understood by those outside the field.
28. (A) (ii) (iii) (i)
29. (A) (iii) (i) (ii) (iv)
30. (A) (iii) (ii) (i)

Assertion-Reason Questions

1. (C) Directing facilitates introduction of needed changes in the organisation.
2. (A) Both Assertion (A) and Reason (R) are true and Reason (R) is the correct explanation of Assertion (A)
3. (C) Providing feedback to workers is a crucial part of supervision.
4. (A) Both Assertion (A) and Reason (R) are true and Reason (R) is the correct explanation of Assertion (A)
5. (A) Both Assertion (A) and Reason (R) are true and Reason (R) is the correct explanation of Assertion (A)

6. (B) Both Assertion (A) and Reason (R) are true, but Reason (R) is not the correct explanation of Assertion (A)
7. (A) Both Assertion (A) and Reason (R) are true and Reason (R) is the correct explanation of Assertion (A)
8. (A) Both Assertion (A) and Reason (R) are true and Reason (R) is the correct explanation of Assertion (A)
9. (D) In the communication process, the person who conveys or sends the message is known as the sender or communicator, not the receiver.

Correct/Incorrect Statements

1. (A) Directing guides employees to fully realise their potential and capabilities by motivating and providing effective leadership.
2. (B) The directing function of management is indeed a continuous process that involves ongoing guidance, coordination and motivation of employees to achieve organisational objectives.
3. (B) Supervision is indeed a crucial element of the directing function of management.
4. (B) Motives arise out of the needs of individuals.
5. (C) Both statements are correct
6. (A) Motivation is a complex process as the individuals are heterogeneous in their expectations, perceptions and reactions.
7. (C) Both statements are correct
8. (C) Both statements are correct
9. (A) Communication is the sum of all things one person does when he wants to create understanding in the mind of another.

Case Based Questions

1. (i) (D) Directing
   (ii) (D) Employee recognition programme
   (iii) (B) Public acknowledgment and recognition often foster a sense of belongingness and acceptance within the team or organisation, thus addressing the social need for affiliation.
   (iv) (C) Communication
2. (i) (B) Initiate action
   (ii) (C) Democratic
   (iii) (D) The bravery award received by Mr. Diali is a form of employee recognition, which is a non-financial incentive. It acknowledges and appreciates his courageous actions and contributions, boosting his morale and motivation.
   (iv) (C) Esteem needs

Subjective Questions

1. Lilly's incentive involves performance-based pay. By linking the salaries of the insurance agents with the volume of sales, Lilly aims to provide an incentive for them to achieve beyond their assigned monthly targets.

   This approach aligns with performance-based pay structures, where employees are rewarded based on their performance and contributions to the organisation's goals.
2. Following steps should be followed by the manager
   (i) Ensure that the basic physiological needs of employees are met, such as providing a comfortable and safe working environment. Address concerns related to workload, work-life balance and job security.
   (ii) Encourage team building activities and collaborative projects to fulfill social needs. Organise team lunches, outings or virtual events to foster a sense of camaraderie among team members.
   (iii) Address esteem needs by recognising employees' achievements and contributions. Implement an employee recognition programme that acknowledges outstanding performance and milestones.
   (iv) Promote self-actualisation by encouraging employees to pursue their passions and interests within their roles.
3. (i) Incentives given by Shanta Enterprises to its employees are
   (a) **Job Security** It refers to stability about future income and work so that the employees do not feel worried on these aspects and work with greater zeal.
   (b) **Employee Recognition Programmes** It refers to acknowledgement with a show of appreciation so that the employees feel motivated to perform/work at higher level.

(ii) The needs of the employees being met by such incentives as per Maslow's Need Hierarchy Theory are

(a) **Safety/Security Needs** These needs provide security and protection from physical and emotional harm.

(b) **Esteem Needs** These needs include factors such as self-respect, autonomy status, recognition and attention.

4. (i) The style of leadership used by Sandhya is 'democratic leadership'.

A democratic leader takes decisions after consultation and encourages the participation of subordinates. This leadership style is more common and popular, as it ensures achievement of goals, when they are set with the acceptance of the subordinates themselves.

A democratic leader provides freedom of thinking and listens to suggestions, grievances and opinions of the subordinates. This improves the attitude of the employees towards their jobs and the organisation, thereby increasing their morale.

This style is of mutual benefit which allows subordinates to become part of team and help leaders (seniors) to make better decisions. As shown in the figure, the leader involves subordinates in decision-making.

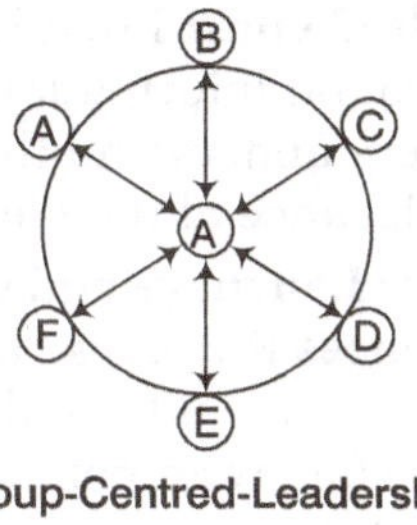

Group-Centred-Leadership
(A is the leader, who consults with the group)

(ii) Two positive effects of informal communication are

(a) Prescribed lines of communication are not followed. Thus, it facilitates quick feedback and spreads information faster.

(b) It provides a sense of belongingness and gives due respect to social and psychological needs.

5. (i) The element of directing applied by the management in this case is indeed motivation.

By offering training, upskilling opportunities, mentorship programmes, and regular performance evaluations, the management is motivating employees to enhance their skills, capabilities and performance.

(ii) No job enrichment and no career advancement opportunity are identified as reasons for the decline in productivity and higher turnover rates. These factors contribute to employees feeling stagnant in their roles and seeing little room for growth or advancement within the company, leading to decreased motivation and job satisfaction.

(iii) Employee recognition programme is the type of incentive used by the company to improve employee performance. By implementing this programme, the company aims to recognise and reward employees for their hardwork and achievements, thereby increasing motivation, job satisfaction and overall engagement.

6. Here are the identified barriers to effective communication in each scenario are

***Scenario 1* Status** In this scenario, the different interpretations of the project's deadline stem from 'team members' diverse status backgrounds. Each team member might have different attitudes towards time, varying work norms and approaches to meeting deadlines, leading to confusion and delays in project execution.

***Scenario 2* Language and Jargon** The use of technical jargon and industry specific terms in the email exchange creates a barrier to effective communication. Some team members may not fully understand the specialised language, leading to misinterpretation of the message and causing misunderstandings and misaligned tasks.

***Scenario 3* Lack of Active Listening** The team member's consistent habit of interrupting others during discussions inhibits open and constructive communication.

This behaviour reflects a lack of active listening, as the individual fails to allow others to express their ideas fully, leading to frustration among team members and hindering effective collaboration.

***Scenario 4* Technological Issues** In this virtual team meeting scenario, poor internet connectivity causing frequent disruptions and audio glitches is a technological issue that acts as a barrier to effective communication.

Some team members may miss crucial information due to the technical problems and the overall efficiency of the meeting is reduced.

7. (i) In Sarah's scenario, potential elements of communication breakdown can be identified as follows

(a) **Sender** Sarah, as the project manager, may be the sender of the messages. However, if she fails to convey information clearly or accurately, it can lead to misunderstandings among team members.

(b) **Message** The subject matter of communication includes project updates, deadlines and expectations. If these messages are unclear, incomplete or inconsistent, it can result in confusion among team members.

(c) **Encoding** Sarah translates the messages into words, gestures or other symbols for transmission. If she fails to encode the messages effectively, team members may not understand the intended meaning.

(d) **Channel** Communication occurs through various channels such as e-mails, video conferences and project management software. If the chosen channels are not suitable for the content or the audience, it can hinder effective communication.

(e) **Receiver** Team members receive the messages from Sarah. If they fail to understand or interpret the messages correctly, it can lead to misinterpretation or misalignment of expectations.

(f) **Decoding** Team members decode the symbols into the intended message. If they misinterpret or misunderstand the encoded messages, it can lead to errors or delays in project execution.

(g) **Feedback** Team members provide responses or feedback to Sarah regarding the messages received.

If Sarah does not actively seek feedback or if team members hesitate to provide feedback, it can hinder the communication process.

(h) **Noise** Obstructions or hindrances in the communication process, such as language barriers, technical issues or cultural differences, can disrupt effective communication.

(ii) To improve communication and ensure effective collaboration and project success, Sarah can take the following steps

(a) **Clarify Objectives** Clearly define project objectives, expectations and roles to ensure that everyone understands their responsibilities.

(b) **Choose Appropriate Channels** Select communication channels that are suitable for the content and the audience, considering factors such as urgency, complexity and accessibility.

(c) **Encourage Feedback** Actively seek feedback from team members to ensure that messages are understood and address any concerns or questions promptly.

(d) **Provide Context** Provide context and background information to help team members understand the significance and relevance of the messages.

(e) **Address Language and Cultural Differences** Recognise and accommodate language and cultural differences to ensure effective communication across diverse teams.

CHAPTER -8

Controlling

Types & Nos. of Questions

Multiple Choice Questions	-	25
Assertion-Reason Questions	-	8
Correct/Incorrect Statements	-	8
Case Based Questions	-	2 Cases, *each with four Questions*
Subjective Questions	-	8

Trend Analysis

On the basis of analysis of last 2 years' papers, it is found that on an average 2 Multiple Choice Questions and 1 Short Answer Type Question (Case Based) are asked from this chapter.

Focus Topics of the Chapter

- Controlling and its Importance
- Relationship between Planning and Controlling
- Process of Controlling

Multiple Choice Questions

No. of Questions : **25** Suggested Time : **40 Minutes**

Direction Each of the question given below is Multiple Choice Question (MCQ) i.e. there are Four Options/Choices for answer, out of which ONLY ONE is correct. You have to select the correct option. A response box is given with each option, mark (✓) in the box of the correct option. For each correct answer you will get 1 mark, while there is no penalty for incorrect answer or missed out questions.

1. Nayan and Shrisha were two employees, who were embezzling an import-export company in Varanasi, where they were working. The finance manager of the company Mr. Kartik Singh became suspicious of the two employees when he realised that their activities were not being performed as per the plans.

   He installed a software program that could secretly log every single stroke of the suspects' computer keys and send an encrypted email report to the cyber police. The police were able to catch the two dishonest employees red-handed and arrest them.

   Identify the function of management being discussed above.

   (A) Staffing ☐
   (B) Coordination ☐
   (C) Controlling ☐
   (D) Organising ☐

2. Radha started a home cooked food delivery Dabba service. Her mother, who is a great cook, decided to help her. They relied on friends and family for orders and then on word of mouth.

   As a step in the process of ensuring that activities are performed as per her plan of supplying healthy, good quality, reasonable food and earning profit, she decided to keep both qualitative and quantitative benchmarks towards which she would strive to work. A function of management is being discussed above.

   An important characteristic of this function of management is

   (A) it is the first function of management ☐
   (B) it is the last function of management ☐
   (C) it is both forward-looking and backward-looking ☐
   (D) it is required only in business organisations ☐

3. Marko Ltd. was excelling in its business from the past 5 years. But over the time, company realised that the employees were taking things easy and it has also resulted in loss of secrecy and confidential information being leaked out.

   To supervise the affairs of the workers, the company decides to install Closed Circuit Televisions (CCTVs), which the employees consider as restriction on their freedom.

   The stigma with employee monitoring is that it negatively impacts employee morale. Employees may fear that monitoring processes would weaponise the work environment.

   Identify the limitation of controlling the company is suffering from.

   (A) Little control on external factors ☐
   (B) Resistance from employees ☐
   (C) Difficulty in setting quantitative standards ☐
   (D) Costly affair ☐

4. "A good control system enables management to verify whether the standards set are accurate and objective."

Identify the importance of controlling discussed above.

(A) Accomplishing organisational goals ☐
(B) Judging accuracy of standards ☐
(C) Making efficient use of resources ☐
(D) Facilitating coordination in action ☐

5. "Controlling provides direction to all activities and efforts for achieving organisational goals."

Identify the importance of controlling from the above statement.

(A) Accomplishing organisational goals ☐
(B) Ensuring order and discipline ☐
(C) Making efficient use of resources ☐
(D) Facilitating coordination in action ☐

6. Umang was working as a 'production manager' at 'LG Papers Ltd.' The company had launched new eco-friendly paper straws in the market. He was given a target of producing 5,000 straws a day, by the general manager. In spite of making the employees work overtime, Umang could not meet the target.

On investigation, it was found that the employees had not received the right training to manufacture these eco-friendly paper straws. So the employees were sent for special training.

The function of management which helped Umang in identifying that he could not meet the target is *[CBSE 2023]*

(A) planning ☐ (B) organising ☐
(C) directing ☐ (D) controlling ☐

7. Himanshu is working as a 'Marketing Manager' in 'Suvidit-Air-Conditioners', a well-known brand in the field of air-conditioners. Till last month the company was able to achieve its sales targets. But this month, Himanshu observed that targets were not being met and the number of air-conditioners sold was decreasing.

He analysed the situation and found that the new salesman appointed last month was not good and for this he took necessary action.

Which of the following function of management helped Himanshu to identify the decrease in sale? *[CBSE 2023]*

(A) Planning ☐
(B) Organising ☐
(C) Directing ☐
(D) Controlling ☐

8. Choose the incorrect statement about the controlling function of management.

(A) Controlling is both backward and forward-looking ☐
(B) Controlling is prescriptive whereas planning is evaluative ☐
(C) Controlling pre-supposes the existence of certain standards ☐
(D) Controlling is a pervasive function of management ☐

9. Choose the incorrect statement from the following

(A) The controlling process starts with setting standards ☐
(B) Taking corrective measures is the final step in the controlling process ☐
(C) Planning and controlling are separate functions of management; therefore, they are not related ☐
(D) The controlling function facilitates coordination ☐

10. Identify the point of importance of controlling that has been tried to achieve in the picture below

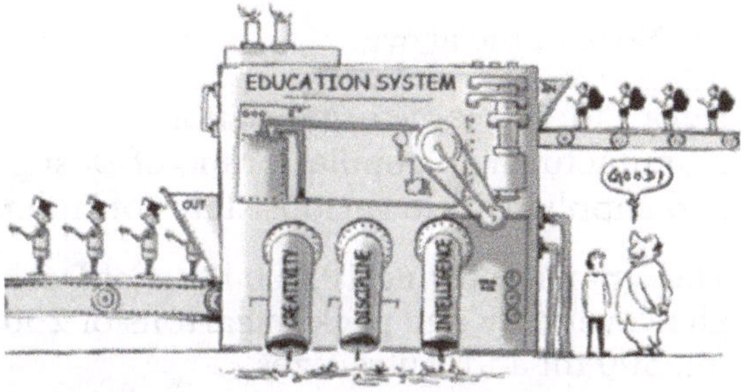

(A) Ensuring order and discipline ☐
(B) Improving employee motivation ☐
(C) Making efficient use of resources ☐
(D) Facilitating coordination in action ☐

11. Match Column I with Column II

	Column I		Column II
A.	Helps in accomplishing organisational goals.	(i)	A restaurant controls food costs by regularly monitoring inventory levels.
B.	Helps in judging accuracy of standards.	(ii)	Controlling ensures the timely completion of a construction project.
C.	Helps in making efficient use of resources.	(iii)	By comparing actual sales figures with projected targets, a retail store determines the accuracy of its sales forecasting methods.

Codes

	A	B	C			A	B	C	
(A)	(ii)	(iii)	(i)	☐	(B)	(iii)	(i)	(ii)	☐
(C)	(i)	(iii)	(ii)	☐	(D)	(ii)	(i)	(iii)	☐

12. Which step of the controlling process is highlighted in the below image?

(A) Setting performance standards ☐
(B) Taking corrective action ☐
(C) Analysing deviations ☐
(D) None of the above ☐

13. Keya Ltd. is a large organisation manufacturing a popular brand of Desi ghee and supplying it to various states of India.

They manufacturing 10,000 litres of Desi ghee everyday and pack in cartons of 250 ml, 500 ml and 1 litre sizes.

The production manager ensures that one out of every ten cartons of each size is checked for quality control everyday.

The step of the controlling process discussed in the above para is *[CBSE 2023]*

(A) Setting performance standards ☐
(B) Measurement of actual performance ☐
(C) Comparison of actual performance with standards ☐
(D) Analysing deviations ☐

14. Ajit Nene, the owner of a newly established food delivery outlet, 'Food and Snacks' in Maharashtra instructed the Human Resource Manager of the firm, to establish qualitative benchmarks of performance, as he wanted to assess the motivation, skill and satisfaction level of his employees.

The sales manager was asked to set quantitative benchmarks of performance in terms of volume of sales made on a daily basis. Identify the step performed by Ajit Nene in the process of controlling.

(A) Measurement of performance ☐
(B) Analysing deviations ☐
(C) Setting performance standards ☐
(D) Taking corrective action ☐

15. ……………… is the step in the controlling process where standards may have to be revised in case the deviation cannot be corrected through managerial action. *[CBSE 2024]*

(A) Setting performance standards ☐
(B) Measurement of actual performance ☐
(C) Comparing actual performance with standards and analysing deviations ☐
(D) Taking corrective action ☐

16. Some employees have been assigned the job of measuring the output in an objective and reliable way. They are applying different techniques for achieving this aim.

Some of these are personal-observation, sample-checking, etc.

They are also keeping the units of measurement same as that of the units in the standards.

Name the step of controlling process applicable in the above paragraph.

(A) Analysing deviations ☐

(B) Comparing actual performance with standards ☐

(C) Establishing standards ☐

(D) Measurement of actual performance ☐

17. An important project at AMB Consultants is running behind schedule by a month. This has upset their clients and might affect the reputation of the company in the long-run. No managerial action like assigning more workers, equipment or giving overtime has been able to solve the problem.

What managerial action may now be taken by the company to avoid such a situation from arising in the future?

(A) Revise the schedule ☐

(B) Assigning additional workers and equipment to the project ☐

(C) Get permission for further overtime work ☐

(D) Both (b) and (c) ☐

18. No project manager likes to see his/her project falling behind schedule, especially if it affects the quality, scope or budget of the deliverables. But sometimes, despite your best efforts, things go wrong and you need to take action to get your project back on track.

It is, therefore, important to determine the acceptable range of deviations. It is neither economical nor easy to keep a check on each and every activity in an organisation.

But once you have a clear picture of the current status and the root causes of the delay, you need to prioritise and reschedule your project activities. It is important to focus on areas which are critical to the success of an organisation.

Identify the method of managerial control highlighted above.

(A) Management by exception ☐

(B) Critical point control ☐

(C) Both (A) and (B) ☐

(D) Budgetary control ☐

19. In order to ensure that the classroom teaching is effective, Mrs. Anju Kapoor, the principal of Golden Public School, carries out classroom teaching observations herself.

Identify the step involved in the controlling process being described in the above lines.

(A) Setting of standards ☐

(B) Measurement of actual performance ☐

(C) Taking corrective action ☐

(D) Analysing the deviations ☐

20. Calculation of certain ratios like gross profit ratio, net profit ratio, return on investment, etc., at periodic intervals is an example of

(A) comparing actual performance with standard ☐

(B) measurement of a company's performance ☐

(C) analysing deviations ☐

(D) setting performance standards ☐

21. Which of the following signifies causes of deviation?

(A) Structural drawbacks ☐

(B) Unrealistic standards ☐

(C) Both (A) and (B) ☐

(D) Sample checking ☐

22. While PV sales overall reached a new all-time high, it was a different story for March, 2024.

Passenger vehicle sales shrunk 6.17 percent year on year to 3,22,345 units from 3,43,527 units a year ago. Sales were also down compared to February, 2024 which stood at 3,30,107 units.

"The PV sector encountered challenges, with a MoM decrease of 2% and a YoY fall of 6%. The downturn was influenced by heavy discounting and selective financing further affected by economic worries and the electoral climate.

Nonetheless, positives such as improved vehicle availability, increased stock levels and new model launches did stimulate demand in certain areas. The impact of election activities and changes in festival dates also played a role in sales dynamics."

FADA adopted a cautious outlook for the near term highlighting that the unchanged lending rate, upcoming elections and continued inflationary trend could dampen auto sales in the coming months.

The dealer body however added that new product launches, improved vehicle supply, favourable government policies and a good monsoon could help revive demand over the course of the year.

Relating the above case to controlling, identify the step of controlling process undertaken to revive demand.

(A) Measurement of performance ☐
(B) Analysing deviations ☐
(C) Setting performance standards ☐
(D) Taking corrective action ☐

23. Choose the incorrect statement about the controlling function of management.

(A) Deviations include unrealistic standards, defective process, inadequacy of resources ☐
(B) Standards may not need some modification to be realistic in the changed business environment ☐
(C) Deviations may have multiple causes for their origin ☐
(D) Performance should be measured in an objective and reliable manner ☐

24. Match the Column I with Column II in the following information

	Column I		Column II
A.	Defective material	(i)	Repair the existing machine or replace the machine if it cannot be repaired.
B.	Defective machinery	(ii)	Undertake technological upgradation of machinery.
C.	Obselete machinery	(iii)	Modify the existing process.
D.	Defective process	(iv)	Change the quality specification for material used.

Codes

	A	B	C	D	
(A)	(i)	(ii)	(iii)	(iv)	☐
(B)	(iv)	(ii)	(i)	(iii)	☐
(C)	(iv)	(i)	(ii)	(iii)	☐
(D)	(iii)	(i)	(ii)	(iv)	☐

25. Match Column I with Column II

	Column I		Column II
A.	Setting performance standards	(i)	Use of measurement techniques.
B.	Analysing deviations	(ii)	Initial step of controlling.
C.	Measurement of actual performance	(iii)	Final step of controlling.
D.	Taking corrective actions	(iv)	Identifying differences in actual and standard performance.

Codes

	A	B	C	D	
(A)	(iii)	(iv)	(i)	(ii)	☐
(B)	(ii)	(i)	(iii)	(iv)	☐
(C)	(iv)	(iii)	(i)	(ii)	☐
(D)	(ii)	(iv)	(i)	(iii)	☐

Assertion-Reason Questions

No. of Questions : **8** Suggested Time : **12 Minutes**

Direction Each of the question given below consist of the two statements; one labelled as **Assertion** (A) and other as **Reason** (R). List of common options applicable for each question is given below

(A) Both Assertion (A) and Reason (R) are true and Reason (R) is the correct explanation of Assertion (A)
(B) Both Assertion (A) and Reason (R) are true, but Reason (R) is not the correct explanation of (A) Assertion
(C) Assertion (A) is true, but Reason (R) is false
(D) Assertion (A) is false, but Reason (R) is true

You have to select the codes as *a, b, c* or *d* as your answer to the question by marking (✓) in the response box given against each option.

1. Assertion (A) Controlling helps in making efficient use of resources.

Reason (R) An efficient control system keeps a check on the changes taking place in the organisation and in the environment and helps to review and revise the standards in light of changes.

(A) ☐ (B) ☐ (C) ☐ (D) ☐

2. Assertion (A) Controlling aims to ensure that resources are used effectively and efficiently to achieve pre-determined goals.

Reason (R) Controlling is both a backward-looking as well as forward-looking function.

(A) ☐ (B) ☐ (C) ☐ (D) ☐

3. Assertion (A) Controlling is not a costly process.

Reason (R) Controlling helps in judging the accuracy of standards set by the management.

(A) ☐ (B) ☐ (C) ☐ (D) ☐

4. Assertion (A) Planning and controlling are inseparable twins of management.

Reason (R) Planning and controlling are two separate functions but are closely-related to each other.

(A) ☐ (B) ☐ (C) ☐ (D) ☐

5. Assertion (A) Controlling can prevent deviations.

Reason (R) Controlling helps to minimise deviations by taking actions and decisions that reduce their recurrence.

(A) ☐ (B) ☐ (C) ☐ (D) ☐

6. Assertion (A) The nature of corrective action required depends upon the extent of deviation from the standards.

Reason (R) Controlling is a prerequisite for planning.

(A) ☐ (B) ☐ (C) ☐ (D) ☐

7. Assertion (A) Controlling is regarded as goal-oriented process.

Reason (R) Controlling ensures that an organisation's resources are effectively and efficiently utilised for achievement of goal.

(A) ☐ (B) ☐ (C) ☐ (D) ☐

8. Assertion (A) Deviations in the key areas of business needs to be attended at an urgent basis.

Reason (R) Critical point control and management by exception should be adopted for such deviations.

(A) ☐ (B) ☐
(C) ☐ (D) ☐

Correct/Incorrect Statements

No. of Questions : **8** Suggested Time : **12 Minutes**

Direction Each of the question given below consist of the two statements. List of common options applicable for each question is given below

(A) Statement I is correct and Statement II is incorrect
(B) Statement I is incorrect and Statement II is correct
(C) Both statements are correct
(D) Both statements are incorrect

You have to select the codes as *a, b, c* or *d* as your answer to the question by marking (✓) in the response box given against each option.

1. **Statement I** Controlling is only forward-looking.

   Statement II Controlling is goal-oriented in nature.

   (A) ☐ (B) ☐ (C) ☐ (D) ☐

2. **Statement I** Controlling involves selecting objectives and frame ways to achieve them.

   Statement II Controlling is the process of assuring that actions are in line with plans.

   (A) ☐ (B) ☐ (C) ☐ (D) ☐

3. **Statement I** Qualitative standards are difficult to define.

   Statement II Provision of congenial and protective working environment can help labour absenteeism.

   (A) ☐ (B) ☐ (C) ☐ (D) ☐

4. **Statement I** Standards should be flexible enough to be modified whenever required.

   Statement II Due to changes taking place in the internal and external business environment, standards may need some modification to be realistic in the changed business environment.

   (A) ☐ (B) ☐ (C) ☐ (D) ☐

5. **Statement I** Standards are the criteria against which actual performance would be measured.

   Statement II Standards serve as benchmarks towards which an organisation strives to work.

   (A) ☐ (B) ☐ (C) ☐ (D) ☐

6. **Statement I** A moderate corrective action is required when the deviations are within acceptable limits.

   Statement II Control is often welcomed by employees in the organisation.

   (A) ☐ (B) ☐ (C) ☐ (D) ☐

7. **Statement I** Standards are set at the time of controlling the activities.

   Statement II Standards help in finding deviations in the performance.

   (A) ☐ (B) ☐ (C) ☐ (D) ☐

8. **Statement I** Planning based on facts makes controlling easier and effective.

   Statement II Public relations and leadership qualities of management are examples of quantitative standards.

   (A) ☐ (B) ☐ (C) ☐ (D) ☐

Case Based Questions

No. of Questions : **2** | Suggested Time : **10 Minutes**

Direction This section contains 2 cases each having 4 Questions of 1 mark each. You have to write the answer of each question based on the context of the related case.

Case 1 GRSE is a shipbuilding company based in India that specialises in building warships and other vessels for the Indian Navy and Indian Coast Guard. With a modern shipbuilding infrastructure, state of the art Virtual Reality Lab and a strong design team, GRSE is recognised as a 'Master Builder' for amphibious ships in India.

The company is doing well but the employees keep on complaining as they say there are no standards to judge the state of mind of the employees, their motivation and job satisfaction levels. For some, it's extra money, it may be focus on developing a positive work culture, foster recognition and appreciation within the company, offer flexible scheduling or set clear and measurable goals.

The HR department is trying to see to the problems which have recently occurred with the employees. In other areas, however, company has set some standards and is trying to effect the control mechanism but implementing and maintaining them can be expensive. All this has not been so easy.

Employees in other departments like manufacturing, purchase, marketing, etc. have time and again resisted to the installation of computer monitoring systems and CCTVs. They say that it is against their freedom. Despite all these great efforts made by the company, it had to face losses last year. Even though all the control mechanisms are in place, there is an entry of competitors with better technology. This has given some bad time to the company despite its alertness in putting proper controlling in execution.

Questions

(i) Which concept of management has been highlighted in the above case?

(A) Planning ☐
(B) Organising ☐
(C) Controlling ☐
(D) Directing ☐

(ii) "The company is doing well but the employees keep on complaining as they say there are no standards to judge the state of mind of the employees, their motivation and job satisfaction levels."

Identify the limitation of controlling highlighted in the above statement.

(A) Resistance from employees ☐
(B) Difficult to set quantitative standards ☐
(C) Controlling is costly ☐
(D) Little control on external factors ☐

(iii) "Employees in other departments like manufacturing, purchase, marketing, etc. have time and again resisted to the installation of computer monitoring systems and CCTVs. They say that it is against their freedom."

How does installation of CCTVs help in controlling function?

(A) Improving employee motivation ☐
(B) Ensuring order and discipline ☐
(C) Facilitating coordination in action ☐
(D) Judging accuracy of standards ☐

(iv) Which corrective action can be best applied in the above situation to overcome from the crisis?

(A) Training of employees ☐
(B) Assigning of additional workers ☐
(C) Motivation of employees ☐
(D) Permission for overtime work ☐

Case 2 On 28th January, 1986, the Space Shuttle Challenger broke apart 73 seconds into its flight, killing all seven crew members aboard. Tightly controlled management processes don't happen by accident, they're never complete but always ongoing. As NASA heartbreakingly realised in 1986 with the explosion of the Space Shuttle Challenger, every process, whether major or minor, converges to form the whole.

The cause of the disaster was the failure of the primary and secondary redundant O-ring seals in a joint in the shuttle's right Solid Rocket Booster (SRB). The record-low temperatures on the morning of the launch had stiffened the rubber O-rings, reducing their ability to seal the joints.

As a result of this disaster, NASA established the Office of safety, reliability, and quality assurance and arranged for deployment of commercial satellites.

In the wake of the Challenger disaster and subsequent commission report, NASA invested $2 billion in nearly 400 improvements before the first post-Challenger Shuttle flight on 29th September, 1988, seeking to upgrade equipment, enlarge its safety corps and inject new accountability into shuttle management.

Control management is critical to making sure processes and systems are running effectively within your organisation.

Questions

(i) Which function of management was instrumental in NASA's response to the challenger disaster, leading to investments in safety improvements and enhanced accountability measures?

(A) Planning ☐

(B) Organising ☐

(C) Controlling ☐

(D) Directing ☐

(ii) "Control management is critical to making sure processes and systems are running effectively within your organisation."

Which limitation of controlling is reflected from the above statement?

(A) Resistance from employees ☐

(B) Difficult to set quantitative standards ☐

(C) Controlling is costly ☐

(D) Little control on external factors ☐

(iii) "Tightly controlled management processes don't happen by accident, they're never complete but always ongoing."

Identify the feature of controlling reflected in the above statement.

(A) Controlling is a primary function ☐

(B) Controlling is a continuous process ☐

(C) Controlling is goal-oriented ☐

(D) Controlling is pervasive ☐

(iv) "In the wake of the Challenger disaster and subsequent commission report, NASA invested $2 billion in nearly 400 improvements before the first post-Challenger shuttle flight on 29th September, 1988, seeking to upgrade equipment, enlarge its safety corps, and inject new accountability into shuttle management."

Which step of controlling process is discussed in the above statement?

(A) Setting performance standards ☐

(B) Measurement of actual performance ☐

(C) Comparing actual performance with standards and analysing deviations ☐

(D) Taking corrective action ☐

Subjective Questions

Free Response Questions, Open-ended Questions etc.

No. of Questions : **8** Suggested Time : **60 Minutes**

1. Paul, the Manager of a manufacturing unit in Noida, employed various strategies to address the production shortfall of 850 balls out of the 1,000 balls target.

   Furthermore, what crucial initial steps he might have overlooked during the process of analysing deviations and implementing corrective measures?

2. Some outlets consistently exceed sales targets, while others struggle to meet their goals. To address these disparities, the regional manager aims to implement two management techniques for analysing deviations. Explore these two techniques in detail.

3. Kunal is working in an MNC. He has created an atmosphere of enforcement of disciplinary actions. Through careful monitoring of raw material usage, labour costs and overhead expenses, he has been able to identify areas of inefficiency and implement cost saving measures.

   He constantly checks dishonest behaviour of employees and takes a stern action immediately. Recently he has installed CCTV cameras to keep vigil on the employees.

   (i) In the above case, which importance of controlling has been implemented by Kunal?

   (ii) How has Kunal's implementation of controlling measures contributed to the overall efficiency and discipline within the MNC?

   (iii) Can you suggest one more way by which Kunal could have implemented controlling?

4. "Without planning, organisations risk drifting aimlessly and reacting to events rather than shaping their own destiny. Without controlling, plans become mere wishful thinking, lacking the feedback mechanisms needed to guide actions and ensure accountability."

   In the light of the above statement, discuss the relationship between planning and controlling.

5. "While one principle focuses on identifying and monitoring key stages or processes where deviations can have significant impacts, the other provides a framework for prioritising attention and resources to areas requiring immediate intervention or decision-making."

   Identify the principles of control and differentiate between the two.

6. Piyush is the production manager of a shoe company 'Comforty'. He has 1,000 workers under him in his department. Piyush booked a special order for 300 pairs of gents shoes at an estimated cost price of ₹ 500 per pair plus a 20% profit margin.

   This order is to be completed within 10 days. After completion of the order, Piyush found out that the production cost of one pair of shoes was ₹ 700. He tried to find out the reason but he couldn't.

   He reported it to the chief executive officer. For this, the chief executive officer appointed Abhay, who was not only a specialised cost accountant, but also a qualified human resource manager. After two days, Abhay reported that the set target could have been completed by only 800 workers.

   This revealed that there was overmanning in the organisation. The organisation was not utilising the human resources optimally which had led to high labour cost.

   The above case highlights an important function of management.

   (i) Identify the function of management discussed above.

   (ii) State any three points of importance of the function identified in (i) above. *[CBSE 2024]*

7. 'B & G' is a large company engaged in assembly of pharmaceuticals. It was concluded by the observation that on an average, a worker can meet the production target of 1,000 units in a day. The company is providing attractive allowances to reduce labour turnover and absenteeism. All the workers are happy. But the workers were facing difficulties in meeting the production target and were able to produce 800 units only.

   To find out the reason, the company compared actual performance of each worker and observed through CCTV that some of the workers were busy in gossiping.

   (i) Identify the function of management discussed above.

   (ii) State the steps in the process of the function identified which are discussed in the above paragraph.

8. Manufacturing Company Zorba Ltd. operates in a highly competitive industry, producing consumer electronics. Despite having a strong product lineup, the company has been facing challenges in meeting production targets, maintaining quality standards and controlling costs.

   Management recognises the need to implement effective measures to address these issues and ensure the company's long-term success.

   By introducing stringent quality control measures at each stage of the production process, including regular inspections and employee training programmes, Company Zorba has significantly reduced product defects and customer complaints.

   (i) Identify the management function to rectify the above situation.

   (ii) Briefly state the procedure followed by the company so that the actual production may come up to the target production.

   (iii) What other measures can be adopted by the company?

Answers

If your answer matches with the answer given here then put (✓) in the box otherwise put (✗). In case you did not attempt the question leave the box blank.

Multiple Choice Questions

1. C ☐	2. C ☐
3. B ☐	4. B ☐
5. D ☐	6. D ☐
7. D ☐	8. B ☐
9. C ☐	10. C ☐
11. A ☐	12. C ☐
13. B ☐	14. C ☐
15. D ☐	16. D ☐
17. A ☐	18. B ☐
19. B ☐	20. B ☐
21. C ☐	22. D ☐
23. B ☐	24. C ☐
25. D ☐	

Your Score__________ *(No. of Correct Answers)*

Assertion-Reason Questions

1. B ☐	2. B ☐	3. D ☐
4. A ☐	5. D ☐	6. C ☐
7. A ☐	8. A ☐	

Your Score__________ *(No. of Correct Answers)*

Correct/Incorrect Statements

1. B ☐	2. B ☐	3. C ☐
4. C ☐	5. C ☐	6. D ☐
7. A ☐	8. A ☐	

Your Score__________ *(No. of Correct Answers)*

Case Based Questions

1. (i) C ☐ (ii) B ☐
   (iii) B ☐ (iv) C ☐
2. (i) C ☐ (ii) D ☐
   (iii) B ☐ (iv) D ☐

Your Score__________ *(No. of Correct Answers)*

Explanations

Multiple Choice Questions

1. (C) Controlling is the management function that involves monitoring activities to ensure they are being performed as planned and taking corrective action when necessary.
2. (C) Controlling is forward-looking because it involves setting future performance standards and ensuring that future activities align with these standards. Controlling is also backward-looking because it involves evaluating past performance and comparing.
3. (B) Resistance from employees
4. (B) Judging accuracy of standards
5. (D) Facilitating coordination in action
6. (D) controlling
7. (D) Controlling
8. (B) Planning is prescriptive whereas controlling is evaluative
9. (C) Planning and controlling are closely related functions of management.
10. (C) Making efficient use of resources
11. (A) (ii) (iii) (i)
12. (C) "Analysing deviations" in controlling refers to the process of examining differences between actual performances and the established standards or expectations.
13. (B) Measurement of actual performance
14. (C) Setting performance standards
15. (D) Taking corrective action
16. (D) Measurement of actual performance
17. (A) Revise the schedule
18. (B) Critical point control
19. (B) Measurement of actual performance
20. (B) measurement of a company's performance
21. (C) Structural drawbacks within an organisation, such as inefficient processes, inadequate resources or poor communication channels, can contribute to deviations from established standards.

    Setting standards that are too ambitious or unattainable can also lead to deviations.
22. (D) Taking corrective action involves implementing measures to address deviations from desired performance levels.

    In this case, the FADA and the dealer body are considering various strategies and initiatives to counteract the downturn in sales and stimulate demand.
23. (B) In reality, standards may indeed need modification to remain realistic in a changed business environment.

    Changes in market conditions, technology, regulations or other factors may necessitate adjustments to standards to ensure they remain relevant and achievable.
24. (C) (iv) (i) (ii) (iii)
25. (D) (ii) (iv) (i) (iii)

Assertion-Reason Questions

1. (B) Both Assertion (A) and Reason (R) are true, but Reason (R) is not the correct explanation of Assertion
2. (B) Both Assertion (A) and Reason (R) are true, but Reason (R) is not the correct explanation of Assertion
3. (D) Controlling may involve costs associated with monitoring, data collection, analysis and implementation of corrective actions.
4. (A) Both Assertion (A) and Reason (R) are true and Reason (R) is the correct explanation of Assertion (A)
5. (D) While controlling can help to minimise deviations, it cannot entirely prevent them.
6. (C) Planning is pre-requisite for controlling
7. (A) Both Assertion (A) and Reason (R) are true and Reason (R) is the correct explanation of Assertion (A)
8. (A) Both Assertion (A) and Reason (R) are true and Reason (R) is the correct explanation of Assertion (A)

Correct/Incorrect Statements

1. (B) Controlling is not only forward-looking but also backward-looking function.
2. (B) Controlling is the process of monitoring performance, comparing it with goals and taking corrective action as needed.
3. (C) Both statements are correct
4. (C) Both statements are correct
5. (C) Both statements are correct
6. (D) No corrective action is required when the deviations are within acceptable limits. Control is often resisted by employees in the organisation
7. (A) Standards provide a basis for evaluating performance but do not directly help in finding deviations.
8. (A) Public relations and leadership qualities of management are examples of qualitative standards.

Case Based Questions

1. (i) (C) Controlling

   (ii) (B) The statement indicates that employees complain about the lack of standards to judge their state of mind, motivation and job satisfaction levels.
   These aspects are often qualitative and subjective, making it challenging to establish clear and measurable quantitative standards for them.

   (iii) (B) The installation of CCTVs primarily helps in ensuring order and discipline within the organisation.

   (iv) (C) By addressing the concerns of employees, fostering a positive work culture, recognising and appreciating their contributions and offering flexible scheduling or clear and measurable goals, the company can improve employee morale and motivation.

2. (i) (C) In the case of NASA's response to the challenger disaster, controlling played a crucial role in identifying the shortcomings in safety measures and management practices.

   (ii) (D) While controlling helps in ensuring internal processes run effectively, it may have limited control over external factors such as market conditions, regulatory changes or natural disasters.

   (iii) (B) Controlling is not a one time activity but rather an ongoing process that requires constant monitoring, evaluation and adjustment to ensure organisational effectiveness.

   (iv) (D) NASA took corrective action by investing in improvements to upgrade equipment, enhance safety measures and introduce new accountability measures in response to the challenger disaster.

Subjective Questions

1. Initial steps that the manager may have overlooked are

   (i) **Setting Performance Standards** The first step in the controlling process is to set the performance standards. Standards are those criteria, on which the actual performances are measured. These standards serve as a benchmark towards which an organisation strives to work.

   (ii) **Measurement of Actual Performance** After the establishment of standards, the next step is measuring the actual performance with the set standards. This can be done by opting several methods like personal observation, sample checking, performance reports, etc.

   (iii) **Comparison of Actual Performance with Standards** In this step, the actual performances are compared with the established standards. Such comparisons reveal the deviation between planned and actual results.

2. By implementing critical point control and management by exception, the regional manager can effectively analyse deviations in sales performance among different stores to enhance operational efficiency and maximise profits.
   These are as follows

   (i) **Critical Point Control** This technique involves identifying critical points or thresholds that signify significant deviations from expected performance.
   e.g. The manager can set critical points for sales targets, profit margins or inventory levels.
   When a store's performance deviates beyond these critical points, it triggers immediate attention and action from the manager.

(ii) **Management by Exception** This technique involves focusing managerial attention on exceptional cases or deviations that require intervention, rather than micro-managing every aspect of store performance. The manager sets predefined criteria or standards for acceptable performance, such as sales targets or profit margins.

Stores that meet or exceed these standards are considered exceptions and require minimal managerial intervention, allowing the manager to focus resources on addressing underperforming stores or significant deviations.

3. (i) Controlling ensures proper order and discipline in the organisation.

(ii) Kunal's implementation of controlling measures has contributed to the overall efficiency and discipline within the MNC by enforcing disciplinary actions, monitoring expenses and installing CCTV cameras to ensure compliance with company policies and maintain order in the workplace.

(iii) Another way in which Kunal could have implemented controlling is by implementing performance evaluations and setting performance standards for employees. By establishing clear performance expectations and regularly evaluating employee performance against these standards, Kunal can ensure that employees are meeting organisational goals and objectives effectively.

4. The relationship between controlling and planning is described below

(i) **Planning and Controlling are Inseparable Twins of Management** Planning provides the basis for controlling. The desired standards are set in the process of planning in clear and specific terms.

In the process of controlling, the actual performance is measured and compared with these standards and the deviations if any are identified and appropriate corrective action is taken.

However, in the absence of any standards, it would not be possible to gauge the actual performance. Thus, planning without controlling is meaningless and controlling without planning is blind.

(ii) **Planning is Prescriptive whereas Controlling is Evaluative** Planning is an intellectual activity which is concerned with thinking, articulating and analysing various alternative course of actions and prescribing the best possible alternative in order to achieve the desired goals efficiently and effectively.

Controlling, on the other hand, is concerned with ensuring that events conform to plans. Thus, it involves monitoring and measuring the extent to which the desired goals have been realised.

(iii) **Planning is Looking Ahead and Controlling is Looking Back** Planning is futuristic in nature as it involves chalking out the future Course of action. It bridges the gap between where we are and where we want to go. Thus, it is deemed to be a forward looking function of management.

Controlling, on the other hand, involves postmortem of the past activities to find out deviations from the standards. Therefore, controlling is said to be a backward looking function of management.

5. The principles of control described in the statement are 'critical point control' and 'management by exception'.

Difference between them is as follows

Principle	Critical Point Control	Management by Exception
Focus	Identifying and monitoring key stages or processes where deviations can have significant impacts.	Prioritising attention and resources to areas requiring immediate intervention or decision-making.
Approach	Setting critical points or thresholds to signify deviations from expected performance.	Setting predefined criteria or standards for acceptable performance.
Trigger Point	Performance deviating beyond critical points triggers immediate attention and action.	Deviations falling outside predefined standards are considered exceptions and require managerial intervention.

6. (i) The function of management discussed here is 'controlling'.

(ii) Importance of controlling can be highlighted through the following points

(a) **Making Efficient Use of Resources** By exercising control, a manager seeks to reduce wastage and spoilage of resources. Each activity is performed in accordance with predetermined standards and norms, which helps in effective and efficient utilisation of resources.

(b) **Improving Employee Motivation** It helps employees in realising well in advance, what they are expected to do and what are the standards of performance, on the basis of which they will be appraised. This motivates them to perform better.

(c) **Ensuring Order and Discipline** By keeping a check on the activities of the employees, controlling creates an atmosphere of order and discipline among them.
It also helps to keep a check on the dishonest behaviour of employees and minimise undesirable activities.

7. (i) Controlling

(ii) Following steps of controlling are identified in the given para

(a) Setting performance standards which are the criteria against which the actual performance would be measured.

(b) Measurement of actual performance with the standards in an objective and reliable manner.

(c) Comparing actual performance with standards to find out any deviations.

8. (i) The controlling function of management is needed to rectify the above situation.

(ii) The procedure followed by the company to ensure that actual production meets the target production involves introducing stringent quality control measures. This includes implementing regular inspections at each stage of the production process and conducting employee training programmes to enhance their skills and knowledge.

By ensuring strict adherence to quality standards and providing necessary training, the company aims to minimise product defects and improve production efficiency.

(iii) Other measures that Company Zorba can adopt include

(a) Implementing advanced production technologies to streamline processes and improve efficiency.

(b) Conducting regular performance evaluations to identify areas for improvement and address any shortcomings.

(c) Investing in research and development to innovate and develop new products that meet customer demands and stay ahead of competitors.

(d) Enhancing supply chain management to ensure timely delivery of raw materials and components, reducing production delays.

(e) Implementing cost control measures to optimise expenditure and improve profitability.

PART B

Business Finance and Marketing

CHAPTER -9

Financial Management

Types & Nos. of Questions

Multiple Choice Questions	-	30
Assertion-Reason Questions	-	8
Correct/Incorrect Statements	-	8
Case Based Questions	-	2 Cases, *each with four Questions*
Subjective Questions	-	6

Trend Analysis

On the basis of analysis of last 2 years' papers, it is found that on an average 3 Multiple Choice Questions and 2 Short Answer Type Questions (Case Based) are asked from this chapter.

Focus Topics of the Chapter

- Financial Decisions
- Financial Planning
- Capital Structure
- Fixed and Working Capital

Multiple Choice Questions

No. of Questions : **30** Suggested Time : **45 Minutes**

Direction Each of the question given below is Multiple Choice Question (MCQ) i.e. there are Four Options/Choices for answer, out of which ONLY ONE is correct. You have to select the correct option. A response box is given with each option, mark (✓) in the box of the correct option. For each correct answer you will get 1 mark, while there is no penalty for incorrect answer or missed out questions.

1. "It is a process that allocates or directs funds available for investment into their most productive instrument opportunity". This is known as *[CBSE 2024]*

(A) financial planning ☐
(B) financial intermediation ☐
(C) allocative function ☐
(D) capital budgeting ☐

2. 'Temptations' is a food joint in Imperial Mall in Bengaluru. It is becoming popular among students and working people due to healthy, on-the-go dishes on its menu like 'Paneer Wrap', 'Chickpeas Salad', 'Grilled Sandwiches', etc.

It has now decided to open two new branches in other parts of Bengaluru. Which financial decision has been discussed in the above case?

(A) Long-term investment decision ☐
(B) Short-term investment decision ☐
(C) Dividend decision ☐
(D) Financing decision ☐

3. Pazero is a mid-sized company that specialises in producing automotive parts. Over the past few years, the company has experienced steady growth in revenue but despite increasing sales, Pazero finds itself in a cash crunch. While revenue is growing, cash reserves are dwindling, leading to difficulties in meeting operational expenses and investing in growth opportunities.

Identify the factor affecting financing decision highlighted in the above case.

(A) Cost ☐
(B) Risk ☐
(C) Cash flow position ☐
(D) Floatation cost ☐

4. Identify the correct statement from the following

(A) Financial management is concerned with both usage and procurement of funds ☐
(B) The primary objective of financial management is to maximise profits for a company ☐
(C) The role of financial management does not include deciding the composition of fixed assets ☐
(D) All of the above ☐

5. Vikrant joins his father's business of Organic masalas, near Kotgarh in Himachal after completing his MBA. In order to capture a major share of the market, he decided to sell the product in small attractive packages by using the latest packaging technology.

His father suggested that they hire financial consultants to estimate the amount of funds that would be required for the purpose and timings when it would be required.

The concept being discussed by Vikrant's father, links which financial decision with the investment decision?

(A) Dividend decision ☐
(B) Financial planning ☐
(C) Capital structure decision ☐
(D) Financing decision ☐

6. Capgemin Corporation is a multinational conglomerate operating in various sectors, including technology, manufacturing and retail. The company's board of directors recently encountered challenges in distributing dividends to its shareholders due to constraints embedded in its debt agreements.

Despite strong financial performance and ample retained earnings, Capgemin Corporation faces limitations on distributing dividends to shareholders as outlined in its debt covenants.

Identify the factor affecting dividend decision highlighted above.

(A) Legal constraints ☐
(B) Contractual constraints ☐
(C) Shareholder's preference ☐
(D) Cash flow position ☐

7. The cost of debt is lower than the cost of equity for a firm because

(A) lender's risk is more than the equity shares ☐
(B) lender's risk is lower than the equity share's risk ☐
(C) equity shareholder's risk is more than the lender's risk ☐
(D) None of the above ☐

8. Identify the correct statement from the following

(A) Capital structure of a firm only affects its financial risk ☐
(B) Regulatory framework do not influence a company's financing decisions ☐
(C) Net working capital is the difference between the current assets and current liabilities ☐
(D) The nature of business has no impact on its working capital ☐

9. If the benefit from a decision exceeds the cost involved, the market price

(A) remains same ☐ (B) decreases ☐
(C) increases ☐ (D) None of these ☐

10. Which type of financial decision is depicted in the below image?

(A) Investment decision ☐
(B) Financing decision ☐
(C) Dividend decision ☐
(D) None of the above ☐

11. "This is the amount of capital invested in fixed assets". What is it called?

(A) Fixed capital ☐
(B) Working capital ☐
(C) Net working capital ☐
(D) Capital structure ☐

12. Identify the incorrect statement.

(A) If the stock markets are bullish, equity shares are more easily sold even at a higher price ☐
(B) Decision to invest in current asset once taken is irrevocable except at a huge loss ☐
(C) A public issue of equity may reduce the managements' holding in the company and make it vulnerable to takeover ☐
(D) A firm's ability to borrow at a lower rate increases its capacity to employ higher debt ☐

13. Match the Column I with Column II in the following information

	Column I		Column II
A.	Process of raising resources also involves some cost.	(i)	Contractual constraints
B.	While granting loans to a company, sometimes the lender may impose certain restrictions on the payment of dividends in future.	(ii)	Legal constraints

	Column I		Column II
C.	Certain provisions of the Companies Act place restrictions on payouts as dividend. Such provisions must be adhered to while declaring the dividend.	(iii)	Floatation cost

Codes

	A	B	C	
(A)	(iii)	(i)	(ii)	☐
(B)	(iii)	(ii)	(i)	☐
(C)	(i)	(ii)	(iii)	☐
(D)	(ii)	(iii)	(i)	☐

14. 'Dovex' was a large company with a renowned name in healthcare industry, specialising in the development and production of life saving medications and medical devices. With a strong reputation for ethical practices, 'Dovex' attracted a large number of investors who had great faith in the company's future.

This allowed 'Dovex' to raise capital easily from the market whenever expansion or new projects were to be undertaken. As a result, it could pay high dividends to the shareholders. The factor affecting dividend decision discussed above, which allowed 'Dovex' to pay high dividends to the shareholders is *[CBSE 2024]*

(A) cash flow position ☐
(B) stock market reaction ☐
(C) legal constraints ☐
(D) access to capital market ☐

15. Bellatrix Aerospace has been experiencing steady growth over the past few years and is now looking to expand its operations internationally.

The company's management team has identified several opportunities for expansion into new markets, including emerging economies in Asia and Latin America.

It developed detailed financial forecasts for each target market, including projected sales revenues, expenses and cash flows to ensure that enough funds are available at right time.

Identify the concept discussed above.

(A) Financial management ☐
(B) Financial planning ☐
(C) Capital structure ☐
(D) Trading on equity ☐

16. Identify the concept illustrated below.

(A) Financial management ☐
(B) Financial planning ☐
(C) Capital structure ☐
(D) Trading on equity ☐

17. Match the Column I with Column II in the following information

	Column I		Column II
A.	It helps in avoiding business shocks and surprises and helps the company in preparing for the future.	(i)	Capital structure
B.	Mix between owners and borrowed funds.	(ii)	Trading on equity
C.	Chance that a firm would fail to meet its payment obligations.	(iii)	Financial planning
D.	Increase in profit earned by the equity shareholders due to the presence of fixed financial charges like interest.	(iv)	Financial risk

Codes

	A	B	C	D	
(A)	(iii)	(i)	(iv)	(ii)	☐
(B)	(iv)	(ii)	(i)	(iii)	☐
(C)	(iv)	(i)	(ii)	(iii)	☐
(D)	(iii)	(i)	(ii)	(iv)	☐

18. "Stock owners expect a rate of return from the equity which is commensurate with the risk they are assumimg." This can be termed as ....

(A) capital structure ☐
(B) financial risk ☐
(C) cost of equity ☐
(D) cost of debt ☐

19. Groupon Ltd. extends favourable credit terms to customers to maintain strong customer relationships and facilitate sales.

The working capital requirement of Groupon Ltd. will be

(A) high ☐
(B) low ☐
(C) Nil ☐
(D) None of the above ☐

20. Golden Gate Ventures specialises in the production of industrial machinery. It replaces the technology faster and avoid obsolete assets. The company has been in operation for over two decades and has established a strong reputation for delivering high quality products to its customers.

Identify the factor affecting fixed capital requirement highlighted in the above case.

(A) Scale of operation ☐
(B) Nature of business ☐
(C) Growth opportunities ☐
(D) Choice of technique ☐

21. Vedant Ltd. is a company with a decreasing EBIT. The company has a significant amount of debt in the form of debentures and further borrowing through debentures could exacerbate the situation. Which factor determining the capital structure, is the CFO of Vedant Ltd. primarily concerned about?

(A) Cost of debt ☐
(B) Return on investment ☐
(C) Interest coverage ratio ☐
(D) Debt service coverage ratio ☐

22. Aarti Steel Limited is a large creditworthy company manufacturing steel. The company seeks to enter the Asian market and therefore wants to raise additional funds of ₹1 crore from the primary market. The finance manager of the company Mr. Sundaram has suggested raising funds by issuing debentures, in order to take advantage of 'trading on equity.'

Identify the factor which is an important determinant of the company's ability to use the 'trading on equity' and thus the capital structure.

(A) Return on investment ☐
(B) Cost of debt ☐
(C) Cost of equity ☐
(D) Risk consideration ☐

23. Accenture Electronics is a leading manufacturer and retailer of consumer electronics products with a global presence. In an effort to stimulate sales and gain a competitive edge in the market, the company offers extended credit terms to its customers.

By offering generous credit terms, Accenture Electronics attracts more customers and drives higher sales volumes. The flexibility in payment terms encourages purchasing behaviour and enhances customer satisfaction, leading to repeat business and positive word of mouth referrals.

However this may lead to higher credit risk, as customers may delay payments or default on their obligations. This poses challenges in managing accounts receivable and collecting outstanding debts, potentially impacting cash flow and profitability.

Identify the factor affecting working capital highlighted above.

(A) Credit allowed ☐
(B) Credit availed ☐
(C) Growth prospects ☐
(D) Level of competition ☐

24. Advicure is a start-up specialising in developing cutting edge artificial intelligence solutions for businesses. The company was founded by a group of experienced software engineers who have identified several growth opportunities in the market.

Advicure aims to expand the customer base and increase market penetration for its existing product, develop new AI powered solutions to address emerging market needs and industry trend and establish strategic partnerships and explore opportunities for international expansion into new geographic markets.

Identify the factor affecting fixed capital requirement of Advicure.

(A) Technology upgradation ☐
(B) Level of collaboration ☐
(C) Growth prospects ☐
(D) Collaboration ☐

25. During the Covid-19 pandemic, the restaurant industry faced many challenges. The slowdown led to huge decrease in demand. From April 2022, the effect of Covid started reducing. The economy started picking up and boom was noticed in the restaurant industry. As a result, larger amount of working capital was required with increased production and sales.

The factor affecting the working capital requirement discussed above is *[CBSE 2023]*

(A) Seasonal factor ☐
(B) Production cycle ☐
(C) Operating efficiency ☐
(D) Business cycle ☐

26. Identify the factor affecting fixed capital requirement reflected in the picture below

(A) Growth prospects ☐
(B) Diversification ☐
(C) Level of collaboration ☐
(D) Technology upgradation ☐

27. Match the Column I with Column II in the following information

	Column I		Column II
A.	It refers to a position when a company is unable to meet its fixed financial charges namely interest payment, preference dividend and repayment obligations.	(i)	Business risk
B.	It depends upon fixed operating costs.	(ii)	Interest coverage ratio
C.	It takes care of the deficiencies referred to in the interest coverage ratio.	(iii)	Financial risk
D.	It refers to the number of times earnings before interest and taxes of a company covers the interest obligation.	(iv)	Debt service coverage ratio

Codes

	A	B	C	D	
(A)	(iii)	(i)	(iv)	(ii)	☐
(B)	(iv)	(ii)	(i)	(iii)	☐
(C)	(iv)	(i)	(ii)	(iii)	☐
(D)	(iii)	(i)	(ii)	(iv)	☐

28. Match the factors affecting fixed capital requirements given in the Column I with explanations given in Column II *[CBSE 2023]*

Column I		Column II
A. Nature of business	(i)	A trading organisation needs lower investments in fixed assets as compared to a manufacturing organisation.
B. Technology upgradation	(ii)	A textile manufacturing company is installing a cement manufacturing plant and thus is investments in fixed assets is increasing.

Column I		Column II
C. Diversification	(iii)	A capital-intensive organisation requires higher investments in fixed assets as compared to labour-intensive organisation.
D. Choice of techique	(iv)	Mobile phones became obsolete faster or many other assets. Hence these type of businesses require more fixed capital.

Codes

	A	B	C	D
(A)	(i)	(iv)	(ii)	(iii)
(B)	(ii)	(iii)	(iv)	(i)
(C)	(iii)	(ii)	(i)	(iv)
(D)	(iv)	(i)	(iii)	(ii)

29. Identify the incorrect statement.
(A) A capital intensive organisation requires less investment in plant and machinery as it relies less on manual labour
(B) A developed financial market may provide leasing facilities as an alternative to outright purchase
(C) Certain business organisations share each other's facilities
(D) Higher growth of an organisation generally requires higher investment in fixed assets

30. "It is the part of the total capital which is required for holding current assets." This is known as
(A) fixed capital
(B) working capital
(C) capital structure
(D) financial structure

Assertion-Reason Questions

No. of Questions : **8** Suggested Time : **12 Minutes**

Direction Each of the question given below consist of the two statements; one labelled as **Assertion** (A) and other as **Reason** (R). List of common options applicable for each question is given below

(A) Both Assertion (A) and Reason (R) are true and Reason (R) is the correct explanation of Assertion (A)
(B) Both Assertion (A) and Reason (R) are true, but Reason (R) is not the correct explanation of (A) Assertion
(C) Assertion (A) is true, but Reason (R) is false
(D) Assertion (A) is false, but Reason (R) is true

You have to select the codes as *a, b, c* or *d* as your answer to the question by marking (✓) in the response box given against each option.

1. **Assertion (A)** Financial management is concerned with optimal procurement as well as the usage of finance.
Reason (R) Different available sources of finance are identified and compared in terms of their costs and associated risks.
(A) (B)
(C) (D)

2. **Assertion (A)** Financial planning takes into consideration the growth, performance, investments and requirement of funds for a given period.
Reason (R) Financial management helps in forecasting what may happen in future under different business situations.
(A) (B) (C) (D)

3. **Assertion (A)** Financial planning enables the management to foresee the fund requirements for both i.e. the quantum as well as the timing.

   Reason (R) If excess funds are available, financial planning will unnecessarily add to the cost and may encourage wasteful expenditure.

   (A) ☐ (B) ☐ (C) ☐ (D) ☐

4. **Assertion (A)** The market price of a company's shares is linked to the financial decisions.

   Reason (R) A company's funds belong to the shareholders and the manner in which they are invested and the return earned by them determines their market value and price.

   (A) ☐ (B) ☐ (C) ☐ (D) ☐

5. **Assertion (A)** A firm's ability to borrow at a lower rate increases its capacity to employ higher debt.

   Reason (R) Less debt can be used if debt can be raised at a lower rate.

   (A) ☐ (B) ☐ (C) ☐ (D) ☐

6. **Assertion (A)** Better sales effort may reduce the average time for which finished goods inventory is held.

   Reason (R) Such efficiencies may increase the level of raw materials, finished goods and debtors resulting in more requirement of working capital.

   (A) ☐ (B) ☐ (C) ☐ (D) ☐

7. **Assertion (A)** Insufficient investment in current assets may make it more difficult for an organisation to meet its payment obligations.

   Reason (R) An asset is more liquid if it can be converted into cash quicker and without reduction in value.

   (A) ☐ (B) ☐ (C) ☐ (D) ☐

8. **Assertion (A)** Amount of earnings is a major determinant of the decision about dividend.

   Reason (R) Dividends are paid out of current and past earnings. *[CBSE 2024]*

   (A) ☐ (B) ☐
   (C) ☐ (D) ☐

Correct/Incorrect Statements

No. of Questions : **8** Suggested Time : **12 Minutes**

Direction Each of the question given below consist of the two statements. List of common options applicable for each question is given below

(A) Statement I is correct and Statement II is incorrect
(B) Statement I is incorrect and Statement II is correct
(C) Both statements are correct
(D) Both statements are incorrect

You have to select the codes as *a*, *b*, *c* or *d* as your answer to the question by marking (✓) in the response box given against each option.

1. **Statement I** Good financial management aims at mobilisation of financial resources at a lower cost and deployment of these in most lucrative activities.

   Statement II Shareholders' funds involve commitment regarding the payment of returns or the repayment of capital.

   (A) ☐ (B) ☐ (C) ☐ (D) ☐

2. **Statement I** Financial planning ensures that unnecessary funds are not raised.

Statement II The objective of financial planning is to ensure the availability of funds whenever required.

(A) ☐ (B) ☐ (C) ☐ (D) ☐

3. **Statement I** Investment decisions are concerned about the quantum of finance to be raised from short-term sources.

Statement II Financing decisions are concerned how the funds are invested in different assets.

(A) ☐ (B) ☐ (C) ☐ (D) ☐

4. **Statement I** Business risk depends upon fixed operating costs.

Statement II Decision to invest in fixed assets must be taken very carefully as such decisions once taken are irrevocable.

(A) ☐ (B) ☐ (C) ☐ (D) ☐

5. **Statement I** Business risk is the chance that a firm would fail to meet its payment obligations.

Statement II A capital structure will be said to be optimal when the proportion of debt and equity is such that it results in an increase in the value of the equity share.

(A) ☐ (B) ☐ (C) ☐ (D) ☐

6. **Statement I** If tax on dividend is higher, it is better to pay more by way of dividends.

Statement II An increase in dividend may have a negative impact on the share prices in the stock market.

(A) ☐ (B) ☐
(C) ☐ (D) ☐

7. **Statement I** Higher amount of debt means higher interest expense in future.

Statement II Expansion of business, which is a result of capital budgeting decision, do not affect virtually all items in the profit and loss account of the business.

(A) ☐ (B) ☐ (C) ☐ (D) ☐

8. **Statement I** Duration of production cycle, affects the amount of funds required for raw materials and expenses.

Statement II A useful guideline in the capital structure planning is the debt-equity ratio of other companies in the different industry.

(A) ☐ (B) ☐ (C) ☐ (D) ☐

Case Based Questions

No. of Questions : **2** Suggested Time : **10 Minutes**

Directions This section contains 2 cases each having 4 Questions of 1 mark each. You have to write the answer of each question based on the context of the related case.

Case 1 Sunrises Ltd. dealing in readymade garments, is planning to expand its business operations in order to cater to international market. For this purpose the company needs additional ₹ 80,00,000 Lakhs for replacing machines with modern machinery of higher production capacity. It involves committing the finance on a long term basis.

These decisions are very crucial for any business since they affect its earning capacity in the long-run. The company wishes to raise the required funds by issuing debentures. The debt can be issued at an estimated cost of 10%. The EBIT for the previous year of the company was ₹ 8,00,000 lakh and total capital investment was ₹ 1,00,00,000 crore. Instead of issuing 10% Debenture the Company can issue Equity Shares for raising the fund. The financial manager of the company would normally opt for a source which is the cheapest. *[CBSE QB]*

Questions

(i) What is the other name of long-term decision?

(A) Capital budgeting ☐
(B) Gross working capital ☐
(C) Financial management ☐
(D) Working capital ☐

(ii) A decision for replacing machines with modern machinery of higher production capacity is a

(A) financing decision ☐
(B) working capital decision ☐
(C) investment decision ☐
(D) None of the above ☐

(iii) A decision for raising fund of ₹ 80,00,000 lakh either from 10% debentures or equity shares is a

(A) financing decision ☐
(B) dividend decision ☐
(C) investment decision ☐
(D) None of the above ☐

(iv) The financing decisions are affected by various factors. Which one of the following factors is discussed in the above case?

(A) Cash flow position of the company ☐
(B) Cost ☐
(C) Amount of earnings ☐
(D) Taxation policy ☐

Case 2 Sri Anal Fireworks (SAF) is one of the leading fireworks manufacturers of India. SAF has done well in recent 5 years and sales have grown over the recent years. Nevertheless, the changing mindset of the customer towards environment friendliness have resulted in reducing demand year by year and increased the problem of skilled workers. Therefore, the company wants to start a new business based on existing funds.

SAF now faces the dilemma as to how to arrange working capital for the same to facilitate smooth day-to-day operations of the business. Manohar, the manager, believes a firm managing its raw materials efficiently may be able to manage with a smaller balance.

Also, raw materials should have a record of un-interrupted availability. Higher level of competitiveness may also necessitate larger stock of finished goods to meet urgent orders from customers.

Questions

(i) Identify the financial decision, SAF has to take.

(A) Long-term investment decision ☐
(B) Short-term investment decision ☐
(C) Financing decision ☐
(D) Dividend decision ☐

(ii) "Manohar, the manager, believes a firm managing its raw materials efficiently may be able to manage with a smaller balance."
Identify the factor affecting working capital highlighted in the given lines.

(A) Level of competition ☐
(B) Availability of raw materials ☐
(C) Operating efficiency ☐
(D) Inflation ☐

(iii) If the competition is low, a firm requires .... level of stock.

(A) low ☐
(B) high ☐
(C) Nil ☐
(D) None of the above ☐

(iv) Which assets provide liquidity to the business?

(A) Fixed assets ☐
(B) Current assets ☐
(C) Net working capital ☐
(D) Current liabilities ☐

Subjective Questions

Free Response Questions, Open-ended Questions etc.

No. of Questions : **6** Suggested Time : **45 Minutes**

1. Amit is running a dropshipping business and earning a lot by providing service that uses the dropshipping model of buying inventory and fulfillment logistics from a third party.

   Identify the working capital requirements of the company.

2. Gasex Fertilisers Ltd. expected a growth of 10% in the sales in the previous quarter. However, due to the prevailing economic situation around the world, the actual growth in sales was only 5%.

   The company's finance manager was called for an urgent meeting, by the senior management of the company, in which he clarified that he was already prepared for the situation, as he had made a financial blueprint for the future operations.

   He also reassured the management that he knew how to control the expenses, in case the sales were lower than the expectation.

   (i) Identify the concept that enabled the finance manager to tackle the situation discussed above.

   (ii) State any four points highlighting how the concept discussed above can help in smooth functioning of the organisation.

3. Sameer has been given a task of evaluating the financial performance of two companies, Alfa Ltd. and Beltex Ltd. in the same industry. Both companies have been trading on equity as part of their financial strategy. Given is the information that Sameer received. Which company is using trading on equity more effectively?

   Alfa Ltd. total assets ₹ 5,00,000, equity capital ₹ 3,00,000, debt capital ₹ 2,00,000, net income ₹ 50,000.

   Beltex Ltd. total assets ₹ 8,00,000, equity capital ₹ 4,00,000, debt capital ₹ 4,00,000, net income ₹ 60,000.

4. 'Abhishek Ltd.' is manufacturing cotton clothes. It has been consistently earning good profits for many years. This year too, it has been able to generate enough profits. There is availability of enough cash in the company and good prospects for growth in future.

   It is a well-managed organisation and believes in quality, equal employment opportunities and good remuneration practices. It has many shareholders who prefer to receive a regular income form their investments.

   It has taken a loan of ₹ 50 lakh from ICICI Bank and is bound by certain restrictions on the payment of dividend according to the terms of the loan agreement.

   The above discussion about the company leads to various factors which decide how much of the profits should be retained and how much has to be distributed by the company. Quoting the lines from the above discussion, identify and explain any four such factors.

5. Kanav, after passing out of college with specialisation in renewable energy, was determined to start a solar power plant. The venture required heavy investment in plant and machinery and less on manual labour. Kanav invested in the latest solar panel technology and infrastructure and purchased the latest solar panels, inverters and battery storage systems.

   Despite the high risk and substantial investment, Kanav's business had good expansion possibilities.

   The world was increasingly moving towards clean energy solutions and there was a growing demand for sustainable power sources. So, Kanav decided to create a higher capacity to meet the anticipated demand quickly.

This entailed further investment in fixed assets which Kanav was able to arrange.

As the years passed, the solar power plant did very well and played a pivotal role in the city's transition towards a greener and more sustainable future.

Identify and explain the two factors affecting the fixed capital requirements discussed in the above case. [CBSE 2024]

6. Kaysons Ltd. was a reputed company manufacturing automotive parts for electric vehicles. As the demand for the electric vehicles grew, Kaysons Ltd. needed more capital to keep up with the demand for automotive parts.

Atul, the finance manager of Kaysons Ltd. suggested that the company should raise funds through a public issue of shares as the stock market was bullish.

The chief executive officer fully understood that this process of raising funds would not only reduce the managements' holding in the company but would also require considerable expenditure.

Even then he agreed with the finance manager and the public issue of shares was made complying with the guidelines of Securities and Exchange Board of India.

Identify and state four factors affecting choice of capital structure being discussed above. [CBSE 2024]

Answers

If your answer matches with the answer given here then put (✓) in the box otherwise put (✗). In case you did not attempt the question leave the box blank.

Multiple Choice Questions

1. B ☐	2. A ☐
3. C ☐	4. A ☐
5. B ☐	6. B ☐
7. B ☐	8. C ☐
9. C ☐	10. A ☐
11. A ☐	12. B ☐
13. A ☐	14. D ☐
15. B ☐	16. B ☐
17. A ☐	18. C ☐
19. A ☐	20. D ☐
21. C ☐	22. A ☐
23. A ☐	24. C ☐
25. D ☐	26. B ☐
27. A ☐	28. A ☐
29. A ☐	30. B ☐

Your Score__________ (*No. of Correct Answers*)

Assertion-Reason Questions

1. A ☐	2. C ☐	3. A ☐
4. A ☐	5. C ☐	6. C ☐
7. A ☐	8. A ☐	

Your Score__________ (*No. of Correct Answers*)

Correct/Incorrect Statements

1. A ☐	2. C ☐	3. D ☐
4. C ☐	5. B ☐	6. D ☐
7. A ☐	8. A ☐	

Your Score__________ (*No. of Correct Answers*)

Case Based Questions

1.	(i) A ☐	(ii) C ☐
	(iii) A ☐	(iv) B ☐
2.	(i) B ☐	(ii) B ☐
	(iii) A ☐	(iv) B ☐

Your Score__________ (*No. of Correct Answers*)

Explanations

Multiple Choice Questions

1. (B) Financial intermediation refers to the process of channeling funds from savers or investors to borrowers or spenders in an economy.
2. (A) The decision to open two new branches in other parts of Bengaluru involves significant capital expenditure and commitment of resources over a long period. This type of decision pertains to capital budgeting, which is a key aspect of long-term investment decisions.
3. (C) Cash flow position
4. (A) Financial management is concerned with both usage and procurement of funds
5. (B) Financial planning
6. (B) Contractual constraints refer to the limitations set by debt agreements that restrict a company's ability to distribute dividends.
7. (B) The cost of debt is lower than the cost of equity because lenders (debt holders) assume less risk compared to equity shareholders. Debt holders have a higher claim on the company's assets in the event of liquidation and receive fixed interest payments regardless of the company's performance.
8. (C) Net working capital is the difference between the current assets and current liabilities.
9. (C) If the benefit from a decision exceeds the cost involved, it typically indicates a positive outcome for the decision-maker. In a competitive market, such positive outcomes often lead to increased demand for the product or service associated with the decision.
10. (A) Investment decisions in financial management involve allocating resources, usually money, in various assets or projects with the expectation of generating returns in the future.
11. (A) Fixed capital
12. (B) Decision to invest in fixed asset once taken is irrevocable except at a huge loss
13. (A) (iii) (i) (ii)
14. (D) access to capital market
15. (B) Financial planning
16. (B) Financial planning is the process of setting and achieving financial goals through the prudent management of finances. It involves analysing current financial situations, setting goals and creating strategies to achieve those goals.
17. (A) (iii) (i) (iv) (ii)
18. (C) cost of equity
19. (A) Extending favourable credit terms to customer's means that the company will have a higher amount of receivables. This increases the working capital requirement as the company needs to fund these receivables until they are collected.
20. (D) Choice of technique
21. (C) A decreasing EBIT (Earnings before Interest and Taxes) suggests that the company might struggle to cover its interest obligations. The interest coverage ratio, which measures a company's ability to pay interest on its outstanding debt, is a critical factor in such a scenario.
22. (A) Trading on equity refers to the use of debt to boost the return on equity. For a company to successfully engage in trading on equity, its Return on Investment (RoI) must be higher than the cost of debt.
23. (A) Credit allowed
24. (C) As Advicure aims to expand its customer base, develop new products and enter new markets, it will need substantial investment in fixed assets such as technology, infrastructure and R & D facilities.
25. (D) The business cycle refers to the fluctuations in economic activity that an economy experiences over a period of time, typically consisting of expansion (boom) and contraction (recession) phases.
26. (B) Diversification in financial management refers to the strategy of spreading investments across different assets or asset classes to reduce risk and optimise returns.
27. (A) (iii) (i) (iv) (ii)
28. (A) (i) (iv) (ii) (iii)
29. (A) A capital intensive organisation requires higher investment in plant and machinery as it relies less on manual labour
30. (B) working capital

Assertion-Reason Questions

1. (A) Both Assertion (A) and Reason (R) are true and Reason (R) is the correct explanation of Assertion (A)
2. (C) Assertion (A) is true, but Reason (R) is false
3. (A) Both Assertion (A) and Reason (R) are true and Reason (R) is the correct explanation of Assertion (A)
4. (A) Both Assertion (A) and Reason (R) are true and Reason (R) is the correct explanation of Assertion (A)
5. (C) More debt can be used if debt can be raised at a lower rate.
6. (C) Such efficiencies may reduce the level of raw materials, finished goods and debtors resulting in lower requirement of working capital.
7. (A) Both Assertion (A) and Reason (R) are true and Reason (R) is the correct explanation of Assertion (A)
8. (A) Both Assertion (A) and Reason (R) are true and Reason (R) is the correct explanation of Assertion (A)

Correct/Incorrect Statements

1. (A) Shareholders' funds involve no commitment regarding the payment of returns or the repayment of capital.
2. (C) Both statements are correct
3. (D) Investment decisions involve determining where to allocate funds for acquiring assets or projects that will generate returns for the company.

   Financing decisions relates to how the quantum of funds required will be acquired.
4. (C) Both statements are correct
5. (B) Financial risk is the chance that a firm would fail to meet its payment obligations
6. (D) If tax on dividend is higher, it is better to pay less by way of dividends.

   A decrease in dividend may have a negative impact on the share prices in the stock market.
7. (A) Expansion of business, which is a result of capital budgeting decision, is likely to affect virtually all items in the profit and loss account of the business.
8. (A) A useful guideline in the capital structure planning is the debt equity ratio of other companies in the same industry.

Case Based Questions

1. (i) (A) Capital budgeting

   (ii) (C) investment decision

   (iii) (A) financing decision

   (iv) (B) The case mentions that the company can issue debentures at an estimated cost of 10%. Cost is a critical factor in financing decisions as it influences the overall cost of capital and affects the company's profitability and financial stability.
2. (i) (B) SAF needs to arrange working capital for the new business to facilitate its day-to-day operations. Working capital management involves short-term investment decisions related to managing current assets and liabilities to ensure smooth operations.

   (ii) (B) Availability of raw materials

   (iii) (A) In a low competition environment, firms typically face less pressure to maintain high levels of stock to meet urgent orders from customers.

   Therefore, they can operate with a lower level of stock without risking stockouts or losing market share to competitors.

   (iv) (B) Current assets

Subjective Questions

1. Dropshipping business service typically requires lower amount of working capital as an order fulfillment method that does not require a business to keep products in stock.

   Instead, the store sells the product and passes on the sales order to a third party supplier, who then ships the order to the customer.
2. (i) Financial planning

   (ii) Financial planning helps in smooth functioning of the organisation in following manner

   (a) **Helps in Forecasting** It provides or detailed plan of action and helps the firm to face the future and helps in smooth running of the business. eg. A growth of 35% in sales is expected but it may happen that growth rate turns out to be 15% or 20%.

   So in these three situations many expenses will be different. So management should prepare a blueprint of financial plans for these.

(b) **Helps in avoiding Business Shocks and Enterprises** Financial planning reduces uncertainty (shocks and surprises) and helps a company in preparing for the future as best as preparing for the future as best as possible.

(c) **Helps in Coordination** It helps in achieving coordination between various functions. e.g. Sales and production functions, can be coordinate by providing clear policies and procedures.

(d) **Helps to Allocate Funds where they can be Best Applied Eliminate Wasteful Activities** It provides a detailed plan of action so there is no duplication of efforts and reduces wasteful activities (wastage of resources such as time, goodwill and other financial resources) and gaps in planning (funds are made available only for resources which are actually required for business activities).

3. To determine which company is using trading on equity more effectively, compare their Return on Equity (RoE) ratios. RoE is a key financial ratio that measures how efficiently a company is using its shareholders' equity to generate profits. RoE is calculated as follows

$$\text{RoE} = \frac{\text{Net Income}}{\text{Average Shareholders' Equity}} \times 100$$

Calculate the RoE for both companies

For Alfa Ltd.

RoE = (50,000/(3,00,000 + 0)/2) × 100

RoE = 50,000/3,00,000 × 100

RoE = 0.1667 × 100

RoE = 16.67%

For Beltex Ltd

RoE = (60,000/(4,00,000) + 0 /2) × 100

RoE = 60,000 / 400,000 × 100

RoE = 0.15 × 100

RoE = 15.00%

Based on the calculated financial data above, Alfa is using trading on equity more effectively than Beltex. Alfa's higher RoE of 16.67% indicates that it is generating a better return on its shareholders' equity compared to Beltex, which has an RoE of 15.00%.

This suggests that Alfa is utilising its equity more efficiently to generate profits, making its trading on equity strategy more effective.

4. The factors identified in the above lines are given below

(i) The line 'It has been consistently earning goods profits for many years' indicated 'Stability of earnings'.

Stability of earnings of a business unit also affects the dividend decision. A company having stable earnings can declare higher dividend whereas a company having unstable earnings is likely to pay smaller dividend.

(ii) The line 'This year too, it has been able to generate enough profits' indicates 'Earnings' as a factor affecting dividend decision.

Companies generally have a policy of stabilising dividends, i.e. increase in dividend is only done when the earning potential of the company has gone up and not just the current year's earnings. Thus, dividend per share is not altered when the change is small or temporary in nature.

(iii) The line 'There is availability of enough cash in the company and good prospects for growth in future' indicates 'Growth opportunities'.

Companies which are intended to grow, generally pay less dividend and retain more money out of profits to invest in profitable projects. On the contrary, companies which are not intended to grow and have enough earnings and cash, can pay higher dividends.

(iv) The line 'It has many shareholders who prefer to receive a regular income from their, investments' indicates 'Shareholders' Preference'.

While declaring dividends, management must keep in mind the preferences of the shareholders in this regard. If the shareholders in general desire that at least a certain amount is paid as dividend, the companies are likely to declare the same. There are always some shareholders who depend upon a regular income from their investments.

5. The factors affecting the fixed capital requirements discussed is the case are

(i) **Technology Upgradation** Industries in which assets becomes obsolete sooner due to technology upgradation, need higher investment in fixed assets to replace older assets.

While companies whose assets are not or least affected by technology upgradation, needs lesser investment.

(ii) **Growth Prospects** Higher growth of an organisation requires higher investment in fixed assets.

A company expecting such growth may expand its production capacity in order to meet the anticipated higher demand quickly.

This entails larger investment in fixed assets and consequently, larger fixed capital.

6. The factors affecting choice of capital structure being discussed are

(i) **Stock Market Condition** If the stock market is rising, i.e. bullish period, then it is easy to raise funds through issue of shares as more people invest in equity.

However, depressed capital market, i.e. bearish period, may make issue of equity shares difficult for any company and the company has to opt for debt financing.

(ii) **Control** Issue of more equity leads to dilution of shareholders' control over the business. Debt financing has no such implication.

Thus, if existing shareholders do not want to lose control, then they can prefer more of debt in capital structure and *vice-versa*.

(iii) **Floatation Cost** It is the cost involved in issue of securities such as underwriting fees, stamp duty, brokerage, etc. If the floatation cost is higher, the source of finance becomes less attractive and *vice-versa*.

e.g. Issue of shares, debentures requires more floatation cost, whereas getting a loan from financial institutions involve less cost.

(iv) **Regulatory Framework** The Companies Act and SEBI guidelines must be observed while raising funds from the public.

e.g. Public issue of shares and debentures have to be made as per the SEBI guidelines.

Borrowings from banks and other financial institutions require fulfilment of certain norms, which has an impact on the choice of the source of finance. The company prefers that source of finance which have less and flexible legal requirements.

CHAPTER - 10

Financial Markets

Types & Nos. of Questions

Multiple Choice Questions	-	26
Assertion-Reason Questions	-	8
Correct/Incorrect Statements	-	9
Case Based Question	-	1 Case, *with four Questions*
Subjective Questions	-	6

Trend Analysis

On the basis of analysis of last 2 years' papers, it is found that on an average 4 Multiple Choice Questions are asked from this chapter. No case based question is asked but may be asked in coming exams.

Focus Topics of the Chapter

- Money Market and Capital Market
- Stock Exchange
- Securities and Exchange Board of India (SEBI)

Multiple Choice Questions

No. of Questions : **26** Suggested Time : **40 Minutes**

Direction Each of the question given below is Multiple Choice Question (MCQ) i.e. there are Four Options/ Choices for answer, out of which ONLY ONE is correct. You have to select the correct option. A response box is given with each option, mark (✓) in the box of the correct option. For each correct answer you will get 1 mark, while there is no penalty for incorrect answer or missed out questions.

1. In the .... market, prices are determined and decided by the management of the company. *[CBSE 2024]*

(A) primary ☐
(B) secondary ☐
(C) money ☐
(D) stock ☐

2. It consists of a series of channels through which savings of the community are made available for industrial and commercial enterprises and for the public in general. Identify the market.

(A) Capital market ☐
(B) Money market ☐
(C) Primary market ☐
(D) Secondary market ☐

3. The essential function of this market is to facilitate the transfer of investible funds from savers to entrepreneurs seeking to establish new enterprises or to expand existing ones through the issue of securities for the first time. Identify the market.

(A) Capital market ☐
(B) Money market ☐
(C) Primary market ☐
(D) Secondary market ☐

4. Adapting to a change in consumer preference towards online shopping, 'Fast Service' started a grocery delivery app. It is a platform that ensures 10 minutes deliveries of groceries. Because of this service, 'Fast Service' earned huge profit within a year. It planned to expand its operations and decided to raise funds by directly issuing its securities to investors. The market through which 'Fast Service' has decided to raise funds for its expansion is *[CBSE 2023]*

(A) money market ☐
(B) primary market ☐
(C) secondary market ☐
(D) Both (B) and (C) ☐

5. It enables the raising of short-term funds for meeting the temporary shortages of cash and obligations and the temporary deployment of excess funds for earning returns. Identify the market.

(A) Capital market ☐
(B) Primary market ☐
(C) Money market ☐
(D) Secondary market ☐

6. The building in the image is associated with which type of market?

(A) Secondary market ☐
(B) Money market ☐
(C) Capital market ☐
(D) Primary market ☐

7. Identify the correct statement from the following.
   (A) Brokers act as a link between depositories and investors ☐
   (B) Physical certificates are converted into electronic form by demutualisation ☐
   (C) A depository participant interacts with the investors ☐
   (D) The first step of trading is to place an order ☐

8. Match the various terms of financial markets Column I with their respective statements in Column II

	Column I		Column II
A.	Financial market	(i)	It is also known as the stock market.
B.	Primary market	(ii)	It is a market for creation and exchange of financial assets.
C.	Secondary market	(iii)	It is also known as new issue market.

Codes

	A	B	C			A	B	C	
(A)	(ii)	(iii)	(i)	☐	(B)	(i)	(iii)	(ii)	☐
(C)	(iii)	(ii)	(i)	☐	(D)	(i)	(ii)	(iii)	☐

9. Rahul wants to buy shares of 'Rexter Ltd' which are being traded at the National Stock Exchange. He feels that the share prices will go up in the future. Which market should he approach for this purpose? *[CBSE 2023]*
   (A) Money market ☐
   (B) Primary market ☐
   (C) Secondary market ☐
   (D) Both (B) and (C) ☐

10. XYZ Corporation, a leading financial institution, urgently requires funds to meet its short-term financial obligations. With a focus on maintaining liquidity and managing cash flows efficiently, XYZ is considering accessing the financial market for financing.

    As a prominent player in the financial sector, XYZ aims to utilise various instruments available in the money market to secure the necessary funds for duration of up to one year.

    Which market should XYZ Corporation approach to meet its short-term financial obligations?
   (A) Stock market ☐
   (B) Primary market ☐
   (C) Money market ☐
   (D) Foreign exchange market ☐

11. ABC Ltd., a growing manufacturing company, plans to expand its production capacity by purchasing new machinery and building a larger facility. To fund this expansion, the company needs to raise a significant amount of medium to long-term capital.

    The finance team at ABC Ltd. is considering different options and decides to approach the capital market to raise the necessary funds. They aim to attract both individual and institutional investors by issuing a combination of equity shares and debentures.

    Which of the following features of the capital market is most relevant to ABC Ltd.'s decision to raise funds for their expansion?
   (A) Providing short-term funds to manage cash flows ☐
   (B) Acting as a link between savers and investment opportunities ☐
   (C) Involving instruments such as treasury bills and commercial paper ☐
   (D) Limiting participation to individual investors only ☐

12. Choose the incorrect statement from the following about functions of a stock exchange. *[CBSE 2024]*
   (A) Provides liquidity and marketability to new securities ☐

(B) Ensures safety of transactions ☐

(C) Contributes to economic growth ☐

(D) Provides scope for speculation ☐

13. Which of the following statement is incorrect?

(A) Capital market securities are considered less liquid investments ☐

(B) Money market instruments enjoy a higher degree of liquidity than capital market securities ☐

(C) Financial transactions are in the form of creation of financial assets only ☐

(D) Banks and financial markets are competing intermediaries in the financial system ☐

14. Sound of Music, an electronics store specialising in high fidelity stereos, was founded in 1966, pulling in $1 million in revenue and about $ 58,000 in profits in its first year. In annual general meeting, it decided to declare bonus issue of equity shares to its shareholders.

Rocky one of the directors took the advantage of this secret internal information and purchased 20,000 shares from market at ₹ 40 per share and sold them at ₹ 100 per share as bonus issue was declared and made capital gain of ₹ 10,00,000.

Identify the function of SEBI which prohibits the insiders in doing so.

(A) Protective function ☐

(B) Regulatory function ☐

(C) Development function ☐

(D) All of the above ☐

15. SEBI received a Financial Reporting Quality Review Report (FRQRR) from National Financial Reporting Authority in the matter of PSIL on 14th February, 2022, wherein it noted serious lapses with respect to accounting and auditing standards of the company.

SEBI has slapped penalties totalling ₹ 12 lakh on Prabhu Steel Industries Ltd (PSIL), its promoters including Harish Gangaram Aggarwal, Dinesh Gangaram Aggarwal and Akshita Harish Aggarwal for flouting regulatory norms.

The regulator has imposed a fine of ₹ 3 lakh each on these entities. They have to pay the penalty within 45 days, SEBI said in its order on Wednesday.

Identify the function of SEBI which prohibits the insiders in doing so?

(A) Prohibition of fraudulent and unfair trade practices like making misleading statements, manipulations, price rigging, etc–Protective function ☐

(B) Calling for information by undertaking inspection, conducting enquiries and audits of stock exchanges and intermediaries–Regulatory function ☐

(C) Controlling insider trading and imposing penalties for such practices–Protective function ☐

(D) Conducting research and publishing information useful to all market participants–Development function ☐

16. Raghav's friend Raman works as a Chartered Accountant in Solutions Ltd. Raman in a meeting with the Board of Directors of the Company came to know that the firm would soon be declaring a bonus issue which would result in increase in the price of shares.

Considering this, Raman advised Raghav to purchase the shares of Solutions Ltd., who acted on his advice and bought the shares before time.

Which function of SEBI can control such malpractices?

(A) Protective function ☐

(B) Regulatory function ☐

(C) Development function ☐

(D) All of the above ☐

17. MFC, operates in the information technology sector. The company provides various IT services, consulting and business solutions, which has helped it become the second largest Indian company in market capitalisation.

Some of the rectors have associated themselves with some bulls and bears and pass on company's vital information to sensitise the prices of the shares of their company to make personal gains.
It has come to the notice of the SEBI. Action has been initiated against the errant board of directors.

Name the term used for trading malpractice done by the rectors.

(A) Insider trading ☐

(B) Manipulations ☐

(C) Misleading statement ☐

(D) Price rigging ☐

18. Zenith Securities is a well-established stock exchange recognised under the Securities Contracts (Regulation) Act, 1956. It plays a crucial role in the financial market by assisting, regulating and controlling the business of buying and selling securities.

Zenith Securities provides various benefits to investors and the economy, including offering liquidity and marketability of existing securities, aiding in the pricing of securities, contributing to economic growth, spreading equity culture, providing a platform for speculation and ensuring the safety of transactions.

Which of the following is not a function of Zenith Securities as described in the case?

(A) Providing liquidity and marketability of existing securities ☐

(B) Pricing of securities ☐

(C) Limiting speculation to ensure stability ☐

(D) Contributing to economic growth ☐

19. Which of the following statements accurately represents one of the protective functions of SEBI in real life scenarios?

(A) It is responsible for managing government budgets and allocating funds for various developmental projects ☐

(B) It ensures the safety and security of data transmitted during online trading transactions ☐

(C) It promotes and regulates the insurance industry to safeguard policyholders' interests ☐

(D) It monitors and regulates the securities market to protect investors and maintain market integrity ☐

20. SEBI called for information and issued a show cause notice to NSE and its 14 officials seeking explanation on the preferential access allegations at the exchange's colocation facility.

State the related function of SEBI in the given case.

(A) Protective function ☐

(B) Regulatory function ☐

(C) Development function ☐

(D) All of the above ☐

21. "To promote orderly and healthy growth of securities market and protection of investors, SEBI was set up." Identify the objective of SEBI in the given statement.

(A) Fair and proper functioning ☐

(B) Prevention of malpractices ☐

(C) Protection to the investors ☐

(D) All of the above ☐

22. Which step of the trading process is highlighted in the below image?

(A) Opening demat account ☐

(B) Selecting a broker ☐

(C) Settlement ☐

(D) Placing the order ☐

23. Identify the correct statement from the following

(A) SEBI was established by Indian government in 1968. ☐

(B) SEBI was established under the administrative control of the defense ministry. ☐

(C) One of the reasons for setting up SEBI was the delay in delivery of shares. ☐

(D) SEBI is not functioned to develop a code of conduct for the stock exchanges. ☐

24. Match the Column I with Column II in the following information *[CBSE 2024]*

	Column I		Column II
A.	Training of intermediaries of securities markets	(i)	Regulatory function
B.	Regulation of takeover bids by companies	(ii)	Protective function
C.	Controlling insider training and imposing penalties for such practices	(iii)	Development function

Codes

	A	B	C			A	B	C	
(A)	(ii)	(iii)	(i)	☐	(B)	(i)	(ii)	(iii)	☐
(C)	(iii)	(i)	(ii)	☐	(D)	(iii)	(ii)	(i)	☐

25. Match the Column I with Column II in the following information

	Column I		Column II
A.	It helps to save time, effort and money that both buyers and sellers of a financial asset would have to otherwise spend to try and find each other.	(i)	Allocative function
B.	It is a process by which allocation of funds is done.	(ii)	Financial market
C.	It allocates or directs funds available for investment into their most productive investment opportunity.	(iii)	Financial intermediation

Codes

	A	B	C	
(A)	(ii)	(i)	(iii)	☐
(B)	(i)	(iii)	(ii)	☐
(C)	(ii)	(iii)	(i)	☐
(D)	(iii)	(ii)	(i)	☐

26. Match the Column I with Column II in the following information

	Column I		Column II
A.	It is assigned to each transaction by the stock exchange and is printed on the contract note.	(i)	Depository
B.	It is a technology driven electronic storage system.	(ii)	Depository Participant (DP)
C.	It is either a bank, broker or financial services company, may be identified.	(iii)	Unique Order Code number

Codes

	A	B	C	
(A)	(ii)	(i)	(iii)	☐
(B)	(iii)	(i)	(ii)	☐
(C)	(ii)	(iii)	(i)	☐
(D)	(iii)	(ii)	(i)	☐

Assertion-Reason Questions

No. of Questions : **8** Suggested Time : **12 Minutes**

Direction Each of the question given below consist of the two statements; one labelled as **Assertion** (A) and other as **Reason** (R). List of common options applicable for each question is given below

(A) Both Assertion (A) and Reason (R) are true and Reason (R) is the correct explanation of Assertion (A)

(B) Both Assertion (A) and Reason (R) are true and Reason (R) is not the correct explanation of (A) Assertion

(C) Assertion (A) is true, but Reason (R) is false

(D) Assertion (A) is false, but Reason (R) is true

You have to select the codes as *a, b, c* or *d* as your answer to the question by marking (✓) in the response box given against each option.

1. **Assertion** (A) Scarce resources are allocated to those firms which have the highest productivity for the economy.

   Reason (R) By mobilising of savings into investments, the financial markets perform allocative function.

   (A) ☐ (B) ☐ (C) ☐ (D) ☐

2. **Assertion** (A) Only the buying of securities by general public (investors) can take place in a primary market.

   Reason (R) Both buying and selling of securities takes place in secondary market.

   (A) ☐ (B) ☐ (C) ☐ (D) ☐

3. **Assertion** (A) There is very low degree of liquidity in the money market.

   Reason (R) The investment required in money market is huge as the instruments are quite expensive.

   (A) ☐ (B) ☐ (C) ☐ (D) ☐

4. **Assertion** (A) A stock exchange is a mechanism of constant valuation through which the prices of securities are determined.

   Reason (R) It is a truth that speculations are illegal and there is no scope for it in the stock exchange.

   (A) ☐ (B) ☐ (C) ☐ (D) ☐

5. **Assertion** (A) The stock exchange spreads equity cult by regulating new issues and taking effective steps in educating the public about investments.

   Reason (R) The stock exchange was established by the government of India as an interim administrative body to promote orderly and healthy growth of securities.

   (A) ☐ (B) ☐ (C) ☐ (D) ☐

6. **Assertion** (A) Ownership of existing securities is exchanged between investors.

   Reason (R) Stock exchange offers liquidity in terms of investment.

   (A) ☐ (B) ☐ (C) ☐ (D) ☐

7. **Assertion** (A) Screen based trading ensures transparency as it allows participants to see the securities.

   Reason (R) Securities are bought and sold on the floor of stock exchange through shouting of prices under screen based trading.

   (A) ☐ (B) ☐ (C) ☐ (D) ☐

8. **Assertion** (A) SEBI meets the needs of issuers, investors and depositories.

   Reason (R) SEBI also aims to stimulate competition and encourage innovation.

   (A) ☐ (B) ☐ (C) ☐ (D) ☐

Correct/Incorrect Statements

No. of Questions : **9** Suggested Time : **15 Minutes**

Direction Each of the question given below consist of the two statements. List of common options applicable for each question is given below

(A) Statement I is correct and Statement II is incorrect
(B) Statement I is incorrect and Statement II is correct
(C) Both statements are correct
(D) Both statements are incorrect

You have to select the codes as *a, b, c* or *d* as your answer to the question by marking (✓) in the response box given against each option.

1. **Statement I** Financial market allocates or directs funds available for investment into their most productive investment opportunity.

   Statement II Banks and financial markets are competing intermediaries in the financial system.

   (A) ☐ (B) ☐ (C) ☐ (D) ☐

2. **Statement I** In the financial market, the business firms are suppliers of funds and households represent the demand.

   Statement II The interaction between them helps to establish a price for the financial asset which is being traded in that particular market.

   (A) ☐ (B) ☐ (C) ☐ (D) ☐

3. **Statement I** Capital market instruments are considered riskier both with respect to returns and principal repayment.

   Statement II Capital market investment generally yields a higher return for investors. *[CBSE 2023]*

   (A) ☐ (B) ☐ (C) ☐ (D) ☐

4. **Statement I** The process of economic development is facilitated by the existence of a well functioning capital market.

   Statement II It is essential that financial institutions are sufficiently developed and that market operations are free, fair, competitive and transparent.

   (A) ☐ (B) ☐ (C) ☐ (D) ☐

5. **Statement I** There is a direct relationship between call rates and other short-term money market instruments.

   Statement II New issue market channelises funds towards the most productive investments through the process in disinvestment and reinvestment.

   (A) ☐ (B) ☐ (C) ☐ (D) ☐

6. **Statement I** A financial market facilitates the transfer of savings from savers to investors.

   Statement II It gives savers the choice of different investments and helps to channelise surplus funds into the most prouductive use. *[CBSE 2024]*

   (A) ☐ (B) ☐ (C) ☐ (D) ☐

7. **Statement I** Dematerialisation enables shares to be transferred to some other account just like cash and ensures settlement of all trades through a single account in shares.

   Statement II These demat securities can even be pledged or hypothecated to get loans.

   (A) ☐ (B) ☐ (C) ☐ (D) ☐

8. **Statement I** Rematerialisation is a process where securities held by the investor in the physical form are cancelled and the investor is given an electronic entry or number so that she/he can hold it as an electronic balance in an account.

Statement II Dematerialisation is a process where physical shares can be converted into electronic form or electronic holdings can be reconverted into physical certificates.

(A) ☐ (B) ☐ (C) ☐ (D) ☐

9. **Statement I** Short-term funds raised by big corporate houses for seasonal and working capital is known as debt financing.

Statement II Trading in securities is done through brokers who are members of the Securities and Exchange Board of India.

(A) ☐ (B) ☐

(C) ☐ (D) ☐

Case Based Question

No. of Question : **1** Suggested Time : **5 Minutes**

Direction This section contains 1 case having 4 questions of 1 mark each. You have to write the answer of each question based on the context of the related case.

Case 1 One fine morning, Mayank woke with the beep sound of Whatsapp message in his mobile. Half woke up thinking it to be some urgent message from his boss, read the message 'Maharaja Holidays will declare a bonus today' from his one friend, Joseph who accidently sent the same to him instead of Sunaina.

Mayank is lawyer by profession and employed with a leading law firm handling the legal matters listed companies. Last year he was also handling a legal case of Maharaja Holidays.

Since Mayank has no interest in the Stock Market without understanding the message further forwarded the same to his friend Sarover (a jobber in stock market).

A few days later Mayank received a call from Sarover inviting him on a party bash at coming Saturday at one of the 5 Star Hotel of the city. To the utter surprise of Mayank, Sarover who never offered a cup of tea to anyone and always in debt is organising such a big party.

Mayank called back Sarover to know the exact reason of organising such party. Sarover expressed there is no special occasion, only few of his friends have been invited as a matter of change from daily life. On Saturday evening, Mayank reached the venue of party where other friend were already there.

On asking what is the reason for this party from all friends, Sarover told he made a huge profit from the stock market and after repaying his old debts now he is buying a small office of his own to work as sub-broker.

During the party after consuming a lot of alcohol, Sarover gone out of control and started shouting it is because Mayank who made him rich. Since earlier one or two occasions Sarover had gone out of control after consuming alcohol, no one paid heed to his loose talks.

Next morning as a daily routine, Mayank was enjoying reading a financial daily. One news catches his attention.

India significantly toughened insider trading rules in early 2015, expanding what constitutes 'unpublished price sensitive information' to include 'any information' that is not 'generally available' and that could have a market impact.

The law also expanded the scope of who constitutes an 'insider' to include 'anyone in possession of or having access to unpublished price sensitive information' regardless of how they came 'in possession of or had access to such information'.

Circulating 'unpublished price sensitive information' can result in penalties of up to 250 million rupees and a jail term of up to 10 years. 'The monetary amount can be higher if it can be proven that an individual traded on such information.'

Although Mayank had no interest in the stock market, but the amount of penalty was enough to further read the news.

Questions

(i) "India significantly toughened insider trading rules in early 2015, expanding what constitutes 'unpublished price sensitive information' to include 'any information' that is not 'generally available' and that could have a market impact."

Identify the function of SEBI to control such malpractices.

(A) Protective function ☐
(B) Regulatory function ☐
(C) Development function ☐
(D) All of the above ☐

(ii) "Circulating 'unpublished price sensitive information' can result in penalties of up to 250 million rupees and a jail term of up to 10 years.

The monetary amount can be higher if it can be proven that an individual traded on such information."

Identify the term used for trading malpractices done incidently by Mayank.

(A) Insider trading ☐
(B) Manipulations ☐
(C) Misleading statement ☐
(D) Price rigging ☐

(iii) The regulatory body which has been established in India to regulate stock exchanges and to protect the interest of investors is

(A) the Reserve Bank of India (RBI) ☐
(B) the Securities and Exchange Board of India (SEBI) ☐
(C) National Stock Exchange (NSE) ☐
(D) Bombay Stck Exchange (BSE) ☐

(iv) According to the scenario described in the case, which term refers to information that, if circulated, can lead to severe penalties under India's insider trading rules?

(A) Restricted data ☐
(B) Insider information ☐
(C) Unpublished price sensitive information ☐
(D) Market confidentiality ☐

Subjective Questions

Free Response Questions, Open-ended Questions etc.

No. of Questions : **6** Suggested Time : **45 Minutes**

1. Neha, a finance manager at a Multinational Corporation, is tasked with optimising the company's short-term investment strategy. With surplus funds available, Neha seeks to explore the features of the money market to ensure efficient allocation of resources.

   She begins her research by delving into the nature of the money market, which deals with short-term funds with maturities of up to one year. Neha identifies various instruments available in the money market, including call money, treasury bills, trade bills, commercial paper and certificates of deposit.

   Additionally, she examines the duration of money market instruments, noting their suitability for meeting short-term financial needs.

   Furthermore, Neha investigates the participants in the money market, recognising the prominent role played by institutional investors such as commercial banks, financial institutions, non-banking finance companies and the Reserve Bank of India.

   Based on the provided content, what are the features of the money market?

2. Rahul, a young investor, is eager to understand the nuances of financial markets to make informed investment decisions. He embarks on a journey to explore the differences between the money market and the capital market.

   In his research, Rahul discovers that the money market primarily deals with short-term funds, facilitating the borrowing and lending of funds for periods of up to one year. On the other hand, the capital market is a network where medium to long-term funds are raised and invested, typically involving periods beyond one year.

   Help Rahul in identifying more differences between money market and capital market.

3. Raghu works as a waiter in a five star hotel in Mumbai. While serving the customer, he overhears him at the table saying that he has made profits higher than expected by investing in the securities market.

   So, Raghu also decided to make a nominal investment from his savings in the stock market in pursuit of higher gains.

   In the context of the above case, as a financial consultant, appraise him of the steps involved in working of a demat account.

4. Stock exchange acts as a regulator of the securities market. It creates a continuous market where the securities are bought and sold. It gives investors the chance to disinvest and reinvest.

   Through this process of disinvestment and reinvestment, savings get channelised into their most productive investment avenues. To ensure that the investing public gets a safe and fair deal in the market, the membership of the stock exchange is well regulated and its dealings are well defined according to the existing legal framework.

   It also ensures wider share of ownership by regulating new issues, better trading practices and taking effective steps in educating the public about investments. Various functions performed by the Stock Exchange are discussed in the above para. By quoting lines from the above para, state any four functions of stock exchange.

5. Demonstrate your understanding of SEBI's regulatory functions by designing the steps SEBI should take to investigate and resolve a suspected case of fraudulent activities by a listed company.

6. Mr Sanjay Nehra was the Chairman of 'Taran Bank'. The bank was earning good profits. Shareholders were happy as the bank was paying regular dividends. The market price of their shares was also steadily rising. The bank was about to announce taking over of 'Vena Bank'.
Mr Sanjay Nehra knew that the share price of 'Taran Bank' would rise on this announcement. Being a part of the bank, he was not allowed to buy shares of the bank. He called one of his rich friends Sudhir and asked him to invest ₹ 5 crore in shares of his bank promising him the capital gains.
As expected the share prices went up by 40% and the market price of Sudhir's shares was now ₹ 7 crore. He earned a profit of ₹ 2 crore.
He gave ₹ 1 crore to Mr Sanjay Nehra and kept ₹ 1 crore with himself. On regular inspection and by conducting enquiries of the brokers involved, Securities and Exchange Board of India (SEBI) was able to detect this irregularity. The SEBI imposed a heavy penalty on Mr Sanjay Nehra.
By quoting the lines from the above para identify and state any two functions that were performed by SEBI in the above case.

Answers

If your answer matches with the answer given here then put (✓) in the box otherwise put (✗). In case you did not attempt the question leave the box blank.

Multiple Choice Questions

1. A ☐
2. A ☐
3. C ☐
4. B ☐
5. C ☐
6. C ☐
7. C ☐
8. A ☐
9. C ☐
10. C ☐
11. B ☐
12. A ☐
13. C ☐
14. A ☐
15. C ☐
16. A ☐
17. A ☐
18. C ☐
19. D ☐
20. B ☐
21. C ☐
22. B ☐
23. C ☐
24. C ☐
25. C ☐
26. B ☐

Your Score__________ *(No. of Correct Answers)*

Assertion-Reason Questions

1. A ☐
2. B ☐
3. D ☐
4. C ☐
5. C ☐
6. B ☐
7. C ☐
8. D ☐

Your Score__________ *(No. of Correct Answers)*

Correct/Incorrect Statements

1. C ☐
2. C ☐
3. C ☐
4. C ☐
5. D ☐
6. C ☐
7. C ☐
8. D ☐
9. D ☐

Your Score__________ *(No. of Correct Answers)*

Case Based Question

1. (i) A ☐ (ii) D ☐
(iii) B ☐ (iv) C ☐

Your Score__________ *(No. of Correct Answers)*

Explanations

Multiple Choice Questions

1. (A) primary
2. (A) Capital market
3. (C) Primary market
4. (B) primary market
5. (C) Money market
6. (C) The National Stock Exchange (NSE) is a crucial component of the capital market in India, providing a regulated platform for trading a diverse array of financial instruments.
7. (C) A depository participant interacts with the investors
8. (A) (ii) (iii) (i)
9. (C) Rahul should approach the secondary market for buying shares of Rexter Ltd, as it is the market where already issued securities, like those of Rexter Ltd, are bought and sold among investors.
10. (C) The money market is specifically designed for short-term borrowing and lending, typically involving financial instruments with maturities of up to one year.
11. (B) The capital market is designed to facilitate the transfer of medium and long-term funds from savers to borrowers, making it a crucial link between saving and investment processes.
12. (A) Provides liquidity and marketability to new securities
13. (C) Financial transactions involve not only the creation but also the exchange and management of financial assets.
14. (A) The protective function of SEBI includes measures to prevent fraudulent and unfair trade practices, such as insider trading, to safeguard the interests of investors and maintain the integrity of the securities market.
15. (C) Controlling insider trading and imposing penalties for such practices–Protective function
16. (A) Protective function
17. (A) Insider trading involves the buying or selling of a security by someone who has access to material, non-public information about the security. In this case, the directors are using sensitive company information to make personal gains in the stock market, which constitutes insider trading.
18. (C) While Zenith Securities provides a platform for speculation, the function described as "limiting speculation to ensure stability" is not listed among the functions of a stock exchange. Instead, stock exchanges provide scope for speculation, which is a recognised function.
19. (D) It monitors and regulates the securities market to protect investors and maintain market integrity
20. (B) In this scenario, SEBI's actions pertain to its regulatory function. By calling for information and issuing a show cause notice, SEBI is exercising its authority to oversee and regulate the activities of stock exchanges and their officials.
21. (C) While SEBI's overall objectives include fair and proper functioning of the market, prevention of malpractices and protection to investors, the primary objective mentioned in the given statement is specifically the protection of investors.
22. (B) Selecting a broker
23. (C) One of the reasons for setting up SEBI was the delay in delivery of shares
24. (C) (iii) (i) (ii)
25. (C) (ii) (iii) (i)
26. (B) (iii) (i) (ii)

Assertion-Reason Questions

1. (A) Both Assertion (A) and Reason (R) are true and Reason (R) is the correct explanation of Assertion (A)
2. (B) In the primary market, new securities are issued and sold by the issuing company to investors.
3. (D) The money market is known for its high liquidity, not low liquidity. The money market instruments are often expensive, requiring substantial investment.
4. (C) A stock exchange indeed serves as a platform where the prices of securities are determined through continuous valuation based on supply and demand dynamics in the market.
5. (C) Assertion (A) is true, but Reason (R) is false

6. (B) Both Assertion (A) and Reason (R) are true, but Reason (R) is not the correct explanation of Assertion (A)
7. (C) Assertion (A) is true, but Reason (R) is false
8. (D) Assertion (A) is false, but Reason (R) is true

Correct/Incorrect Statements

1. (C) Both statements are correct
2. (C) Both statements are correct
3. (C) Both statements are correct
4. (C) Both statements are correct
5. (D) There is no direct relationship between call rates and other short-term money market instruments. The primary market is where new securities are issued and sold to investors for the first time.
6. (C) Both statements are correct
7. (C) Both statements are correct
8. (D) Dematerialisation is a process where securities held by the investor in the physical form are cancelled and the investor is given an electronic entry or number so that she/he can hold it as an electronic balance in an account.
   Rematerialisation is the process of converting electronic holdings into physical share certificates.
9. (D) Short-term funds raised by big corporate houses for seasonal and working capital is known as bridge financing.
   Trading in securities is done through brokers who are members of the stock exchange.

Case Based Question

1. (i) (A) SEBI's protective function involves safeguarding the interests of investors and ensuring fair and orderly conduct in the securities markets.
   (ii) (D) Price rigging involves artificially inflating or deflating the price of securities, often by spreading false or misleading information.
   (iii) (B) the Securities and Exchange Board of India (SEBI)
   (iv) (C) Unpublished price sensitive Information

Subjective Questions

1. Features of money market are as follows
   (i) **Instruments** Money market raises funds by wide variety of short-term securities such as call money, treasury bills, trade bills, commercial paper, certificate of deposit, etc.
   (ii) **Duration** Money market provides funds for a period of less than one year.
   (iii) **Participants** The participants in the money market are large institutional investors such as Reserve Bank of India (RBI), commercial banks, financial institutions, non-banking finance companies, State Government, large corporate houses, etc.
   (iv) **Investment Outlay** Investment in money market entails huge sums of money as the instruments are quite expensive.
   (v) **Liquidity** Money market instruments enjoy a high degree of liquidity as there is a formal arrangement for it.
   (vi) **Expected Return** The expected rate of return of the money market is generally low as money is invested for a short duration.
2. Differences between capital market and money market are

Basis	Capital Market	Money Market
Participants	Individual investors as well as institutional investors like financial institutions, banks, corporate houses and foreign investors participate in the capital market transactions.	The participants are RBI, commercial banks financial institutions, mutual funds and corporate houses. Individual investors do not participate in money market.
Instruments Traded	The instruments of capital market include equity shares, preference shares, bonds, debentures, etc.	Some of the main instruments used in money market are commercial paper, treasury bills, trade bills, certificate of deposit, etc.
Duration of Securities Traded	The capital market deals in medium and long-term securities which are for more than one year.	Money market deals in short-term securities having a maximum tenure of one year.
Expected Return	Higher returns on investment.	There is always a trade off between risk and return. Low risk involved leads to lesser returns.
Safety	Capital market is more risky.	The instruments of money markets are safe, less risky due to short duration and soundness of issuers.

3. As a financial consultant, here are the steps involved in the working of a demat account that Raghu should be aware of
   (i) **Opening an Account** Raghu needs to approach a Depository Participant (DP) or a stockbroker to open a demat account. He will be required to fill out an account opening form and provide necessary documents such as identity proof, address proof and PAN card.
   (ii) **Account Activation** Once the account opening form is submitted along with the required documents, the DP will verify the details and activate Raghu's demat account.
   (iii) **Linking with Bank Account** Raghu needs to link his demat account with his bank account to facilitate seamless transactions. This linkage allows for easy transfer of funds for buying and selling securities.
   (iv) **Securities Depository** After the demat account is activated, Raghu can start depositing his securities in electronic form into the demat account. These securities include stocks, bonds, mutual fund units and other financial instruments.
   (v) **Trading in Securities** With a functioning demat account, Raghu can now engage in buying and selling securities through the stock market. He can place buy or sell orders through his stockbroker and the transactions will be executed electronically.
   (vi) **Settlement of Transactions** Once Raghu executes a buy or sell order, the securities are debited from or credited to his demat account accordingly. Settlement of transactions occurs electronically, typically within two working days from the trade date.
   (vii) **Holding and Monitoring** Raghu can use his demat account to hold and monitor his securities portfolio. He can track the performance of his investments, view transaction history and receive electronic statements from the DP.
   (viii) **Security and Convenience** One of the key advantages of a demat account is its enhanced security and convenience. Raghu's securities are held in electronic form, reducing the risk of loss or theft associated with physical certificates.
   Additionally, demat account offers ease of access and flexibility in managing investments.

4. Functions of stock exchange discussed are
   (i) Provides liquidity and marketability to existing securities "It creates a continuous .... reinvest".
   (ii) Safety of transactions "To ensure that .... legal framework."
   (iii) Contributes to economic growth "Through this process .... investment avenues."
   (iv) Spreading equity cult "It also ensures .... about investments."

5. SEBI should take following steps to investigate and resolve a suspected case of fraudulent activities
   (i) **Preliminary Investigation** SEBI should initiate a preliminary investigation based on the information received about the suspected fraudulent activities by the listed company. This involves gathering initial evidence, identifying potential violations and assessing the gravity of the situation.
   (ii) **Formal Investigation** Upon finding substantial evidence during the preliminary investigation, SEBI should launch a formal investigation. This involves a deeper examination of the company's activities, including financial records, transactions and management practices. The investigation may involve summoning company officials, scrutinising books and seeking expert opinions.
   (iii) **Inspection of Books and Records** As part of its regulatory function, SEBI has the authority to inspect the books and records of listed companies to ensure compliance with securities laws. This step involves a detailed examination of the company's financial records and transactions.

6. The two functions performed by SEBI in the above case are as follows
   (i) **SEBI conducts inspections, enquiries and audit of stock exchanges.**
   It is one of the regulatory functions of SEBI. Lines from the above para which indicate that the above function was performed are
   "On regular inspection .... was able to detect this irregularity."
   (ii) **SEBI controls insider trading and imposes penalty for such practices.**
   It is one of the protective functions of SEBI. Lines from the above para which indicate that the above function was performed by SEBI are
   "SEBI imposed .... on Vikas Mehra."

CHAPTER - 11

Marketing

PRODUCT

PROMOTION

Types & Nos. of Questions

Multiple Choice Questions – 34
Assertion-Reason Questions – 9
Correct/Incorrect Statements – 10
Case Based Questions – 2 Cases, *each with four Questions*
Subjective Questions – 7

Trend Analysis

On the basis of analysis of last 2 years' papers, it is found that on an average 3 Multiple Choice Questions and 1 Long Answer Type Question are asked from this chapter.

Focus Topics of the Chapter

- Concept of Marketing
- Marketing Mix: Product, Pricing, Place/Physical Distribution and Promotion

Multiple Choice Questions

No. of Questions : **34** Suggested Time : **50 Minutes**

Direction Each of the question given below is Multiple Choice Question (MCQ) i.e. there are Four Options/Choices for answer, out of which ONLY ONE is correct. You have to select the correct option. A response box is given with each option, mark (✓) in the box of the correct option. For each correct answer you will get 1 mark, while there is no penalty for incorrect answer or missed out questions.

1. XYZ Ltd. is a leading e-commerce platform that connects buyers and sellers worldwide. It focused on proactive engagement, multichannel support and continuous improvement.

Identify the function of marketing reflected above.

(A) Market research and planning ☐
(B) Market planning ☐
(C) Customer support services ☐
(D) Gathering and analysing market information ☐

2. Singam Ltd. is a multinational corporation known for its innovative and high-quality products in the consumer electronics industry. With a diverse product portfolio spanning smartphones, tablets, laptops and home appliances, the company has established itself as a leader in the market.

Singam Ltd. develops a distinctive visual identity and focuses on enhancing customer loyalty and advocacy.

Identify the function of marketing reflected above.

(A) Branding ☐
(B) Market planning ☐
(C) Pricing ☐ (D) Promotion ☐

3. Company Zonova, a software-as-a-service (SaaS) provider operating in the financial technology sector, specialises in developing software solutions for financial institutions, including banks, credit unions and investment firms.

Company Zonova had a thorough understanding of customer needs, market trends and competitive landscape.

Identify the function of marketing reflected above.

(A) Market planning ☐
(B) Customer support services ☐
(C) Gathering and analysing market information ☐
(D) Product designing and development ☐

4. Benefit(s), a customer may seek to satisfy from the purchase of a product is/are

(A) functional benefits ☐
(B) psychological benefits ☐
(C) social benefits ☐
(D) All of the above ☐

5. 'Roma Ltd' identified the needs of the customers for the successful marketing of their products. This was important for making an analysis of the available opportunities, threats, weaknesses and strengths of the organisation and help in deciding what opportunities can best be pursued by it.

By doing so, which of the following functions of marketing is being performed by 'Roma Ltd' ? *[CBSE 2023]*

(A) Standardisation and grading ☐
(B) Product designing and development ☐
(C) Marketing planning ☐
(D) Gathering and analysing market information ☐

6. Ms. Arundhati, the CEO of Sunlife Ltd., is delivering a speech to a group of investors. She is emphasising the significance of the company's success and achievement, which relies on the support of customers, share-holders, suppliers, and intermediaries.

She also discusses how establishing a positive association with these parties contributes to enhancing the company's public image in the market. What is the primary goal of Ms. Arundhati's speech?

(A) To increase sales ☐
(B) To generate positive publicity ☐
(C) To improve the company's image ☐
(D) To build relationships with stakeholders ☐

7. ………… involves a variety of programme designed of promote or protect a company's image and its individual products in the eyes of the public. *[CBSE 2023]*

(A) Personal selling ☐
(B) Public relations ☐
(C) Sales promotion ☐
(D) Advertising ☐

8. The marketing strategy revolves around creating awareness and generating interest in the product through targeted advertising campaigns, influencer partnerships and social media promotions.

Emphasis is placed on highlighting the unique benefits and value proposition of the fitness tracker compared to competitors. Identify the marketing concept adopted above.

(A) Selling concept ☐
(B) Marketing concept ☐
(C) Product concept ☐
(D) Societal concept ☐

9. Ziavia Ltd. is a multinational corporation operating in the consumer goods industry, with a diverse product portfolio ranging from food and beverages to personal care products.

It initiaties to reduce carbon emissions, promoting ethical sourcing practices, supporting local communities and empowering employees through volunteering opportunities.

Identify the marketing concept adopted above.

(A) Selling concept ☐
(B) Marketing concept ☐
(C) Product concept ☐
(D) Societal concept ☐

10. Daniel and Andrew are two friends engaged in their respective businesses. Daniel concentrates on producing products that meet the needs of producers and sells whatever is produced by any means necessary.

Andrew believes in achieving the firm's goals through understanding the needs of consumers and delivering the right products to them and constantly monitoring competitors.

Which marketing management philosophies do Daniel and Andrew adhere to in their businesses?

(A) Product and selling ☐
(B) Selling and marketing ☐
(C) Marketing and product ☐
(D) Production and product ☐

11. State the incorrect statement.

(A) Marketing orientation implies that focus on satisfaction of customer's needs is the key to the success of any organisation in the market. ☐
(B) Marketing concept is based on development of products or services for satisfying needs of the target market. ☐
(C) Branding ensures that goods belong to a particular quality and helps in realising higher prices for high quality output. ☐
(D) A marketer has to take several crucial, decisions in respect of promotion of the products. ☐

12. One of the important decision areas under the marketing function of .... is managing inventory.
(A) branding ☐
(B) pricing ☐
(C) promotion ☐
(D) physical distribution ☐

13. Para Tech focused on differentiating the Smart Home Hub from competitors by emphasising its user-friendly interface, advanced features and compatibility with a wide range of smart devices.
Identify the element of marketing mix referred here.
(A) Product ☐ (B) Price ☐
(C) Place ☐ (D) Promotion ☐

14. State the incorrect statement.
(A) There is a need for storage of adequate stock of goods to protect against unavoidable delays in delivery or to meet out contingencies in the demand. ☐
(B) Price is the amount of money customers have to pay to obtain the product. ☐
(C) Brand name refers to the name of the whole class of the product. ☐
(D) The brand names should be sufficiently versatile to accommodate new products, which are added to the product line. ☐

15. Which technique of promotion is represented in the below image?

(A) Sales promotion ☐
(B) Public relations ☐
(C) Sample selling ☐
(D) Personal selling ☐

16. Pine Apple, a mobile manufacturing company, known for its design and innovation and how it sets its products apart through unique features and customer experience.
Identify the element of product mix referred above.
(A) Packaging ☐ (B) Branding ☐
(C) Labelling ☐ (D) None of these ☐

17. Zonia Energy Drink prioritised experiential marketing initiatives to provide consumers with first hand experiences of the product. Sampling events were organised at high-traffic locations such as gyms, fitness centers and sporting events, allowing consumers to taste the product and interact with brand ambassadors.
Identify the promotional technique that is used by the company.
(A) Public relations ☐
(B) Sales promotion ☐
(C) Advertising ☐
(D) Personal selling ☐

18.

The symbol which appears on all the 'Elegant' cars and which is not utterable is known as its *[CBSE 2023]*
(A) brand ☐ (B) brand name ☐
(C) brand mark ☐ (D) trademark ☐

19. Identify the correct statement.
(A) A good brand name should be complex and lengthy, so that it is difficult to be copied. ☐

(B) The brand mark is that part of brand which gives it a legal protection. ☐

(C) Brand name is the part of brand that is visible to the customers but not utterable. ☐

(D) A brand is a name, term, sign, symbol, design or some combination of them. ☐

20. Identify the function of packaging reflected below.

(A) Facilitating use of the product ☐

(B) Product promotion ☐

(C) Product identification ☐

(D) Product protection ☐

21. Marbury Biscuits' launched its new range of oat cookies in three varieties. They decided to distribute free samples of their biscuits in schools as a part of their promotional campaign. Identify the tool of promotion used by 'Marbury Biscuits'. *[CBSE 2024]*

(A) Advertising ☐

(B) Personal selling ☐

(C) Sales promotion ☐

(D) Public relations ☐

22. The picture given below is the package of a perfume bottle.

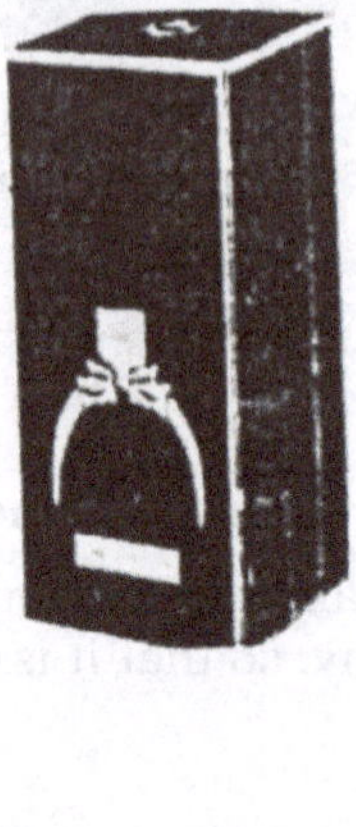

Identify the level of packaging of the box shown above.

(A) Primary package ☐

(B) Secondary packaging ☐

(C) Transportation packaging ☐

(D) Both (a) and (b) ☐

23. Sona Ltd. operates in the personal care sector. It collaborated with renowned design agencies to develop packaging concepts that resonate with their target demographic.

Emphasis was placed on sleek, modern designs that reflect the brand's ethos of sophistication and luxury.

Identify the importance of packaging reflected above.

(A) Product differentiation ☐

(B) Innovational opportunity ☐

(C) Rising standards of health and sanitation ☐

(D) Self service outlets ☐

24. Kumar Pharmaceuticals is a leading pharmaceutical company specialising in the development and manufacturing of innovative medications.

With a diverse product portfolio spanning various therapeutic areas, Kumar Pharmaceuticals operates in a highly competitive market.

The company explored new geographic markets and segments within the pharmaceutical industry, leveraging its expertise to diversify its revenue streams and capture untapped opportunities.

Identify the factor affecting price discussed in the above para.

(A) Utility and demand ☐

(B) Pricing objectives ☐

(C) Extent of competition in the market ☐

(D) Marketing method used ☐

25. Identify the correct statement.

(A) Pricing plays an important role in the marketing of products. ☐

(B) Product prices do not influence the profits of a firm. ☐

(C) The marketing methods used by a firm do not affect the price determination for its products. ☐

(D) Pricing does not help at the time of stiff competition. ☐

26. Munnar Electronics is a multinational electronics retailer known for its wide range of electronic products and excellent customer service.

With an extensive online presence and physical stores in major cities, Munnar Electronics receives thousands of orders daily from customers worldwide.

The company struggled to maintain accurate inventory levels across its multiple warehouses, leading to stockouts and overstock situations.

Which component of physical distribution should be adopted to rectify the situation?

(A) Order processing ☐

(B) Warehousing ☐

(C) Transportation ☐

(D) Inventory control ☐

27. Stereo Electronics sells its products by leveraging e-commerce platforms, digital marketing, customer support and logistics optimisation. The company successfully gained control over its distribution channel, enhanced profitability and improved customer engagement, positioning the company for sustained growth and success in a rapidly evolving market place.

Identify the channel of distribution adopted by Stereo Electronics.

(A) One level ☐ (B) Zero level ☐

(C) Two level ☐ (D) Three level ☐

28. Match the Column I with Column II in the following information

Column I	Column II
A. The main focus is on quantity of product	(i) Product concept
B. The main focus is on existing product	(ii) Production concept
C. The main focus is on quality, performance, features of product	(iii) Marketing concept
D. The main focus is on consumer needs	(iv) Selling concept

Codes

	A	B	C	D	
(A)	(ii)	(iv)	(i)	(iii)	☐
(B)	(iii)	(ii)	(i)	(iv)	☐
(C)	(iii)	(iv)	(i)	(ii)	☐
(D)	(i)	(iv)	(ii)	(iii)	☐

29. Promo Ltd. is a leading manufacturer of automotive components with operations in multiple countries. The company prides itself on its commitment to quality, innovation and customer satisfaction. Promo Ltd. faces a crisis when reports surface of a potential safety defect in one of its flagship products, a braking system used in passenger vehicles.

The defect has led to a series of accidents and injuries, prompting widespread concern among consumers, regulators and the media. This led to the decline in sales.

Identify the promotional technique which can help the company to come out of the crisis.

(A) Public relations ☐

(B) Sales promotion ☐

(C) Advertising ☐

(D) Personal selling ☐

30. Match the Column I with Column II in the following information

Column I		Column II
A. It includes decision related to the quality standards to be used for shape or design of the product and packing.	(i)	Gathering and analysing market information
B. It is a process of producing goods of predetermined standards so as to achieve the uniformity and consistency in products	(ii)	Marketing planning
C. It involves making plans for increasing production and sales, promotion of product, etc and also laying down a course of action for achieving these objectives.	(iii)	Product designing and development
D. This is essential to find out the needs of the customers and to take various decisions regarding successful marketing of products.	(iv)	Standardisation

Codes

	A	B	C	D
(A)	(iii)	(iv)	(ii)	(i)
(B)	(iv)	(ii)	(i)	(iii)
(C)	(iv)	(i)	(ii)	(iii)
(D)	(iii)	(i)	(ii)	(iv)

31. Beenu had a bookstore in Sabad called 'Book-mark'. For years, the bookstore was doing reasonably well but with the rise of digital books and online retailers, her sales had declined. Beenu's daughter, who had just completed her MBA with a specialisation in marketing decided to launch a marketing campaign to revive the bookstore.

The campaign's focus was on the joy of reading books in physical form, the joy of turning pages and the warm atmosphere of the bookstore. She organised story writing and other competitions every weekend. The information of these was given to the parents and children through television, radio, children's magazines, etc. Attractive prizes were offered to the winners.

This increased the footfall of the children and their parents and the bookstore soon became popular.

The tool of communication used by Beenu's daughter to revive the bookstore was *[CBSE 2024]*

(A) advertising ☐

(B) personal selling ☐

(C) sales promotion ☐

(D) public relations ☐

32. Match the Column I with Column II in the following information

Column I		Column II
A. That part of a brand which can be recognised but which is not utterable is called	(i)	Trademark
B. A brand or part of a brand that is given legal protection is called	(ii)	Brand name
C. That part of a brand, which can be spoken, is called	(iii)	Brand mark

Codes

	A	B	C
(A)	(iii)	(i)	(ii)
(B)	(ii)	(i)	(iii)
(C)	(ii)	(iii)	(i)
(D)	(iii)	(ii)	(i)

33. Match the Column I with Column II in the following information

Column I		Column II
A. It refers to the product's immediate container.	(i)	Secondary packaging
B. It refers to additional layers of protection that are kept till the product is ready for use.	(ii)	Transportation packaging
C. It refers to further packaging components necessary for storage, identification or transportation.	(iii)	Primary package

Codes

	A	B	C
(A)	(iii)	(i)	(ii)
(B)	(ii)	(i)	(iii)
(C)	(ii)	(iii)	(i)
(D)	(iii)	(ii)	(i)

34. Match following

Column I	Column II
A. Product	(i) Marketing activities used to communicate benefits of products offered.
B. Price	(ii) Process of transferring products from producer to consumers.
C. Promotion	(iii) Tangible goods offered to customers.
D. Distribution	(iv) Value of goods and services.

Codes

	A	B	C	D	
(A)	(ii)	(iv)	(i)	(iii)	☐
(B)	(iii)	(iv)	(i)	(ii)	☐
(C)	(ii)	(iii)	(iv)	(i)	☐
(D)	(iv)	(iii)	(ii)	(i)	☐

Assertion-Reason Questions

No. of Questions : **9** Suggested Time : **15 Minutes**

Direction Each of the question given below consist of the two statements; one labelled as **Assertion** (A) and other as **Reason** (R). List of common options applicable for each question is given below

(A) Both Assertion (A) and Reason (R) are true and Reason (R) is the correct explanation of Assertion (A)
(B) Both Assertion (A) and Reason (R) are true, but Reason (R) is not the correct explanation of Assertion (A)
(C) Assertion (A) is true, but Reason (R) is false
(D) Assertion (A) is false, but Reason (R) is true

You have to select the codes as *a, b, c* or *d* as your answer to the question by marking (✓) in the response box given against each option.

1. **Assertion** (A) Marketing is not merely a post-production activity.
 Reason (R) It includes many activities that are performed even before goods are actually produced and continue even after the goods have been sold.
 (A) ☐ (B) ☐ (C) ☐ (D) ☐

2. **Assertion** (A) The process of marketing helps individuals and groups in obtaining what they need and want.
 Reason (R) The primary reason or motivation for people to engage in the process of marketing is to satisfy some of their needs and wants.
 (A) ☐ (B) ☐ (C) ☐ (D) ☐

3. **Assertion** (A) Customer's satisfaction becomes the focal point of all decision-making in the organisation.
 Reason (R) The business orientation should not be short-sighted to serve only consumers' needs.
 (A) ☐ (B) ☐
 (C) ☐ (D) ☐

4. **Assertion** (A) The marketing concept, cannot be considered as adequate if we look at the challenges posed by social problems like environmental pollution, deforestation, shortage of resources, population explosion and inflation.

Reason (R) It is so because any activity which satisfies human needs but is detrimental to the interests of the society at large cannot be justified.

(A) ☐ (B) ☐ (C) ☐ (D) ☐

5. **Assertion (A)** The selling concept implies that products and services are bought not merely because of their quality, packing or brand name, but because they satisfy a specific need of a customer.

Reason (R) A pre-requisite for the success of any organisation, therefore, is to understand and respond to customer needs.

(A) ☐ (B) ☐ (C) ☐ (D) ☐

6. **Assertion (A)** Gathering and analysing market information is one of the important functions of a marketer.

Reason (R) This is necessary to identify the needs of the customers and take various decisions for the successful marketing of the products and services.

(A) ☐ (B) ☐
(C) ☐ (D) ☐

7. **Assertion (A)** The design of the product contributes to make the product attractive to the target customers.

Reason (R) Standardisation is particularly necessary for products which are not produced according to predetermined specifications.

(A) ☐ (B) ☐ (C) ☐ (D) ☐

8. **Assertion (A)** Pricing objectives influence the determination of product prices.

Reason (R) Pricing is primarily influenced by the utility and demand of a product.

(A) ☐ (B) ☐ (C) ☐ (D) ☐

9. **Assertion (A)** The intermediaries keep inventory of the firm's products, demonstrate them to potential buyers, negotiate price with buyers, close sales and also service the products after the sale.

Reason (R) The success of a market offer will depend on how well these ingredients are mixed to create superior value for the customers and simultaneously achieve their sale and profit objectives.

(A) ☐ (B) ☐ (C) ☐ (D) ☐

Correct/Incorrect Statements

No. of Questions : **10** Suggested Time : **15 Minutes**

Direction Each of the question given below consist of the two statements. List of common options applicable for each question is given below

(A) Statement I is correct and Statement II is incorrect
(B) Statement I is incorrect and Statement II is correct
(C) Both statements are correct
(D) Both statements are incorrect

You have to select the codes as *a, b, c* or *d* as your answer to the question by marking (✓) in the response box given against each option.

1. **Statement I** Wants are basic to human beings and do not pertain to a particular product.

Statement II Wants are culturally defined objects that are potential satisfiers of needs.

(A) ☐ (B) ☐ (C) ☐ (D) ☐

2. **Statement I** A marketer's job in an organisation is to identify needs of the target customers and develop products and services that satisfy such needs.

Statement II A product will be purchased only if it is perceived to be giving greatest benefit or value for the money.

(A) ☐ (B) ☐ (C) ☐ (D) ☐

3. **Statement I** The process of marketing involves exchange of products and services for money or something considered valuable by the people.

Statement II Market value is referred to as the essence of marketing.

(A) ☐ (B) ☐ (C) ☐ (D) ☐

4. **Statement I** For products requiring long-term storage like agricultural products, the warehouses are located near to the market.

Statement II Higher the level of inventory, higher will be the level of service to customers but the cost of carrying the inventory will also be high.

(A) ☐ (B) ☐ (C) ☐ (D) ☐

5. **Statement I** The marketing management is not only concerned with creating demand but with managing the demand effectively, as per the situation in the market.

Statement II The product quality and availability ensure the survival and growth of firms because of the large number of sellers selling quality products.

(A) ☐ (B) ☐ (C) ☐ (D) ☐

6. **Statement I** Selling is a part of marketing, limited to sale and purchase of goods and services.

Statement II Marketing is a broader concept, including various post sales activities as well.

(A) ☐ (B) ☐ (C) ☐ (D) ☐

7. **Statement I** Product mix concentrates on the important decision regarding the products to be sold.

Statement II A product package has no role in promoting the product.

(A) ☐ (B) ☐ (C) ☐ (D) ☐

8. **Statement I** The direct level of distribution involves producer, retailer and consumer.

Statement II One level channel includes producer and the consumer.

(A) ☐ (B) ☐ (C) ☐ (D) ☐

9. **Statement I** Channel of distribution is important as goods are produced at one place and customers are scattered all over in the nook and corner of the country, so the producer needs to distribute the goods through middlemen.

Statement II Physical movement of goods is transportation of goods from place of production to place of ultimate consumption.

(A) ☐ (B) ☐
(C) ☐ (D) ☐

10. **Statement I** Product publicity is done by organising events like seminars and exhibitions.

Statement II Press relations are arranged to provide true facts about products and companies.

(A) ☐ (B) ☐
(C) ☐ (D) ☐

Case Based Questions

No. of Questions : **2** Suggested Time : **10 Minutes**

Direction This section contains 2 cases each having 4 questions of 1 mark each. You have to write the answer of each question based on the context of the related case.

Case 1 Kalka Electronics, known for its innovative consumer electronics, operates in a competitive market. Kalka Electronics aims to effectively promote its products to target audiences, balancing traditional and digital marketing channels to maximise reach and impact. To maintain competitive prices and profitability, it implemented a comprehensive marketing mix strategy focusing on price, place and promotion.

Adopting a value-based pricing strategy, Kalka positioned its products as premium offerings with advanced features. Market research helped in setting prices, balancing affordability and perceived benefits. The company used a multi-channel distribution strategy, partnering with traditional retailers and e-commerce platforms, and established branded retail stores as well as authorised resellers to enhance the shopping experience.

Promotion tactics included traditional media (TV, print, billboards) and digital marketing (social media, influencer partnerships, email campaigns). Seasonal discounts were also used to boost demand. This approach positioned Kalka's products as premium in the market, increased their accessibility and achieved the company's business objectives.

Questions

(i) "Kalka Electronics aims to effectively promote its products to target audiences, balancing traditional and digital marketing channels to maximise reach and impact."

Which aspect of marketing strategy is emphasised in the statement?

(A) Pricing strategy ☐
(B) Distribution strategy ☐
(C) Promotional strategy ☐
(D) Product positioning ☐

(ii) "Kalka Electronics, known for its innovative consumer electronics, operates in a competitive market."

Identify the element of marketing mix referred here.

(A) Product ☐ (B) Price ☐
(C) Distribution ☐ (D) Promotion ☐

(iii) "The company used a multi-channel distribution strategy, partnering with traditional retailers and e-commerce platforms and established branded retail stores as well as authorised resellers to enhance the shopping experience."

Who are the participants in a multi-level distribution channel?

(A) Only traditional retailers ☐
(B) Only e-commerce platforms ☐
(C) Traditional retailers, e-commerce platforms, branded retail stores and authorised resellers ☐
(D) Branded retail stores and authorised resellers ☐

(iv) "Seasonal discounts were also used to boost demand. This approach positioned Kalka's products as premium in the market, increased their accessibility and achieved the company's business objectives." Which promotion strategy is highlighted in the above statement?

(A) Personal selling ☐
(B) Sales promotion ☐
(C) Public relations ☐
(D) None of the above ☐

Case 2 Sachin and Virag are two enterprising youth completed their MBA in Marketing. They have passed out from well-known, Prominent and Pioneer Institute of Management located in Western Maharashtra.

They thought instead of doing a job, they will launch fresh vegetables in Indian markets. Having learnt of the future conventional foods, they decided to venture into cultivation and marketing of mushrooms. Mushrooms are known to be the best alternative food for vegetarians.

For Sachin and Virag, fund raising was a serious handicap for mass production. However, the first trial batch of mushrooms, that they produced, was bought by three Star Hotel in Kolhapur. Further, the hotel placed orders for supply of 20 kgs every day. Now mushroom industry is run by small entrepreneurs, like Sachin and Virag.

Another big player in Market, M/s Pranava Mushrooms Ltd., equiped with cold storage facility was more interested in the export market. Sachin and Virag have set their sights high. They aim to market and brand mushrooms in a very big way all over India. Mushrooms have a great market potential and is a perishable food.

Questions

(i) "Having learnt of the future conventional foods, they decided to venture into cultivation and marketing of mushrooms."

Which concept of the marketing mix is highlighted in the above statement?

(A) Price ☐ (B) Product ☐

(C) Distribution ☐ (D) Promotion ☐

(ii) Which marketing strategy will be best to be adopted to increase sales?

(A) Samples can be distributed in big malls and variety stores ☐

(B) Hoardings ☐

(C) Banners ☐

(D) Insertions in newspapers ☐

(iii) "Mushrooms have a great market potential and is a perishable food."

For the product having being perishable

(A) company should go for faster and effective distribution network having cold storage facility ☐

(B) distribute through company delivery vans in local market ☐

(C) Both (A) and (B) ☐

(D) distribute through rail or road transport ☐

(iv) "They aim to market and brand mushrooms in a very big way all over India."

Which promotion tool will help to achieve the above target?

(A) Advertising ☐

(B) Sales promotion ☐

(C) Publicity ☐

(D) Public relation ☐

Subjective Questions

Free Response Questions, Open-ended Questions etc.

No. of Questions : 7 | Suggested Time : **55 Minutes**

1. IDEO and the H&M Group created new plastic-free packaging, rallying around a more sustainable packaging solution that's easily customisable. By applying a design led approach that went far beyond hiring a sustainability consultant, the H&M Group managed to reduce its use of plastic.
   (i) Identify the various types of thinking that guided IDEO and the H&M Group in the marketing efforts of their business.
   (ii) State one feature of the thinking identified in (i).

2. McCoy's, made in the United Kingdom by KP Snacks, is a brand of crinkle-cut potato chips. Every item bought is delivered with excess packaging and sometimes even non-biodegradable materials are used.

   Potato chips are packed in plastic bags in a nitrogen atmosphere to prevent from being rancid or oxidised and to protect the product from external factors like air, moisture and light, which could spoil the chips.

   In the context of above case
   (i) Name the other two levels of packaging that the marketers may be using besides the immediate package.
   (ii) Describe briefly any two points highlighting the functions of packaging.
   (iii) State any two factors that should be kept in mind by the marketers while designing the packaging of its products.

3. Drug price watchdog 'National Pharmaceutical Pricing Authority'(NPPA) has decided to cap the prices of the medicines, for which the prices rise by more than 20% in a year.

   This has been done in pursuance of the 'public interest' clause in the drugs law.
   (i) Identify the consideration that is being kept in mind by the NPPA while fixing the price of medicines.
   (ii) State any five other considerations affecting the fixation of price of the product, apart from the one identified above.

4. Coca-Cola has colossal brand recognition as it targets every customer in the market. Its perfect marketing segmentation is a major reason behind its success.

   They use celebrities in their advertisements to attract customers and arrange campaigns in universities, schools and colleges.

   It introduces packaging and sizes priced at various levels to increase affordability and target students, middle class and low income families and individuals.

   Coca-Cola sells its products globally and targets different cultures, customs and climates. The company targets different segments.

   Coca-cola has approximately 500 products. Its soft drinks are offered globally and its product strategy includes a marketing mix. Its beverages like Coca-Cola, Minute Maid, Diet Coke, Light, Coca-Cola Life, Coca-Cola Zero, Sprite Fanta and more are sold in various sizes and packaging. They contribute a significant share and generate enormous profits.

   The company had to make its pricing strategy flexible with the increased competition with competitors like Pepsico.

   The company's bottling partners manufacture, package and ship to the agents. The agents then transport the products by road to the stockist, then to distributors, to retailers and finally to the customer.

Coca-Cola also has an extensive reverse supply chain network to collect left over glass bottles for reuse. Thus, saving costs and resources.

(i) The given case describes the combination of variables used by Coca-Cola to prepare its market offering. By quoting the lines, identify the variables.

(ii) Identify the marketing management philosophy being followed by the Coca-Cola Company.

(iii) State any two market related factors that are likely to affect the decision of a marketer about the choice of channel of distribution.

5. Fast Runners has become one of the most recognised athletic brands in India. It deals in a wide variety of sportswear. However, of late it has been facing difficulty in keeping its inventory under control.

In 2022, the company adopted an inventory management software which helped it to predict items that could sell best and prepare the company to meet their demand.

This has helped the company in providing better customer satisfaction by making the goods physically available to them.

State the three activities Fast Runners should undertake other than the one discussed above, in order to ensure the availability of its products at the right place, at right time and in right quantity.

6. 'X Ltd' is engaged in the manufacturing of cars. The company surveyed the market and found that customers need a car which runs on eco-friendly fuel instead of petrol or diesel. Keeping the needs of customers as well as social, ethical and ecological aspects of marketing in mind, the company launched a new model of car that runs on bio-diesel. The launch event was covered by the top news channels and newspapers.

This was done to disseminate information about the car and build goodwill of the business, 'X Ltd'. understands that it is imperative to manage public opinion and company's relations with the public on a regular basis.

(i) Identify and explain the marketing philosophy involved in the above case.

(ii) Identify and explain the communication tool that was used by the company.

(iii) Explain any two other promotional tools that can be used by 'X Ltd', to achieve its objectives. *[CBSE 2023]*

7. Ayush and Rhea were passionate about sustainable agriculture and healthy living. They wanted to start a business selling organic produce. They had a small farm in a rural area where they began growing fresh organic produce and herbs.

In the beginning, they faced challenges in marketing their organic products. They realised that their high quality produce needed better presentation and a strong identity to stand out in a competitive market.

They named the business 'Earthy Store' which indicated the products' benefits and qualities and reflected the values of the business – sustainablility and health. They chose a 'logo' that incorporated elements of nature and used earthy colours to convey their organic commitment.

They designed and developed eco-friendly biodegradable bags and reusable containers to courier their products to the customers. They also added personal touch by including handwritten notes in each bag.

They also designed and developed product stickers with detailed information about organic certification, nutritional benefits, date of manufacture, date of expiry, etc. The stickers so developed were put on the bags and reusable containers for customers convenience.

'Earthy Store' created a user-friendly website and established strong media presence to inform potential customers about their products and persuading them to buy the same. Within a couple of months, they had built a loyal customer base which made them earn profits even in a competitive environment. In a year, they were able to secure contracts with local grocery stores and restaurants.

Quoting lines from the above paragraph, identify and explain the three functions of marketing discussed in the above case. *[CBSE 2024]*

Answers

If your answer matches with the answer given here then put (✓) in the box otherwise put (✗). In case you did not attempt the question leave the box blank.

Multiple Choice Questions

1. C ☐	2. A ☐
3. C ☐	4. D ☐
5. D ☐	6. D ☐
7. B ☐	8. A ☐
9. D ☐	10. A ☐
11. C ☐	12. D ☐
13. A ☐	14. C ☐
15. A ☐	16. B ☐
17. B ☐	18. C ☐
19. D ☐	20. A ☐
21. C ☐	22. B ☐
23. A ☐	24. B ☐
25. A ☐	26. D ☐
27. B ☐	28. A ☐
29. A ☐	30. A ☐
31. D ☐	32. A ☐
33. A ☐	34. B ☐

Your Score__________ *(No. of Correct Answers)*

Assertion-Reason Questions

1. A ☐	2. A ☐	3. B ☐
4. A ☐	5. A ☐	6. A ☐
7. C ☐	8. B ☐	9. A ☐

Your Score__________ *(No. of Correct Answers)*

Correct/Incorrect Statements

1. B ☐	2. C ☐
3. A ☐	4. B ☐
5. A ☐	6. C ☐
7. A ☐	8. D ☐
9. C ☐	10. C ☐

Your Score__________ *(No. of Correct Answers)*

Case Based Questions

1. (i) C ☐	(ii) A ☐
(iii) C ☐	(iv) B ☐
2. (i) B ☐	(ii) A ☐
(iii) C ☐	(iv) A ☐

Your Score__________ *(No. of Correct Answers)*

Explanations

Multiple Choice Questions

1. (C) Customer support services
2. (A) Branding
3. (C) Company Zonova demonstrates a thorough understanding of customer needs, market trends and the competitive landscape, indica- ting the function of gathering and analysing market information.
4. (D) All of the above
5. (D) Gathering and analysing market information
6. (D) To build relationships with stakeholders
7. (B) Public relations
8. (A) Creating awareness and generating interest through targeted advertising campaigns and promotions, aligns with the selling concept of aggressive sales and promotion efforts to sell products.
9. (D) Ziavia Ltd.'s commitment to ethical sourcing, community support and employee empowerment, reflects the societal marketing concept of fulfilling broader societal needs and responsibilities.
10. (A) Daniel focuses on producing products that meet the needs of producers and sells whatever is produced by any means necessary. This aligns with the production philosophy. Andrew believes in understanding the needs of consumers, delivering the right products to them and constantly monitoring competitors. This aligns with the selling philosophy.
11. (C) Grading ensures that goods belong to a particular quality and helps in realising higher prices for high quality output.
12. (D) Physical distribution
13. (A) The features and compatibility of the Smart Home Hub, falls under the product element of the marketing mix.
14. (C) Genric name refers to the name of the whole class of the product.
15. (A) Sales promotion
16. (B) Branding involves creating a unique identity and image for a product in the minds of consumers, which Pine Apple achieves through its design, innovation and customer experience, setting its products apart from competitors.
17. (B) Sales promotion
18. (C) brand mark
19. (D) A brand is a name, term, sign, symbol, design or some combination of them
20. (A) Packaging plays a crucial role in facilitating the use of products by ensuring their safety, convenience, information accessibility, identification and portion control.
21. (C) By distributing free samples of their new oat cookies in schools, they are engaging in a sales promotion strategy to encourage trial and potentially boost sales.
22. (B) Secondary packaging refers to the packaging materials that surround the primary packaging, providing an additional layer of protection and branding.
23. (A) Product differentiation
24. (B) Pricing objectives
25. (A) Pricing plays an important role in the marketing of products.
26. (D) The issue of inaccurate inventory levels across multiple warehouses suggests that adopting better inventory control methods is necessary to rectify the situation.
27. (B) Zero level
28. (A) (ii) (iv) (i) (iii)
29. (A) To come out of the crisis caused by safety defects, Promo Ltd. can utilise public relations to manage perceptions, rebuild trust and communicate corrective actions effectively to consumers, regulators and the media.
30. (A) (iii) (iv) (ii) (i)

31. (D) In this scenario, Beenu's daughter used public relations techniques by organising story writing and other competitions and then promoting these events through various channels like television, radio and children's magazines.

32. (A) (iii) (i) (ii)
33. (A) (iii) (i) (ii)

34. (B) (iii) (iv) (i) (ii)

Assertion-Reason Questions

1. (A) Both Assertion (A) and Reason (R) are true and Reason (R) is the correct explanation of Assertion (A)
2. (A) Both Assertion (A) and Reason (R) are true and Reason (R) is the correct explanation of Assertion (A)
3. (B) Both Assertion (A) and Reason (R) are true, but Reason (R) is not the correct explanation of Assertion (A)
4. (A) Both Assertion (A) and Reason (R) are true and Reason (R) is the correct explanation of Assertion (A)
5. (A) Both Assertion (A) and Reason (R) are true and Reason (R) is the correct explanation of Assertion (A)
6. (A) Both Assertion (A) and Reason (R) are true and Reason (A) is the correct explanation of Assertion (A)
7. (C) Product design plays a significant role in attracting target customers by enhancing aesthetics, functionality and perceived value.
8. (B) Pricing objectives, such as profit maximisation, sales growth, market share targets and survival, are essential factors that directly impact the determination of product prices.
9. (A) Both Assertion (A) and Reason (A) are true and Reason (A) is the correct explanation of Assertion (A)

Correct/Incorrect Statements

1. (B) Needs are basic to human beings and do not pertain to a particular product.
2. (C) Both statements are correct
3. (A) Exchange is referred to as the essence of marketing
4. (B) Typically, for products requiring long-term storage, such as agricultural products, warehouses are often located near the production areas rather than the market.
5. (A) While product quality and availability are important, they alone do not ensure the survival and growth of firms.
6. (C) Both statements are correct
7. (A) A product package plays a crucial role in promoting the product by attracting customers, providing essential information and enhancing the overall brand image.
8. (D) The direct level of distribution involves only the producer and the consumer, with no intermediaries.

   One level channel includes the producer and one intermediary (e.g., a retailer), who then sells to the consumer.
9. (C) Both statements are correct
10. (C) Both statements are correct

Case Based Questions

1. (i) (C) Promotional strategy

   (ii) (A) Product

   (iii) (C) Traditional retailers, e-commerce platforms, branded retail stores and authorised resellers

   (iv) (B) Sales promotion

2. (i) (B) Product

   (ii) (A) Distributing samples of mushrooms in big malls and variety stores would allow potential customers to taste and experience the product firsthand, increasing the likelihood of purchase.

   (iii) (C) Both (A) and (B)

   (iv) (A) Advertising would be the most suitable promotion tool to help Sachin and Virag achieve their goal of marketing and branding mushrooms extensively across India.

Subjective Questions

1. (i) IDEO and the H&M Group were guided by the product concept, which emphasises continuous product innovation and improvement to meet customer needs effectively.

   Additionally, they embraced the societal concept, which focuses on not only meeting customer needs but also considering broader societal welfare and environmental sustainability in their marketing efforts.

(ii) One feature of the product concept is its emphasis on delivering superior product quality and innovation to satisfy customer demands effectively.

In contrast, the societal concept emphasises the importance of considering how business activities impact society and the environment, leading to more sustainable and socially responsible marketing practices.

2. (i) Besides the immediate package, marketers may use secondary packaging and tertiary packaging to protect the product during storage, transportation and display.

Secondary packaging provides additional protection and branding opportunities, while tertiary packaging (such as corrugated boxes) is used for bulk handling and shipping.

(ii) The functions of packaging in the marketing of goods and services are

(a) **Product Identification** Packaging facilitates the identification of the product with the use of different colours like wrapper of Maggi noodles is red whereas Yippe noodles are sold in orange colour packaging. Also, the shape of different brands of cold drinks bottles is different.

(b) **Product Protection** One of the basic purposes of packaging is to safeguard the contents of a product from any kind of damage due to mishandling, adverse weather conditions, etc. during the activities related to physical distribution like storing, transportation, etc.

(iii) Two factors that should be kept in mind by the marketers while designing the packaging of its products are

(a) **Use of Biodegradable Packaging Material** Marketers should prioritise the use of biodegradable packaging materials to align with environmental sustainability goals. Biodegradable materials break down naturally over time, reducing the environmental impact of packaging waste.

(b) **Enhancement of Product Usability** Packaging design should focus on enhancing the usability and convenience of the product for consumers. This can include features such as easy-open seals, portion control mechanisms and ergonomic designs.

3. (i) The consideration being kept in mind by the NPPA while fixing the price of medicines is 'public interest', as mentioned in the clause of the drugs law.

(ii) Other considerations affecting the fixation of price of the product include

(a) **Cost of Production** Determining the expenses incurred in manufacturing the product.

(b) **Demand and Supply** Analysing the market demand and supply dynamics to set a competitive price.

(c) **Competition** Assessing the pricing strategies of competitors in the market.

(d) **Legal and Regulatory Requirements** Complying with government regulations and laws related to pricing.

(e) **Market Positioning** Setting the price to position the product appropriately in the market related to competitors.

4. (i) The variables of the marketing mix utilised by Coca-Cola Company are as follows

(a) **Product** Its soft drinks are offered globally and its product strategy includes a marketing mix. Its beverages like Coca-Cola, Minute Maid, Diet Coke, Light, Coca-Cola Life, Coca-Cola Zero, Sprite Fanta and more are sold in various sizes and packaging.

(b) **Price** The company had to make its pricing strategy flexible with the increased competition with competitors like Pepsico.

(c) **Place** The company's bottling partners manufacture, package and ship to the agents. The agents then transport the products by road to the stockist, then to distributors, to retailers and finally to the customer.

(d) **Promotion** They use celebrities in their advertisements to attract customers and arrange campaigns in universities, schools and colleges.

(ii) **Selling Concept** They use celebrities in their advertisements to attract customers and arrange campaigns in universities, schools and colleges.

(iii) The market related factors that are likely to affect the decision of a marketer about the choice of channel of distribution are

(a) **Size of Market** If the size of the target market is small, it is advisable that the marketer adopts methods of direct channels of distribution like online selling, mail order house, personal selling, etc. wherein there are no intermediaries between the manufacturer and the consumers.

However, if the marketer intends to target larger markets, he should adopt indirect channels of distribution (one level, two level or three level) by using intermediaries like wholesalers, retailers etc.

(b) **Geographical Concentration of Potential Buyers** If the potential buyers for the firm's product are geographically concentrated at a few specific places, it is advisable for the marketer to adopt direct channels of distribution. If the market for the product is widely scattered, indirect channels of distribution will be more effective.

5. To ensure the availability of its products at the right place, at the right time and in the right quantity, Fast Runners should undertake the following activities

(i) **Efficient Distribution Network** Fast Runners should establish an efficient distribution network that ensures timely delivery of products to various retail outlets and locations where their target customers are located.

This may involve partnering with reliable logistics companies or setting-up their own distribution centers strategically located to cover a wide geographic area efficiently.

(ii) **Demand Forecasting** Implementing robust demand forecasting techniques will enable Fast Runners to anticipate customer demand accurately.

By analysing historical sales data, market trends and other relevant factors, the company can predict future demand for its products. This information can then be used to optimise inventory levels and ensure that the right amount of stock is available at all times.

(iii) **Collaboration with Suppliers** Fast Runners should establish strong relationships with suppliers to ensure a steady and reliable supply of raw materials and finished products. Collaborating closely with suppliers can help the company negotiate favourable terms, minimise lead times and reduce the risk of stockouts.

Additionally, adopting practices such as Vendor-Managed Inventory (VMI) can further streamline the supply chain process and enhance inventory management capabilities.

6. (i) Promotion mix is the marketing philosophy involved in above case. It refers to informing the customers about the product and persuading them to purchase these products.

This job is done by the company through the medium of advertisement, personal selling, sales promotion and public relations. Decisions with regard to all these factors directly influence the sale of the product.

(ii) The communication tool used here is 'Advertising'. It is an impersonal form of communication, which is paid for by the marketers (sponsors) to promote some goods or services. Most common modes of advertising are newspaper, television and radio.

(iii) (a) **Pubic relations** The concept of public relations involves a variety of programmes to promote and protect a company's image or its products.

It is the sustained and planned effort to influence public opinion and to establish and maintain mutual understanding between an organisation and the public.

(b) **Personal selling** It refers to the oral presentation of message in the form of conversation with one or more prospective customers for the purpose of making sales.

Companies appoint sales persons to contact prospective buyers and create awareness about the product and develop product preferences with the aim of making sale.

7. By quoting the lines from the paragraph, the functions of marketing discussed here are as follows

(i) They realised that ……… competitive market.

Marketing Planning After market research, the marketer has to develop an appropriate marketing plan to achieve the marketing objective of the organisation.

e.g. A marketer of LED TV, having 15% of the country's current market share, aims to enhance his market share to 30% in the next two years.

So, he will have to develop a complete marketing plan which will cover various important aspects like plan for increasing the level of production, products promotion, etc and specify the action programmes to achieve these objectives.

(ii) They named ...... their organic commitment.

Branding It refers to the process of giving a name, sign, symbol or a combination of all to a product for creating its identification.

It helps to differentiate the product from other products available in the market. It also helps to build customer's loyalty and promoting its sales.

The important decision areas in respect of branding include deciding the brand strategy, i.e. whether each product will be given a separate brand name such as Kitkat,Milkybar, etc. or the same brand name will be extended to all products, like Whirlpool fridge, Whirlpool LED TV etc.

(iii) They designed .... customer convenience.

Packaging and Labelling Packaging refers to designing and developing the package for a product.

Package refers to the wrapper or container, which not only provides protection to the product, but also acts as a promotional tool for it.

Labelling refers to designing and developing the label to be put on the package. A label is a carrier of information. It may be a simple tag or a complex graphic providing details about the product.

In modern day marketing, packaging and labelling have become so important that these are considered as the pillars of marketing.

CHAPTER-12

Consumer Protection

Types & Nos. of Questions

Multiple Choice Questions - 25
Assertion-Reason Questions - 8
Correct/Incorrect Statements - 8
Case Based Questions - 2 Cases, *each with four Questions*
Subjective Questions - 7

Trend Analysis

On the basis of analysis of last 2 years' papers, it is found that on an average 2 Multiple Choice Questions and 2 Short Answer Type Questions are asked from this chapter.

Focus Topics of the Chapter

- Concept of Consumer Protection
- The Consumer Protection Act, 2019
- Consumer Rights and Responsibilites
- Redressal Agencies

Multiple Choice Questions

No. of Questions : **25** Suggested Time : **40 Minutes**

Direction Each of the question given below is Multiple Choice Question (MCQ) i.e. there are Four Options/Choices for answer, out of which ONLY ONE is correct. You have to select the correct option. A response box is given with each option, mark (✓) in the box of the correct option. For each correct answer you will get 1 mark, while there is no penalty for incorrect answer or missed out questions.

1. "Good and ethical practices encourage firms to realise that it is in their long-term interest to serve the customers in a rightful manner."
Which importance of consumer protection is highlighted from the above statement?
(A) Business associations ☐
(B) Consumer awareness ☐
(C) Self-regulation by business ☐
(D) Consumer organisations ☐

2. Identify the incorrect statement.
(A) Consumer protection has a moral justification for business ☐
(B) In addition to rights, a consumer also has some responsibilities ☐
(C) A legal heir or representative of a deceased customer cannot file a complaint in the appropriate consumer forum ☐
(D) The Consumer Protection Act provides for six consumer rights ☐

3. Identify the incorrect statement.
(A) Consumer includes any user of such goods or beneficiary of services if such use is made with the approval of the buyer ☐
(B) Any person who obtains goods or avails services for resale or commercial purpose is treated as a consumer ☐
(C) If the complaint alleges defect in goods which cannot be determined without proper analysis or test of goods, the commission obtains the sample of goods, seal it and refer to the appropriate authority for analysis ☐
(D) Every order of a district commission, the state commission or the national commission is deemed final if no appeal for such order is made by any of the parties involved in dispute ☐

4. It has a jurisdiction to entertain complaints where value of goods and services paid as consideration exceeds one crore but does not exceed ten crore rupees.
(A) District Commission ☐
(B) State Commission ☐
(C) National Commission ☐
(D) Supreme Court ☐

5. A humble tea vendor, Rajesh Sakre, had ₹ 20,000 in his State Bank of India account and had withdrawn ₹ 10,800. On his next visit to the ATM, however, he realised all his money was gone. When he asked the bank authorities, they blamed it on him.
Identify the right that Rajesh can exercise in the above case.
(A) Right to consumer education ☐
(B) Right to safety ☐
(C) Right to be heard ☐
(D) Right to seek redressal ☐

6. Aarushi purchased a pack of biscuits. When she opened it, she felt the biscuits were stale. She carefully read the label on the pack of biscuits which mentioned
"If you are not satisfied with the product quality, write to our Customer Care Cell at
Bell Foods Pvt. Ltd.
B/321, Jalandhar, Punjab."

The biscuit company has set up its own consumer service and grievance cell to promote and protect the following right

(A) Right to safety ☐
(B) Right to be heard ☐
(C) Right to be informed ☐
(D) Right to consumer education ☐

7. Which of the following is not the function of non-governmental organisations working for consumer protection?

(A) Educating the general public about consumer rights ☐
(B) Carrying out comparative testing of consumer products in accredited laboratories ☐
(C) Carrying out comparative analysis of prices of consumer goods ☐
(D) Providing legal assistance to consumers ☐

8. A case was filed by a consumer against a Body Care programme alleging that even after paying ₹ 10,500 and undergoing the treatment, she did not lose weight.

The District Forum in Bangalore had directed that the money be refunded to the consumer and also a compensation of ₹ 25,000 be paid.
Which right was exercised by the consumer?

(A) Right to be heard ☐
(B) Right to consumer education ☐
(C) Right to safety ☐
(D) Right to seek redressal ☐

9. RK Gupta advertised with impunity, his clinic and claimed that he was offering a sure cure for epilepsy.

In 2000, the Indian Medical Association declared him a quack after a committee had found that he was giving his patients toxic drugs in high doses. Yet, he continued to advertise.

Identify the right which was violated by RK Gupta.

(A) Right to safety ☐
(B) Right to consumer education ☐
(C) Right to choose ☐
(D) Right to seek redressal ☐

10. To protect people from being exploited or affected by misleading advertisements, consumer organisations and NGO's have conducted various training programmes , seminars and workshops.

They publish periodical to warn companies to forbid advertisements from exaggerating the features of a product or service in a manner that leads children to have unrealistic expectations of them, making claims of healthy nutritional benefits, which are not scientifically substained by a recognised organisation.

The consumer right promoted by consumer organisations and NGO is

(A) right to be informed ☐
(B) right to be assured ☐
(C) right to consumer education ☐
(D) right to safety ☐

11. Saurabh, an NGO worker, wants to raise awareness about the rights of consumers and safeguarding them against unfair practices, discrimination and exploitation. He wants to encourage consumers to educate them about their rights and take proactive measures to address grievances.

Identify the right discussed in the above para.

(A) Right to consumer education ☐
(B) Right to be informed ☐
(C) Right to be assured ☐
(D) Right to safety ☐

12. If the market has enough qualities and varieties of product at competitive prices, then buyer have an opportunity of wise selection.

Identify the consumer right highlighted in the above statement.

(A) Right to be assured

(B) Right to be informed

(C) Right to consumer education

(D) Right to safety

13. Lyka Ltd. launched its new range of herbal shampoos at the beginning of the year. As per legal framework, Lyka Ltd. provided the name and address of the manufacturer, the weight, manufacturing date, expiry date, maximum retail price, etc. on the package and label of the herbal shampoo. The consumer right highlighted above is *[CBSE 2024]*

(A) right to choose

(B) right to be informed

(C) right to consumer education

(D) right to safety

14. Which of the following rights of consumers is being fulfilled by the following image?

(A) Right to safety

(B) Right to be heard

(C) Right to seek redressal

(D) Right to consumer education

15. Which consumer right is being highlighted in the below image?

(A) Right to consumer education

(B) Right to be heard

(C) Right to healthy environment

(D) Right to be assured

16. Match the Column I with Column II in the following information

	Column I		Column II
A.	Protection against hazardous goods and services.	(i)	Right to be informed
B.	Setting-up of grievance cells for customer complaints.	(ii)	Right to seek redressal
C.	Proper labeling of products.	(iii)	Right to safety
D.	Customers can register complaints in appropriate forums.	(iv)	Right to be heard

Codes

	A	B	C	D
(A)	(ii)	(iv)	(i)	(iii)
(B)	(iii)	(iv)	(i)	(ii)
(C)	(ii)	(iii)	(iv)	(i)
(D)	(iv)	(iii)	(ii)	(i)

17. While Consumer Protection Act, 1986 is already on way to be amended suitably after earlier three amendments, consumers are also bound to take adequate care while dealing with online and digital purchases in order to safeguard their own interest.

While doing online shopping, one should use strong passwords, take complete information about the e-portal, find out about the e-merchant's privacy policy, keep personal information private, shop only with known e-merchants and review monthly bank and credit card details.

Thus, a high level of consumer awareness and protection in every strata of the society is required so that consumers both at individual or collective level are empowered to exercise their rights and responsibilities consciously.

Identify the responsibility of the consumer reflected in the above lines.

(A) Assert yourself that you get a fair deal ☐

(B) Form consumer societies which would play an active part in educating consumers and safeguarding their interests ☐

(C) Learn about the risks associated with products and services, follow manufacturer's instructions and use the products safely ☐

(D) Be aware about various goods and services available in the market so that an intelligent and wise choice can be made ☐

18. Which consumer responsibility is being fulfilled in the following image?

(A) Read labels carefully ☐

(B) Assert to get a fair deal ☐

(C) Be honest ☐

(D) File complaints in appropriate forums ☐

19. Sarthi purchased five liters of mustard oil from a nearby shop. After using it, she had a doubt that it was adulterated. She sent it for a laboratory test which confirmed her doubt.

She filed a complaint in court and proved her point. What relief will be available to Sarthi?

(A) Refund of the amount paid by her ☐

(B) Stop adulterated products trade practice ☐

(C) Pay an amount to recover the loss caused ☐

(D) All of the above ☐

20. Dipika Pallikal, a squash champion and Arjuna awardee, found herself in an awkward situation when she used her Axis Bank debit card at a hotel in Rotterdam, Netherlands, but the transaction failed. Despite having sufficient funds in her account, the transaction of ₹ 1 lakh could not be completed. As a result, she faced loss of reputation and humiliation. The bank claimed that the incident was due to *'Force Majeure'* (an act of God or something beyond their control).

Where she can file a complaint under Consumer Protection Act?

(A) District Commission ☐

(B) State Commission ☐

(C) National Commission ☐

(D) Supreme Court ☐

21. Sarita bought a flat from Sugan Developers for ₹ 5 crore and was shocked to discover that the quality of construction was bad, roof leaked during the rainy season and plaster was coming off at various places.

Which consumer forum should she approach for redressal of her grievance? *[CBSE 2023]*

(A) District Commission ☐

(B) State Commission ☐

(C) National Commission ☐

(D) Supreme Court ☐

22. Which of the following does not comes under unfair contract?

(A) Requiring manifestly excessive security deposits to be given by a consumer for the performance of contractual obligations ☐

(B) Refusing to accept early repayment of debts on payment of applicable penalty ☐

(C) File a complaint in an appropriate consumer forum in case of a shortcoming in the quality of goods purchased or services availed ☐

(D) Entitling a party to the contract to terminate such contract unilaterally, without reasonable cause ☐

23. Match the Column I with Column II in the following information

Column I	Column II
A. Consumers	(i) Institutions to address grievances.
B. Sellers	(ii) Safeguarding rights of consumers.
C. Consumer protection	(iii) Buying for reselling.
D. Redressal agencies	(iv) Buying for personal use.

Codes

	A	B	C	D
(A)	(ii)	(iv)	(i)	(iii)
(B)	(iii)	(iv)	(i)	(ii)
(C)	(ii)	(iii)	(iv)	(i)
(D)	(iv)	(iii)	(ii)	(i)

24. Payal was working in a multinational company. Her father gifted her a smartphone worth ₹ 40,500 on her birthday. The mobile phone was purchased by her father from his friend's shop.

After few months, the mobile phone started creating problems. Payal tried to contact the manufacturer many times but he did not respond.

Ultimately, Payal decided to file a complaint against the manufacturer.

The appropriate grievance redressal machinery where Payal can file a complaint is *[CBSE 2024]*

(A) District Forum/Commission
(B) State Commission
(C) National Commission
(D) Supreme Court

25. Match the Column I with Column II in the following information

Column I	Column II
A. National Commission	(i) They hear cases involving disputes valued up to one crore rupees.
B. State Commission	(ii) It hears cases involving disputes valued over ten crore rupees.
C. District Commission	(iii) Hear cases involving disputes valued between one crore and ten crore rupees.

Codes

	A	B	C
(A)	(ii)	(iii)	(i)
(B)	(iii)	(ii)	(i)
(C)	(ii)	(i)	(iii)
(D)	(i)	(iii)	(ii)

Assertion-Reason Questions

No. of Questions : **8** Suggested Time : **12 Minutes**

Direction Each of the question given below consist of the two statements; one labelled as **Assertion** (A) and other as **Reason** (R). List of common options applicable for each question is given below

(A) Both Assertion (A) and Reason (R) are true and Reason (R) is the correct explanation of Assertion (A)
(B) Both Assertion (A) and Reason (R) are true, but Reason (R) is not the correct explanation of Assertion (A)
(C) Assertion (A) is true, but Reason (R) is false
(d) Assertion (A) is false, but Reason (R) is true

You have to select the codes as *a*, *b*, *c* or *d* as your answer to the question by marking (✓) in the response box given against each option.

1. **Assertion (A)** Many consumer organisations and some enlighted businesses are taking an active part in educating consumers.

   Reason (R) The consumer has a right to have complete information about the product, he intends to buy.

   (A) ☐ (B) ☐ (C) ☐ (D) ☐

2. **Assertion (A)** It is advisable that business organisations should not resort to exploitative trade practices.

   Reason (R) Businesss organisations engaged in exploitative trade practices would invite government intervention.

   (A) ☐ (B) ☐ (C) ☐ (D) ☐

3. **Assertion (A)** It is important to understand and respond to customer needs.

   Reason (R) The approach followed now is caveat venditor.

   (A) ☐ (B) ☐ (C) ☐ (D) ☐

4. **Assertion (A)** Business organisations have responsibility to supply such products and render such services which are in public interest.

   Reason (R) Satisfied customers not only lead to repeat sales but also provide good feedback to prospective customers helping in increasing the customer base of business.

   (A) ☐ (B) ☐ (C) ☐ (D) ☐

5. **Assertion (A)** It is necessary to educate consumers.

   Reason (R) Consumers are not organised and there are not many consumer organisations.

   (A) ☐ (B) ☐ (C) ☐ (D) ☐

6. **Assertion (A)** The Consumer Protection Act, 2019 provides for five rights of consumers.

   Reason (R) Right to heard means a right to file a complaint in case of dissatisfaction with a good or a service.

   (A) ☐ (B) ☐ (C) ☐ (D) ☐

7. **Assertion (A)** Many enlightened business firms have set-up their own consumer service and grievance cells.

   Reason (R) The consumer has a right to file a complaint and to be heard in case of dissatisfaction with a good or service.

   [CBSE 2024]

   (A) ☐ (B) ☐ (C) ☐ (D) ☐

8. **Assertion (A)** Complaints cannot be filed against the provider of services, if they are deficient in any manner.

   Reason (R) A complaint can be filed against seller, manufacturer or dealer of goods, whose goods are defective.

   (A) ☐ (B) ☐ (C) ☐ (D) ☐

Correct/Incorrect Statements

No. of Questions : **8** Suggested Time : **12 Minutes**

Direction Each of the question given below consist of the two statements. List of common options applicable for each question is given below

(A) Statement I is correct and Statement II is incorrect
(B) Statement I is incorrect and Statement II is correct
(C) Both statements are correct
(D) Both statements are incorrect

You have to select the codes as *a*, *b*, *c* or *d* as your answer to the question by marking (✓) in the response box given against each option.

1. **Statement I** The consumer has a right to seek redressal.

   Statement II The consumer has a right to be protected against goods and services which are hazardous to life and health.

   (A) ☐ (B) ☐ (C) ☐ (D) ☐

2. **Statement I** The right to consumer education asserts that the consumer can choose from various options available.

   Statement II The right to seek redressal provides relief to consumers.

   (A) ☐ (B) ☐ (C) ☐ (D) ☐

3. **Statement I** Black marketing and hoarding leads to scarcity of the product as well as a rise in the price of the same.

   Statement II Consumers might be exploited by unscrupulous, exploitative and unfair trade practices like defective and unsafe products, adulteration, false and misleading advertising, hoarding, black marketing, etc.

   (A) ☐ (B) ☐ (C) ☐ (D) ☐

4. **Statement I** Consumers have a responsibility to learn about various risks associated with products before buying.

   Statement II It is not the consumer responsibility to be aware of different goods and services available. It is the duty of the seller.

   (A) ☐ (B) ☐ (C) ☐ (D) ☐

5. **Statement I** Provision of meditation cell is available at the level of District Commission.

   Statement II Consumer organisations cannot carry out comparative testing of consumer products in accredited laboratories.

   (A) ☐ (B) ☐ (C) ☐ (D) ☐

6. **Statement I** Mannara bought a packet of wheat as an aware customer, she should check the FPO mark.

   Statement II The order of National Commission can be challenged before the Supreme Court.

   (A) ☐ (B) ☐ (C) ☐ (D) ☐

7. **Statement I** The State Government is required to establish a District Commission in each state.

   Statement II The State Commission is set-up by the State Government.

   (A) ☐ (B) ☐ (C) ☐ (D) ☐

8. **Statement I** Central or State Governments cannot file consumer complaints.

   Statement II A state commission does not entertain the complaints filed in a District Commission.

   (A) ☐ (B) ☐ (C) ☐ (D) ☐

Case Based Questions

No. of Questions : **2** Suggested Time : **10 Minutes**

Direction This section contains 2 cases each having 4 questions of 1 mark each. You have to write the answer of each question based on the context of the related case.

Case 1 Piyali purchased an ISI marked heater from Bharti Appliances. She made cash payment, but failed to get a cash memo. While making use of the heater, she observed that it was not working properly. She contacted the shopkeeper immediately and told him the problem.

Shopkeeper paid no heed to her complaint. Rather he marked that the good in question was not bought from his shop. Piyali had no evidence of proving that the heater was purchased from his shop only.

She discussed the problem with her friend Sohini who advised her to approach Consumer Forum and lodge the complaint. Piyali was convinced with the idea of lodging the complaint against the shopkeeper but due to lack of cash memo it was difficult for her to proceed. *[CBSE QB]*

Questions

(i) Identify the right of the consumer as referred to in the above paragraph.

(A) Right to be informed ☐
(B) Right to safety ☐
(C) Right to be heard ☐
(D) Right to be assured ☐

(ii) Identify the responsibility of the consumer referred in the above case.

(A) Quality conscious ☐
(B) Must obtain cash memo ☐
(C) Cautious consumer ☐
(D) Ready to lodge complaint ☐

(iii) Piyali cannot lodge a complaint against the shopkeeper. Why?

(A) She do not have the right ☐
(B) She was aware of the fact ☐
(C) She do not have the cash memo ☐
(D) She was happy with the product ☐

(iv) Under which Act, Piyali can seek to protect the rights being a consumer?

(A) Consumer Protection Act, 2019 ☐
(B) Consumer Protection Act, 1968 ☐
(C) The Indian Contract Act, 1872 ☐
(D) The Competition Act, 2002 ☐

Case 2 Sunder complained before the consumer court, that in order to promote a brand of the bread called 'Bonn', the manufacturer had announced, through advertisements, that each packet of bread would contain a 'scratch and win' coupon.

The advertisement, he complained, implied that every person purchasing a packet of bread would win one of the prizes mentioned in the advertisement. Allured by it, he bought the bread, priced at ₹ 10, but every time he scratched the coupon, he found the words 'Please try again'.

This, he argued, was clearly an unfair trade practice. In response, the manufacturer argued that the scheme was launched without charging any extra amount and it had not given any guarantee that every purchaser of bread will win a prize as alleged.

By its order dated 4th January, 2001, the District Forum held the manufacturer guilty of unfair trade practice and awarded ₹ 5,000 as compensation. Unhappy with this verdict, Sunder filed an appeal for enhancement of the compensation and in response; the Punjab State Commission increased the compensation to ₹ 50,000, through its order delivered in July, 2002. Subsequently, the manufacturer filed a revision petition before the apex consumer court.

The National Commission held that there was no illegality in the order of the State Commission warranting its interference. What it said about the compensation is highly relevant.

Questions

(i) Under which Act Sunder can seek to protect rights of being a consumer?

(A) The Consumer Protection Act, 1986 ☐
(B) The Consumer Protection Act, 2002 ☐
(C) The Consumer Protection Act, 2019 ☐
(D) The Consumer Protection Act, 1872 ☐

(ii) Identify the responsibility of the consumer referred in the above para.

(A) Quality conscious ☐
(B) Must take cash memo ☐
(C) Cautious consumer ☐
(D) Ready to lodge a complaint ☐

(iii) Identify the right of the consumer as referred to in the above para.
(A) Right to be assured ☐
(B) Right to be informed ☐
(C) Right to seek redressal ☐
(D) Right to safety ☐

(iv) Identify the responsibility reflected in the above lines.
(A) File a complaint in an appropriate consumer forum in case of a shortcoming in the quality of goods purchased or services availed ☐
(B) Form consumer societies which would play an active part in educating consumers and safeguarding their interests ☐
(C) Learn about the risks associated with products and services, follow manufacturer's instructions and use the products safely ☐
(D) Be aware about various goods and services available in the market so that an intelligent and wise choice can be made ☐

Subjective Questions

Free Response Questions, Open-ended Questions etc.

No. of Questions : **7** Suggested Time : **55 Minutes**

1. Rajesh Rajan, from Ahmedabad, bought soft drink from a local store and found a packet of gutka floating in it. He sent a legal notice to the company immediately and approached a Consumer Dispute Redressal Forum.

   Moreover, he claimed that there was a deficiency in service that could have caused a health hazard to him. He demanded compensation of ₹ 5 lakh for the same. As an aware consumer, name and explain the right which Rajesh Rajan has exercised.

2. 'MVT Ltd' is a leading cosmetic manufacturing company. It has its own consumer service and grievance redressal centre to address consumer concerns. The mobile phone number of the consumer service and grievance redressal cell is printed on the labels of all its products as a policy to get feedback or complaints form their consumers.

   It also runs various programmes to educate the consumers about their rights and reliefs available to them in case a product or service falls short of their expectations.

   Explain the two rights of the consumers which are being promoted by the company. *[CBSE 2023]*

3. A student was asked to deposit lump sum fees of ₹ 18,734 for coaching of medical entrance examination for the next two years. This amount was deposited by the student in two complete instalments.

   However, the student realised that the quality of the coaching institute was not upto the mark and complained to the director and therefore sought a refund for the remaining period. The director refused to listen to the student, so he lodged a case against coaching institute.

   (i) Name and explain the right that can be exercised by the student.

   (ii) Where can the student file the complaint?

4. Sameeksha is a Class-XII student having business studies as one of her subjects. After studying 'Consumer Protection'as one of the chapters in Business Studies, she tried to apply the acquired knowledge while purchasing and using the goods. She is very fond of cooking and always tries new recipies.

   This time she wants to purchase a 'Bread Maker' to prepare homemade bread.

She checked online about the various brands of 'Bread Maker' available in the market and compared their price, so that an intelligent and wisé choice can be made. Then she went to a near by market to buy it.
Being an informed consumer she looked for the standardisation mark, negotiated the price printed on the label, checked the date of manufacturing and asked for guarantee or warranty of the product.
After satisfying with all the concerned information she purchased the 'Bread Maker' and as a responsible consumer asked for the cash memo. After coming back home she opened the packaging of the 'Bread Maker' and found an instruction booklet inside.

She carefully read all the instructions and operated the Bread Maker step-by-step and succeeded in making nice 'Atta Bread' for her family.

Sameeksha has fulfilled many responsibilities of a consumer while purchasing and using the 'Bread Maker'.

State any four responsibilities fulfilled by Sameeksha besides asking for a cash memo. *[CBSE 2023]*

5. Nishi had gone to a grocery store to make routine purchases. On reaching home, as she took out Binx tomato chips packet from the bag to give it to her son, she felt that it was underweight.

She checked its weight on the kitchen weighing scale and found that it weighed 60 grams whereas the label on the chips packet mentioned the weight of the packet as 100 grams. She approached the manufacturer and complained about it.

The manufacturer offered her a gift hamper and requested her not to disclose this to anyone. Nishi refused to accept the gift hamper and took the issue to a redressal agency.

(i) State two responsibilities discharged by Nishi, as a consumer, in the above case.

(ii) State any two reliefs which can be granted to Nishi, if the consumer court is satisfied with the genuineness of the complaint. *[CBSE 2024]*

6. Anuj, after a lot of research, paid 'SS Developers' an advance of ₹ 2 crore to build a lavish house for him. They promised to deliver the property within 18 months. At the end of 18 months, Anuj asked for the delivery of the property many times but the developer did not respond.

Anuj realised that 'SS Developers' was not in a positioin to hand over the property to him. Anju asked for a refund of the money with interest, which 'SS Developers' refused. Anuj approached the consumer court with his complaint.

(i) Which grievance redressal agency had Anuj approached?

(ii) State any three reliefs Anuj is likely to get, if the consumer court is satisfied with the complaint. *[CBSE 2024]*

7. An NGO, 'Hope Horizon,' operates in a developing country, focusing on providing education and healthcare to marginalised communities. Over the years, it has gained significant funding from international donors and built a reputation for its humanitarian work.

While the NGO claims to empower local communities, there are reports of staff members exploiting beneficiaries for personal gain.

The NGO is found to engage in unethical practices such as employing underage workers in its projects, violating labour laws and international conventions.
Suman, a degree holder in Entrepreneurship, came to know about the exploitation of the workers. He decided to set up an organisation for the protection and promotion of the consumer interest of the villagers.

List and explain the role that a consumer organisation or association plays.

Answers

If your answer matches with the answer given here then put (✓) in the box otherwise put (✗). In case you did not attempt the question leave the box blank.

Multiple Choice Questions

1. C ☐	2. C ☐
3. B ☐	4. B ☐
5. C ☐	6. B ☐
7. C ☐	8. D ☐
9. A ☐	10. C ☐
11. A ☐	12. A ☐
13. B ☐	14. D ☐
15. D ☐	16. B ☐
17. C ☐	18. A ☐
19. D ☐	20. A ☐
21. B ☐	22. C ☐
23. D ☐	24. A ☐
25. A ☐	

Your Score________ *(No. of Correct Answers)*

Assertion-Reason Questions

1. B ☐	2. A ☐	3. A ☐
4. B ☐	5. A ☐	6. D ☐
7. B ☐	8. D ☐	

Your Score________ *(No. of Correct Answers)*

Correct/Incorrect Statements

1. C ☐	2. B ☐	3. C ☐
4. A ☐	5. D ☐	6. B ☐
7. C ☐	8. D ☐	

Your Score________ *(No. of Correct Answers)*

Case Based Questions

1. (i) B ☐ (ii) B ☐
   (iii) C ☐ (iv) A ☐
2. (i) C ☐ (ii) D ☐
   (iii) C ☐ (iv) A ☐

Your Score________ *(No. of Correct Answers)*

Explanations

Multiple Choice Questions

1. (C) Good and ethical practices encourage firms to serve customers in a rightful manner, emphasising the role of self-regulation by businesses in consumer protection.
2. (C) The Consumer Protection Act allows for the representation of the deceased consumer's interests through legal heirs or representatives.
3. (B) Any person who obtains goods or avails services for resale or commercial purpose is not treated as a consumer
4. (B) State Commission
5. (C) The right to be heard ensures that consumers have the opportunity to raise complaints and concerns about a product or service and that their complaints will be considered at appropriate forums.
6. (B) Right to be heard
7. (C) Carrying out comparative analysis of prices of consumer goods
8. (D) The consumer exercised the right to seek redressal by filing a complaint and receiving a directive for a refund and compensation.
9. (A) By offering harmful treatments, RK Gupta violated consumers' right to safety, which ensures that products and services do not pose any significant risk to health or life.
10. (C) right to consumer education
11. (A) Right to consumer education
12. (A) Right to be assured
13. (B) The right to be informed ensures that consumers have access to accurate and sufficient information about a product, including details such as the name and address of the manufacturer, weight, manufacturing date, expiry date and maximum retail price.
14. (D) Right to consumer education
15. (D) Right to be assured
16. (B) (iii) (iv) (i) (ii)

17. (C) Learn about the risks associated with products and services, follow manufacturer's instructions and use the products safely
18. (A) Reading labels carefully is essential for consumers to exercise their right to be informed and make educated decisions about the products they purchase.
19. (D) All of the above
20. (A) District Commission
21. (B) Since Sarita's flat is worth ₹ 5 crore, which falls in the range that the State Commission handles (₹ 1 crore to ₹ 10 crore), she should approach the State Commission for redressal of her grievance.
22. (C) Filing a complaint in an appropriate consumer forum is a consumer right and does not constitute an unfair contract.
23. (D) (iv) (iii) (ii) (i)
24. (A) District Forum/Commission
25. (A) (ii) (iii) (i)

Assertion-Reason Questions

1. (B) Both Assertion (A) and Reason (R) are true, but Reason (R) is not the correct explanation of Assertion (A)
2. (A) Both Assertion (A) and Reason (R) are true and Reason (R) is the correct explanation of Assertion (A)
3. (A) Both Assertion (A) and Reason (R) are true and Reason (R) is the correct explanation of Assertion (A)
4. (B) Both Assertion (A) and Reason (R) are true, but Reason (R) is not the correct explanation of Assertion (A)
5. (A) Both Assertion (A) and Reason (R) are true and Reason (R) is the correct explanation of Assertion (A)
6. (D) Consumer Protection Act, 2019 actually provides for six rights of consumers.
7. (B) Both Assertion (A) and Reason (R) are true, but Reason (R) is not the correct explanation of Assertion (A)
8. (D) Consumers have the right to file complaints against service providers if their services are deficient or unsatisfactory.

Correct/Incorrect Statements

1. (C) Both statements are correct
2. (B) Right to consumer education is about providing consumers with information and resources to make informed choices.
3. (C) Both statements are correct
4. (A) Sellers do have a responsibility to provide accurate information about their products, but consumers also have to actively seek information and educate themselves about the market offerings to make wise choices.
5. (D) Provision of meditation cell is available at the level of all commissions.

   Consumer organisations can carry out comparative testing of consumer products in accredited laboratories.
6. (B) Mannara bought a packet of wheat as an aware customer, she should check the agmark.
7. (C) Both statements are correct
8. (D) Central or State Governments can file consumer complaints if they are consumers themselves. Additionally, a State Commission can entertain complaints filed in a District Commission.

Case Based Questions

1. (i) (B) Right to safety

   (ii) (B) Must obtain cash memo

   (iii) (C) She do not have the cash memo

   (iv) (A) Consumer Protection Act, 2019
2. (i) (C) The Consumer Protection Act, 2019

   (ii) (D) Ready to lodge a complaint

   (iii) (C) Right to seek redressal

   (iv) (A) File a complaint in an appropriate consumer forum in case of a shortcoming in the quality of goods purchased or services availed

Subjective Questions

1. The right exercised by Rajesh Rajan in this scenario is the 'right to safety'.

   The 'right to safety' entitles consumers for protection against goods and services that could potentially endanger their health or safety.

   In Rajesh Rajan's case, finding a packet of gutka floating in a soft drink bottle indicates a serious breach of this right.

   The presence of gutka, a harmful and banned substance, in a consumable product like soft drink poses a significant health risk to consumers. By exercising his right to safety, Rajesh took legal action against the company and demanded compensation for the potential health hazard caused by the contaminated product.

Rajesh's action highlights his awareness of his rights as a consumer and his commitment to hold businesses accountable for providing safe and reliable products.

2. Right being promoted by the company are
   (i) **Right to Consumer Education** The consumer has a right to acquire knowledge and to be a well informed consumer throughout life. Many consumer organisations and some business are actively educating consumers. He should be aware about his rights and the reliefs available to him in case of a product or service falls short of his expectations.
   (ii) **Right to Seek Redressal** CPA has provided consumers reliefs including replacement of product, removal of defect of product, compensation to be paid for any loss or injury suffered by the consumer.

3. (i) **Right to be Heard** This right allows consumers to raise their complaints and have their concerns addressed by the seller or service provider.
   (ii) The student can file the complaint in the appropriate consumer forum. In this case, since the transaction involves amount of ₹ 18,734, the student can file the complaint in the District Consumer Disputes Redressal Forum (District Forum) as per the provisions of the Consumer Protection Act, 2019.

4. The responsibilites fulfilled by Sameeksha are
   (i) A consumer should be aware about the various goods and services available in the market, so that she can make a wise choice by comparing their features and prices.
   (ii) A consumer must always buy standardised goods as they provide quality assurance. Thus, look for ISI mark on electrical goods, FPO mark on food products, hallmark on jewellery, etc.
   (iii) A consumer must learn about the various risks associated with the use and maintenance of goods must follow the manufacturer's instructions carefully.
   (iv) A consumer must read the labels carefully, so as to have complete information about the price, quantity, ingredients, usage, contents, expiry date, etc.

5. (i) Responsibilities discharged by Nishi are
   (a) Read labels carefully so as to have information about prices, net weight, manufacturing and expiry dates, etc.
   (b) File a complaint in an appropriate consumer forum in case of a shortcoming in the quality of goods purchased or services availed. Do not fail to take an action even when the amount involved is small.
   (ii) Reliefs available are
   (a) To replace the defective product with a new one, free from any defect.
   (b) To refund the price paid for the product, or the charges paid for the service.

6. (i) Anuj had approached to 'State Commission'.
   (ii) If the consumer court is satisfied about the genuineness of the complaint, it can issue one or more of the following directions to the opposite party (any three)
   (a) To refund the price paid for the product or the charges paid for the service.
   (b) To pay a reasonable amount of compensation for any loss suffered by the consumer due to the negligence of the opposite party.
   (c) To pay punitive damages in appropriate circumstances.
   (d) To discontinue the unfair/restrictive trade practice and not to repeat it in the future.

7. Suman has set-up an NGO or consumer organisation in the village for the protection and promotion of the consumer interests.

   The key functions highlighting the role of a consumer association are listed below
   (i) Educating the general public about consumer rights by conducting training programmes, conferences and workshops.
   (ii) Publishing periodicals and other publications to give knowledge about consumer problems, legal reporting, reliefs available and other matters of interest.
   (iii) Carrying out comparative testing of consumer products in accredited laboratories to test relative qualities of competing brands and publishing the test results for the benefit of consumers.
   (iv) Encouraging consumers to strongly protest and take an action against unscrupulous, exploitative and unfair trade practices of sellers.
   (v) Providing legal assistance to consumers by way of providing aid, legal advice, etc. in seeking legal remedy.
   (vi) Filing complaints in appropriate consumer courts on behalf of the consumers.

